THE KINGDOM OF GOD NOW

J. C. Hedgecock

Published by:
J. C. Hedgecock Publications
P. O. Box 702981
Tulsa, Oklahoma 74170 USA

Unless otherwise noted, Scripture taken from
THE AMPLIFIED BIBLE, Old Testament
copyright © 1965, 1987 by The Zondervan Corporation.
The Amplified New Testament copyright © 1958, 1987
by The Lockman Foundation. Used by permission.

Scripture noted as (KJV) is quoted from
THE HOLY BIBLE, KING JAMES VERSION.

The Kingdom of God Now
Copyright © 2001 by J. C. Hedgecock.
P. O. Box 702981 Tulsa, Oklahoma 74170

Published by J. C. Hedgecock Publications.
P. O. Box 702981 Tulsa, Oklahoma 74170

ALL RIGHTS RESERVED.
No part of this book may be reproduced in any form
without written permission from the Publisher.

ISBN 0-945255-75-6

Dedication

This book has been many years in the making. This is not a work that was taken lightly. I know that God's heart is for every one of his children to receive their full inheritance. He grieves every time satan robs from any one of you. The Bible says we perish from a lack of knowledge. This book is dedicated to you who are God's children. Through the knowledge in this book, you will be able to receive much more of your inheritance and stop the thief.

A special thanks to Aaron and Patricia Ross for their tireless work in editing. Also, thanks to the Servants of the Lord Ministry team for their support.

Contents

<u>Descriptions of the Kingdom</u>

Chapter 1	The Kingdom of God	1
Chapter 2	The Kingdom of Heaven	10
Chapter 3	The Kingdom of Christ (The Millennial Reign of Christ)	32
Chapter 4	The Final Recorded Stage of the Kingdom of God	52

<u>Living in the Kingdom Now</u>

Chapter 5	The Kingdom of God Now	59
Chapter 6	Why Do We Need the Kingdom Now?	72
Chapter 7	What Are the Conditions for Living in the Kingdom Now?	78
Chapter 8	What Are Some of the Benefits Now?	89
Chapter 9	What Are Some of the Benefits in the Future?	99
Chapter 10	Why Has the Kingdom of God Been So Hard for Some to Understand?	114
Chapter 11	How Does Our Enemy, Satan, See the Kingdom of God Now?	128
Chapter 12	What Should I Do to See the Kingdom of God Now?	143
Chapter 13	If I Embrace the Kingdom of God Now, How Will That Affect My Life?	150
Chapter 14	If I Reject the Kingdom of God Now, How Will That Affect My Life?	155

God's Plan for You

Chapter 15	God Has a Plan	161
Chapter 16	God Has a Place for You in His Plan	169
Chapter 17	Jesus is the Author and Finisher of God's Plan in and for You	176
Chapter 18	How Do I Get Started?	184
Chapter 19	Getting in His Kingdom Now and Growing Up	187

Reigning with Christ

Chapter 20	Qualifying to Reign with Christ	198
Chapter 21	Enjoying God Manifesting You as His Child	211
Chapter 22	Being Part of the Solution and Not Part of the Problem	218
Chapter 23	Being an Eye-Witness to the Destruction of Satan's Kingdom on This Earth	222
Chapter 24	Being an Eye-Witness to the Establishment of God's Kingdom on This Earth (The Millennial Reign of Christ)	228

The Kingdom of God Now

Chapter 25	God's Kingdom: A More Excellent Way	233
Chapter 26	Summary	237
Chapter 27	Conclusion	246

Introduction

Many Christians are confused about God's kingdom. There are different titles throughout the Bible that refer to God's kingdom. It is called the kingdom of heaven (Matthew 3:2), the kingdom of Christ (Ephesians 5:5), the kingdom of our Lord (2 Peter 1:11), and his heavenly kingdom (2 Timothy 4:18), as well as the kingdom of God.

We are told by Jesus in Matthew 6:10 to pray that the Father's kingdom would come and his will would be done on earth as it is in heaven. We are told about Jesus reigning on the earth during the millennium. Many scriptures refer to God's kingdom and his throne, and Revelation 3:21 says the saints will sit with Jesus on his throne just as he sits on his Father's throne. Revelation 11:15 says the kingdoms of this world are to become the kingdoms of our Lord.

These references can become very confusing and many questions arise that seem to lead to additional questions. Satan is the author of confusion. Jesus is truth and the Holy Spirit was sent to lead us into all truth. (John 16:13) I believe God authorized me to write this book with the guidance of the Holy Spirit in order to clear up the confusion and stop the lies of the enemy. As you study this book, many questions will be answered truthfully and clearly. Each description and dispensation of the kingdom of God will be clarified with specific attention being given to the kingdom of God <u>now</u>. We need to be prepared for what is coming, but we also need to know what is available to us now as God's children. This book is being presented during a critical time in history. Don't miss God's timing! **Now is the time to get prepared to be part of God's kingdom.** Now is the time to study to show yourself approved unto God. (2 Timothy 2:15)

Chapter 1

The Kingdom of God

In examining the kingdom of God now, we are first going to look at several different descriptions of God's kingdom. The first truth you must understand is that everything begins with our Father, God Almighty. Our Father existed before anything was created. Everything that exists (including creation) was brought about at the direction of our Father even though the actual creation was done by Jesus. (John 1:1-3) The Son came from the Father. Once we realize that everything begins with the Father and ultimately ends with the Father, we can get other truths lined up in the right perspective. The Father placed everything in heaven and earth under Jesus' authority, except for God himself. (1 Corinthians 15:27)

Sometimes when we read the Bible, we take things out of context or forget to harmonize all parts of the Word of God. We can get a distorted view of the different phases of God's kingdom and God's will being fulfilled in the universe. In these first chapters, I will describe each stage of the kingdom of God. However, the purpose of this book is to bring more understanding about the kingdom of God <u>now</u> and what is available in the time in which we are now living.

God's Kingdom

Let's start with some simple basics. God has a kingdom and he is in charge. He rules from his throne in heaven. The location of God's throne is described as being in the new Jerusalem in the third heaven. In 2 Corinthians 12:2, Paul described a time when he was caught up into the third heaven. He said, *"I know a man in Christ who fourteen years ago-whether in the body or out of the body I do not know, God knows-was caught up to the third heaven."* Paul went on to describe many things that happened to him on that journey. Some of what he saw was so awesome, he could not even speak of it.

In the book of Revelation, John was also caught up to the third heaven and given a vision of what is to come. One of the things he saw was the new Jerusalem, which he described as a bride, beautified and adorned for her husband. (Revelation 21:2)

God's throne is located in the new Jerusalem within the third heaven, but where is the third heaven? The first heaven is the atmosphere around the earth. The universe, which includes our solar system and galaxy, makes up the second heaven. The third heaven and the city of God are somewhere beyond our universe. Scientists have now realized that our universe is immensely larger than we originally thought. The third heaven is a long way out there!

One day God will destroy the heavens and the earth and create new ones. (Revelation 21:1) We have not been able to comprehend how he could do this. However, with the recent scientific discovery of black holes deep in space, we can at least see the possibility of how it might be done.

We need to realize that there is an awesomeness to God that we do not encounter in our day-to-day Christian walk. As we go to church, in our prayer time and in our encounters with God, we barely get a glimpse of the magnitude of who God is. This is proven by the attitude many Christians have toward him. Their insolence, arrogance and rebellion are clues that they are not walking anywhere close to his kingdom. If they were, all wrong attitudes would be gone in an instant. There would be nothing but awesome reverence and fear of the One who is sitting on the heavenly throne.

God is getting closer all the time, because his city is on the move. (Revelation 3:12b) After Christ's millennial reign, the new Jerusalem will arrive. At that point, everyone will stand before God to give an account for what they have done in this life. (Romans 14:12) There is a day of judgment coming. It will be initiated from the throne of God in his kingdom in the new Jerusalem. He will judge each one of us and then destroy the heavens and the earth. New heavens and a new earth will be created. All this will be authorized from the kingdom of God and the throne of God in the new Jerusalem. (Revelation 20:7-21:1)

The New Jerusalem

In Revelation 21:10-22:2, John was caught up to heaven and shown this city. *"Then in the Spirit He conveyed me away to a vast and lofty mountain and exhibited to me the holy (hallowed, consecrated) city of Jerusalem descending out of heaven from God, Clothed in God's glory [in all its splendor and radiance]. The luster of it resembled a rare and most precious jewel, like jasper, shining clear as crystal. It had a massive and high wall with twelve [large] gates, and at the gates [there were stationed] twelve angels, and [on the gates] the names of the twelve tribes of the sons of Israel were written: On the east side three gates, on the north side three gates, on the south side three gates, and on the west side three gates.*

And the wall of the city had twelve foundation [stones], and on them the twelve names of the twelve apostles of the Lamb. And he who spoke to me had a golden measuring reed (rod) to measure the city and its gates and its wall. The city lies in a square, its length being the same as its width. And he measured the city with his reed-12,000 stadia (about 1,500 miles); its length and width and height are the same. He measured its wall also-144 cubits (about 72 yards) by a man's measure [of a cubit from his elbow to his third fingertip], which is [the measure] of the angel. The wall was built of jasper, while the city [itself was of] pure gold, clear and transparent like glass.

The foundation [stones] of the wall of the city were ornamented with all of the precious stones. The first foundation [stone] was jasper, the second sapphire, the third chalcedony (or white agate), the fourth emerald, The fifth onyx, the sixth sardius, the seventh chrysolite, the eighth beryl, the ninth topaz, the tenth chrysoprase, the eleventh jacinth, the twelfth amethyst. And the twelve gates were twelve pearls, each separate gate being built of one solid pearl. And the main street (the broadway) of the city was of gold as pure and translucent as glass. I saw no temple in the city, for the Lord God Omnipotent [Himself] and the Lamb [Himself] are its temple. And the city has no need of the sun nor of the moon to give light to it, for the splendor and radiance (glory) of God illuminate it, and the Lamb is its lamp.

The nations shall walk by its light and the rulers and leaders of the earth shall bring into it their glory. And its gates shall never be closed by day, and there shall be no night there. They shall bring the glory (the splendor and majesty) and the honor of the nations into it. But nothing that defiles or profanes or is unwashed shall ever enter it, nor anyone who commits abominations (unclean, detestable, morally repugnant things) or practices falsehood, but only those whose names are recorded in the Lamb's Book of Life.

Then He showed me the river whose waters give life, sparkling like crystal, flowing out from the throne of God and of the Lamb Through the middle of the broadway of the city; also, on either side of the river was the tree of life with its twelve varieties of fruit, yielding each month its fresh crop; and the leaves of the tree were for the healing and the restoration of the nations."

This passage gives you a description of the city and its amazing structure. It is <u>so</u> amazing, we might actually doubt if it could be real. This city has a width and breadth equalling 1,500 miles square. The measurement that is the most difficult to comprehend is its height, because it is also 1,500 miles high! So you see, we're talking about a <u>huge</u> city. Its walls are made of pure diamond (jasper). That is a lot of diamonds when you consider that the city's perimeter is 6,000 miles! This city only has three entrances per side and the gates are made of one single pearl each. They must either be very small gates or very large pearls! The streets are paved with pure gold, so pure it is translucent. That is hard for most of us to imagine.

Revelation 4:1-11, *"After this I looked, and behold, a door standing open in heaven! And the first voice which I had heard addressing me like [the calling of] a war trumpet said, Come up here, and I will show you what must take place in the future. At once I came under the [Holy] Spirit's power, and behold, a throne stood in heaven, with One seated on the throne! And He Who sat there appeared like [the crystalline brightness of] jasper and [the fiery] sardius, and encircling the throne there was a halo that looked like [a rainbow of] emerald. Twenty-four other thrones surrounded the throne, and seated on these thrones were twenty-four elders (the members of the heavenly Sanhedrin), arrayed in white clothing, with crowns of gold upon their heads. Out from the throne came flashes of lightning and rumblings and peals of thunder, and in front of the throne seven blazing torches burned, which are the seven Spirits of God [the seven-fold Holy Spirit];*

And in front of the throne there was also what looked like a transparent glassy sea, as if of crystal. And around the throne, in the center at each side of the throne, were four living creatures (ones, beings) who were full of eyes in front and behind [with intelligence as to what is before and at the rear of them]. The first living creature (one, being) was like a lion, the second living creature like an ox, the third living creature had the face of a man, and the fourth living creature [was] like a flying eagle. And the four living creatures, individually having six wings, were full of eyes all over and within [underneath their wings]; and day and night they never stop saying, Holy, holy, holy is the Lord God Almighty (Omnipotent), Who was and Who is and Who is to come.

And whenever the living creatures offer glory and honor and thanksgiving to Him Who sits on the throne, Who lives forever and ever (through the eternities of the eternities), The twenty-four elders (the members of the heavenly Sanhedrin) fall prostrate before Him Who is sitting on the throne, and they worship Him Who lives forever and ever; and they throw down their crowns before the throne, crying out, Worthy are You, our Lord and God, to receive the glory and the honor and dominion, for You created all things; by Your will they were [brought into being] and were created."

<u>Jesus, the Son of God</u>

Chapter 1 of Hebrews helps us understand the Son's place in his Father's kingdom. There is an order within the Trinity. Reigning within our Father's kingdom is his first born Son. The Son was begotten of the Father. (John 3:16) Even though Jesus is God's Son, he was always with the Father. Jesus created everything except himself. (John 1:1-3) All of creation came into being at the Father's initiative.

Jesus had to meet certain conditions to attain his position in the Father's kingdom. Two thousand years ago, Jesus came to earth and took on the form of man. He took all the sins of the world on himself and paid the price for those sins on the cross. He was made the curse for us. (Galatians 3:13) He did this in order to redeem us to God the Father. By doing this, he earned a place of honor beyond what he already possessed, and he was <u>highly honored</u> from the beginning.

Hebrews 1:1-14, *"In many separate revelations [each of which set forth a portion of the Truth] and in different ways God spoke of old to [our] forefathers in and by the prophets, [But] in the last of these days He has spoken to us in [the person of a] Son, Whom He appointed Heir and lawful Owner of all things, also by and through Whom He created the worlds and the reaches of space and the ages of time [He made, produced, built, operated, and arranged them in order]. He is the sole expression of the glory of God [the Light-being, the out-raying or radiance of the divine], and He is the perfect imprint and very image of [God's] nature, upholding and maintaining and guiding and propelling the universe by His mighty word of power. When He had by offering Himself accomplished our cleansing of sins and riddance of guilt, He sat down at the right hand of the divine Majesty on high,*

[Taking a place and rank by which] He Himself became as much superior to angels as the glorious Name (title) which He has inherited is different from and more excellent than theirs. For to which of the angels did [God] ever say, You are My Son, today I have begotten You [established You in an official Sonship relation, with kingly dignity]? And again, I will be to Him a Father, and He will be to Me a Son? Moreover, when He brings the firstborn Son again into the habitable world, He says, Let all the angels of God worship Him. Referring to the angels He says, [God] Who makes His angels winds and His ministering servants flames of fire;

But as to the Son, He says to Him, Your throne, O God, is forever and ever (to the ages of the ages), and the scepter of Your kingdom is a scepter of absolute righteousness (of justice and straightforwardness). You have loved righteousness [You have delighted in integrity, virtue, and uprightness in purpose, thought, and action] and You have hated lawlessness (injustice and iniquity). Therefore God, [even] Your God (Godhead), has anointed You with the oil of exultant joy and gladness above and beyond Your companions. And [further], You, Lord, did lay the foundation of the earth in the beginning, and the heavens are the works of Your hands. They will perish, but You remain and continue permanently; they will all grow old and wear out like a garment. Like a mantle [thrown about one's self] You will roll them up, and they will be changed and replaced by others. But You remain the same, and Your years will never end nor come to failure. Besides, to which of the angels has He ever said, Sit at My right hand [associated with Me in My royal dignity] till I make your enemies a stool for your feet? Are not the angels all ministering spirits (servants) sent out in the service [of God for the assistance] of those who are to inherit salvation?"

Because Jesus was willing to cleanse our sins, God said, *"...sit at My right hand in My throne till I make Your enemies Your footstool."* Acts 7:49a (KJV) says, *"Heaven is my throne, and earth is my footstool."* When Jesus returns, the Father is going to make all of Jesus' enemies his footstool and put them under him. He will have sole authority to put down all rebellion, destroy all his enemies and set up his throne on this earth to reign for one thousand years. We have the opportunity to sit with Jesus on his throne and reign with him. This is a place of honor just as he has a place of honor at the right hand of the Father. The Father has turned over all authority to his Son, but God hasn't retired and stepped off his throne of authority.

As I said before, everything begins with the Father. When Jesus' throne is established on this earth and we're sitting with him on that throne, the Father's throne will still be in the new Jerusalem. During the millennium, all authority will come from Jesus and we will do exactly what he wants. Jesus' authority comes from the Father and everything he does will be exactly the way the Father wants it done.

In Matthew 6:10 (KJV) Jesus was teaching the disciples to pray. He said, *"Thy kingdom come. Thy will be done in earth, as it is in heaven."* Jesus was telling the disciples to pray that the Father's kingdom would come and his will would be done <u>in this earth</u> as it is in heaven. The Father will never come to the earth as we know it to rule and reign, so why is Jesus telling us to pray this prayer? We are praying to the Father, but he is not coming to this earth. He is going to send his Son instead. The kingdom of Christ will be established, but it is still the kingdom of God. Once again, the Father has put all things in heaven and in earth under his Son with the only exception being the Father himself. (1 Corinthians 15:27) Everything Jesus does is done to fulfill the will of his Father.

In John 14:8 and 9, Philip asked Jesus to show them the Father. Jesus wasn't being arrogant when he told them, "...*Have I been with all of you for so long a time, and do you not recognize and know Me yet, Philip? Anyone who has seen Me has seen the Father. How can you say then, Show us the Father?*"

Jesus also said in John 5:30, "*I am able to do nothing from Myself [independently, of My own accord-but only as I am taught by God and as I get His orders]. Even as I hear, I judge [I decide as I am bidden to decide. As the voice comes to Me, so I give a decision], and My judgment is right (just, righteous), because I do not seek or consult My own will [I have no desire to do what is pleasing to Myself, My own aim, My own purpose] but only the will and pleasure of the Father Who sent Me.*"

We are told to be imitators of Jesus, just as Jesus is an imitator of the Father. When we seek God for direction and he speaks to us with correction, exhortation and revelation, his goal is to make us like his first born Son. We don't have the capacity in this life to reach the fullness of the measure of the stature of Christ. It is an ongoing work, but old things should be passing away and all things should become new so we can be like Christ. (2 Corinthians 5:17)

It is imperative that you begin to understand the magnitude of <u>who you are in God's kingdom</u> as well as the awesomeness of the kingdom itself. God's kingdom is not like the kingdoms of this world. They will pass away, but God's kingdom will endure forever.

Chapter 2

The Kingdom of Heaven

In the previous chapter, we looked at Matthew 6:10. The Lord said to pray that our Father's kingdom would come and his will would be done on earth as it is in heaven. In this chapter, we will be focusing on the kingdom of heaven. As I shared previously, everything concerning "the kingdom" refers to God's kingdom. Matthew primarily uses the phrase "the kingdom of heaven", while John uses the phrase "the kingdom of God".

Parables About the Kingdom

I'm now going to elaborate on several parables Jesus relayed concerning the kingdom of heaven. Mark 4:10-12, *"And as soon as He was alone, those who were around Him, with the Twelve [apostles], began to ask Him about the parables. And He said to them, To you has been entrusted the mystery of the kingdom of God [that is, the secret counsels of God which are hidden from the ungodly]; but for those outside [of our circle] everything becomes a parable. In order that they may [indeed] look and look but not see and perceive, and may hear and hear but not grasp and comprehend, lest haply they should turn again, and it [their willful rejection of the truth] should be forgiven them."*

A parable uses natural illustrations to portray spiritual truths. When Jesus was teaching, parables were given to those who did not have ears to hear. The truth behind the parables was given only to those who were close to Jesus. This is still true today. Ask the Lord to give you ears to hear the deeper truths. As you read the Word of God or hear a divine word from him directly, apply that truth or revelation in your own life. Let the Holy Spirit search your heart to see if you are embracing and obeying it.

The Sower and the Seed

Let's look at Matthew 13:1-12. *"That same day Jesus went out of the house and was sitting beside the sea. But such great crowds gathered about Him that He got into a boat and remained sitting there, while all the throng stood on the shore. And He told them many things in parables (stories by way of illustration and comparison), saying, A sower went out to sow. And as he sowed, some seeds fell by the roadside, and the birds came and ate them up. Other seeds fell on rocky ground, where they had not much soil; and at once they sprang up, because they had no depth of soil. But when the sun rose, they were scorched, and because they had no root, they dried up and withered away. Other seeds fell among thorns, and the thorns grew up and choked them out. Other seeds fell on good soil, and yielded grain-some a hundred times as much as was sown, some sixty times as much, and some thirty. He who has ears [to hear], let him be listening and let him consider and perceive and comprehend by hearing.*

Then the disciples came to Him and said, Why do You speak to them in parables? And He replied to them, To you it has been given to know the secrets and mysteries of the kingdom of heaven, but to them it has not been given. For whoever has [spiritual knowledge], to him will more be given and he will be furnished richly so that he will have abundance; but from him who has not, even what he has will be taken away."

The Lord is saying that the one who has spiritual knowledge will be given more so that he has an abundance, but he who has not, even what he has will be taken away. How could that be fair? God is no respecter of persons. (Acts 10:34b) The explanation is given in Matthew 13:13-16, *"This is the reason that I speak to them in parables: because having the power of seeing, they do not see; and having the power of hearing, they do not*

11

hear, nor do they grasp and understand. In them indeed is the process of fulfillment of the prophecy of Isaiah, which says: You shall indeed hear and hear but never grasp and understand; and you shall indeed look and look but never see and perceive. For this nation's heart has grown gross (fat and dull), and their ears heavy and difficult of hearing, and their eyes they have tightly closed, lest they see and perceive with their eyes, and hear and comprehend the sense with their ears, and grasp and understand with their heart, and turn and I should heal them. But blessed (happy, fortunate, and to be envied) are your eyes because they do see, and your ears because they do hear."

It is critical, as you are reading this book, that you have ears to hear and eyes to see what the Spirit is saying. **Make sure you prepare yourself to study this book.** Don't just read and acquire more knowledge, then disregard the parts that are bothersome to you. Many believers do that. They skip over every part that makes them uncomfortable and search for things that tickle their ears. They look for the blessings, but they never want the corresponding responsibilities that go with the blessings. If you do that, you will only deceive yourself. **It is imperative that you have ears to hear "the hard sayings" because they will make the most dramatic changes in your life.** They are the truths that will qualify you to live in the kingdom of God.

Matthew 13:17, *"Truly I tell you, many prophets and righteous men [men who were upright and in right standing with God] yearned to see what you see, and did not see it, and to hear what you hear, and did not hear it."* This is an important point. Part of your heritage is the gift to understand the mysteries of the kingdom of God. Many of the old prophets yearned to see what you can see now, but they never got the chance you have been given. Yet most children of God in the world today still don't see or hear clearly because they disregard God's commands. They become dull of hearing and allow satan to steal their inheritance.

The Lord explained this parable to the disciples because of

their submissive attitude toward him. Because they honored him as the Son of God and did what he commanded them to do, he gave them ears to hear and eyes to see. He explained things to them so their understanding was opened and they started seeing what the mysteries were. He related parables to everyone else.

Only the Lord, through the Holy Spirit, can reveal spiritual truth and make it clear. Sometimes when we read the spiritual interpretation of a parable, we still don't get the full meaning of what Jesus is saying. If it makes us uncomfortable, we may even disregard what he says. We may prefer the mysteries we don't understand. That way we have an excuse for our disobedience. There is no excuse for disobedience, because you have the Holy Spirit living in you if you are a child of God. His job is to lead you into all truth. (John 16:13)

Matthew 13:18-23, *"Listen then to the [meaning of the] parable of the sower: While anyone is hearing the Word of the kingdom and does not grasp and comprehend it, the evil one comes and snatches away what was sown in his heart. This is what was sown along the roadside. As for what was sown on thin (rocky) soil, this is he who hears the Word and at once welcomes and accepts it with joy; Yet it has no real root in him, but is temporary (inconstant, lasts but a little while); and when affliction or trouble or persecution comes on account of the Word, at once he is caused to stumble [he is repelled and begins to distrust and desert Him Whom he ought to trust and obey] and he falls away. As for what was sown among thorns, this is he who hears the Word, but the cares of the world and the pleasure and delight and glamour and deceitfulness of riches choke and suffocate the Word, and it yields no fruit. As for what was sown on good soil, this is he who hears the Word and grasps and comprehends it; he indeed bears fruit and yields in one case a hundred times as much as was sown, in another sixty times as much, and in another thirty."*

Let's examine again the meaning of the parable of the sower.

Anyone who hears the word of the kingdom and does not comprehend it, the evil one comes and snatches away what was sown in his heart. This is the seed that was sown along the roadside.

Thin, rocky soil has never been broken up very deeply. This represents one who hears the word and at once welcomes it with joy, yet it has no real root in him. It is temporary and only lasts a little while. When affliction, trouble or persecution come because of the word, that person stumbles. He begins to distrust and desert him whom he ought to trust and obey. **When God convicts you repeatedly of sin and you repent of the fruit yet never let God go down to the root of <u>why</u> you continue to sin, this kind of ground is produced.** You never humble yourself enough to allow God to break up the ground of your heart so that when he does plant something, the root will go deep.

As for that which was sown among thorns, this is the person who hears the word, but the cares of the world and the deceitfulness of riches choke out the word so that it yields no fruit. This person tries to embrace the word and let it grow, but the cares of the world (which are very common in our generation) choke it out. The seed that is sown never produces any lasting fruit.

It doesn't make any difference how good the seed is. The yield that seed will produce is determined by the quality of the ground in which it is sown. I can give you an abundance of seed, but I have no control over your ground. I can only expose the fact that your ground is not in the condition it should be, just as this parable does.

Your heart is like one (or more) of the types of ground in these scriptures. I encourage you to get before God and repent until your heart has "good soil". If you don't do that, it doesn't make any difference how good the seed is. It is not going to bear any lasting fruit.

Remember, a good tree bears good fruit, but a bad tree bears bad fruit. (Matthew 7:19) Godly fruit manifesting in your life proves that the seed went into good ground. If you don't bear good fruit, you are good for nothing except to be thrown into the fire.

Matthew 13:23 explains that the person who has the good soil got the same seed the others did. Their ground wasn't shallow nor was it full of thorns. It didn't have rocks or other things that would choke out the seed. The difference was having an open, repentant heart so the seed produced fruit. This person hears the Word of God and grasps what God is saying <u>within their spirit</u>. **They listen to the Spirit of God instead of their natural reasoning**. They understand and obey what God says and they do not disregard his word. They become a faithful doer of the word and it produces fruit in their life; some a hundred, some sixty and some thirty fold.

In this passage, the Lord is talking about the seed of revelation about his kingdom which is sown in you. It is amazing how we have turned that around. Today, it is often preached that we will get a yield based on what we have sown in somebody else, and it is usually taught about sowing and reaping money. You sow money into somebody else and you are going to reap money back.

These scriptures are very clear. **You reap from what is sown in you, not what you sow into somebody else.** Please don't misunderstand me. You <u>are</u> to sow into other people's lives, but let's examine exactly what this passage says. This is the only passage in the Bible that talks about the thirty, sixty and one hundred fold return. The same parable is related in Luke 8 with minor differences. It refers to what God sows in you or a word from God about his kingdom. A word from God that goes into your spirit will bring forth fruit based on the <u>condition of your heart</u>. That's what affects your yield!

Today, this is often taught as if my yield is dependent upon how much faith I have in God to give me more back. The reality is that your yield is determined by the quality of your ground and how well you receive what God sows into your life and what you do with it. You must allow God to prepare the ground.

For the most part, we are missing God because of our "ground preparation". With a good yield, you have seed to sow to somebody else. The seed you sow into someone else gives them the chance to receive and put seed into their ground so that they get a good yield. They can then give it to someone else.

<u>The Wheat and The Darnel</u>

Matthew 13:24-30, *"Another parable He set forth before them, saying, The kingdom of heaven is like a man who sowed good seed in his field. But while he was sleeping, his enemy came and sowed also darnel (weeds resembling wheat) among the wheat, and went on his way. So when the plants sprouted and formed grain, the darnel (weeds) appeared also. And the servants of the owner came to him and said, Sir, did you not sow good seed in your field? Then how does it have darnel shoots in it? He replied to them, An enemy has done this. The servants said to him, Then do you want us to go and weed them out? But he said, No, lest in gathering the wild wheat (weeds resembling wheat), you root up the [true] wheat along with it. Let them grow together until the harvest; and at harvest time I will say to the reapers, Gather the darnel first and bind it in bundles to be burned, but gather the wheat into my granary."*

Again, Jesus didn't explain this parable to the multitudes. However, his disciples were given the explanation in Matthew 13:36-43. *"Then He left the throngs and went into the house. And His disciples came to Him saying, Explain to us the parable of the darnel in the field. He answered, He Who sows the good seed is the Son of Man. The field is the world, and the good seed means the children of the kingdom; the darnel is the children of the evil one, And the enemy who sowed it is the devil. The harvest is the close and consummation of the age, and the reapers are angels. Just as the darnel (the weeds, the wild wheat) is gathered and burned with fire, so it will be at the close of the age. The Son of Man will send forth His angels, and they will gather out of His kingdom all causes of offense [persons by whom others are drawn into error or sin] and all who do iniquity and act wickedly, And will cast them into the furnace of fire; there will be weeping and wailing and grinding of teeth. Then will the righteous (those who are upright and in right standing with God) shine forth like the sun in the kingdom of their Father. Let him who has ears [to hear] be listening, and let him consider and perceive and understand by hearing."*

This is a very sobering passage. There is a time coming when God will send his Son back to set up his literal kingdom. Those who were willing to suffer for his name's sake and are in right standing with God will rule and reign with Jesus Christ. They will sit down with him on his throne, just as Jesus sits at the right hand of our Father on his throne. Every person who has led anyone into error or sin, acted wickedly or committed iniquity without repenting is going to be removed. Even those who said, "Lord, Lord" that he never knew are going to be removed. (Matthew 7:21-23)

God will set up his kingdom. The righteous who have kept their robes white and have stayed humble before God are going to shine forth like the sun in the kingdom of their Father. The Lord concludes this passage with a warning, *"Let him who has ears [to hear] be listening, and let him consider and perceive and understand by hearing."*

The Mustard Seed

Let's go back to Matthew 13:31 and 32 and look at the parable of the mustard seed. *"Another story by way of comparison He set forth before them, saying, The kingdom of heaven is like a grain of mustard seed, which a man took and sowed in his field. Of all the seeds it is the smallest, but when it has grown it is the largest of the garden herbs and becomes a tree, so that the birds of the air come and find shelter in its branches."*

God placed the seed of his Spirit within you when you were

born again. Sometimes you may feel like you don't have much, but if you yield to the gardener (the Father) and allow him to do what he wants to do in you, that little seed can grow to become greater than all the other herbs in the field. **As you yield to the Lordship of Jesus Christ, the spiritual "seed" (the kingdom of God) will grow in you until it overcomes everything else and provides life for others.**

Leavening

In Matthew 13:33b, Jesus told the people another parable. *"...The kingdom of heaven is like leaven (sour dough) which a woman took and covered over in three measures of meal or flour till all of it was leavened."* A little bit of leaven can leaven a whole loaf. That's what God did in us. He put the seed of faith and his Spirit in each of us. If you will yield to the Master, that little bit of leaven will change you completely. Your spirit, soul and body will become holy and in right standing with God.

The Importance of Parables

Matthew 13:34 and 35, *"These things all taken together Jesus said to the crowds in parables; indeed, without a parable He said nothing to them. This was in fulfillment of what was spoken by the prophet: I will open My mouth in parables; I will utter things that have been hidden since the foundation of the world."* Parables are very important and they contain great revelation. The problem is people not "seeing" because they process everything through their human reasoning which cannot understand the things of God. The things of God must be spiritually discerned. (1 Corinthians 2:14) If you have never been trained in the ways of righteousness, you do not know how to communicate with God, fellowship with him or hear his voice. You don't have spiritual ears or spiritual eyes.

Jesus trained the disciples to have ears to understand, just as he is training us. If you process the truth quickly and continue to let God open your eyes and ears as we go through this teaching, you will have understanding and insight into the kingdom of God by the time you reach the end of this book. You can meet the conditions to walk in the kingdom of God now, as well as when Jesus comes back and throughout eternity.

Other Parables

Matthew 13:44, *"The kingdom of heaven is like something precious buried in a field, which a man found and hid again; then in his joy he goes and sells all he has and buys that field."* **Does the kingdom of heaven have that kind of value to you?** Do you have eyes to see and ears to hear what a precious blessing the kingdom of God is? Would you be willing to sell everything you have to get it? Do you seek the kingdom of God first? (Matthew 6:33) **If the kingdom of God is not your first priority, then you really don't see its value.** Once you have eyes to see and ears to hear the value of the kingdom of God and the privilege you've been given, everything this world has to offer will pale in comparison. **If there are things in your life that have priority over the kingdom of God, then you do not hear and see at the level that God wants you to see and hear.**

Matthew 13:45-50, *"Again the kingdom of heaven is like a man who is a dealer in search of fine and precious pearls, Who, on finding a single pearl of great price, went and sold all he had and bought it. Again, the kingdom of heaven is like a dragnet which was cast into the sea and gathered in fish of every sort. When it was full, men dragged it up on the beach, and sat down and sorted out the good fish into baskets, but the worthless ones they threw away. So it will be at the close and consummation of the age. The angels will go forth and separate the wicked from the righteous (those who are upright and in right standing with God) And cast them [the wicked] into the furnace of fire; there will be weeping and wailing and grinding of teeth."* Notice that the angels will separate the righteous from those who are wicked.

Are you in right standing with God? Do you live a life that is consistently righteous? If you do, then you are living in the presence of God. You have fullness of joy, and you are getting to know God. The fruit of the Spirit listed in Galatians 5:22 will start appearing in your life if you are consistently righteous. You will have ears to hear when God speaks, and you will also understand what he says to you. You will embrace it and have fruit proving you are obeying it.

Forgiveness

Matthew 18:23-35, *"Therefore the kingdom of heaven is like a human king who wished to settle accounts with his attendants. When he began the accounting, one was brought to him who owed him 10,000 talents [probably about $10,000,000], And because he could not pay, his master ordered him to be sold, with his wife and his children and everything that he possessed, and payment to be made. So the attendant fell on his knees, begging him, Have patience with me and I will pay you everything. And his master's heart was moved with compassion, and he released him and forgave him [cancelling] the debt. But that same attendant, as he went out, found one of his fellow attendants who owed him a hundred denarii [about twenty dollars]; and he caught him by the throat and said, Pay what you owe! So his fellow attendant fell down and begged him earnestly, Give me time, and I will pay you all! But he was unwilling, and he went out and had him put in prison till he should pay the debt.*

When his fellow attendants saw what had happened, they were greatly distressed, and they went and told everything that had taken place to their master. Then his master called him and said to him, You contemptible and wicked attendant! I forgave and cancelled all that [great] debt of yours because you begged me to. And should you not have had pity and mercy on your fellow attendant, as I had pity and mercy on you? And in wrath his master turned him over to the torturers (the jailers), till he should pay all that he owed. So also My heavenly Father will deal with every one of you if you do not freely forgive your brother from your heart his offenses."

I don't know how to get it much plainer than that. Our Father has forgiven us because of the price Jesus paid. We were full of sin and bound for hell. We owed a debt we could never repay. All we had to look forward to was an eternity of torment. When we were totally alienated from God, he loved us so much that he gave his only Son to die for us so that our debt could be cancelled. There is no way that any person could owe us anything close to what we owe God yet he forgave our debt freely. He doesn't even remember our sins. (Hebrews 8:12)

The Father will deal with every one of us in the same way as in this parable. **If you want complete forgiveness from God, you must forgive your brother from your heart.** Don't hold it against him unless you want to be treated in the same way by God.

The master in this parable forgave ten million dollars, but he also had the power to reinstate the debt because he was the king. You may say, "God forgave my sins. He can't undo what he already did." No, he won't reinstate the penalty for what you have <u>genuinely</u> repented of (not as the man in the parable who was only sorrowful because he got caught), but what about the sins you are committing now and the next ones you will commit? God said if you don't freely forgive your brother, then he will not forgive your sin. The refusal to forgive others is an indication that you do not have a truly repentant heart yourself.

I shared earlier in Matthew 6:10 about praying that God would send his kingdom and that his will would be done on earth as it is in heaven. He said we are to pray that he would forgive us our debts <u>as we forgive our debtors</u>. Matthew 7:2 says that as we measure, so it will be measured back unto us. As we forgive, so will we be forgiven. **We can determine the measure of forgiveness we receive from God by how readily we forgive those**

who have sinned against us.

If you are unforgiven, you cannot enter the kingdom of God. That may upset many of you and you may defend your doctrines about this, but I didn't say it. Jesus said it! We think we have God locked in a box. We think we've got him in a legal bind because of our doctrines. You better read the fine print. Jesus said if you don't freely forgive your brothers, then neither is the Father going to forgive you of your debts. If you don't have forgiveness from God, you will never enter the kingdom of God because sin cannot enter into his presence. Think about this seriously before you go on!

The Workers in the Field

Matthew 20:1-16, *"For the kingdom of heaven is like the owner of an estate who went out in the morning along with the dawn to hire workmen for his vineyard. After agreeing with the laborers for a denarius a day, he sent them into his vineyard. And going out about the third hour (nine o'clock), he saw others standing idle in the marketplace; And he said to them, You go also into the vineyard, and whatever is right I will pay you. And they went. He went out again about the sixth hour (noon), and the ninth hour (three o'clock) he did the same. And about the eleventh hour (five o'clock) he went out and found still others standing around, and said to them, Why do you stand here idle all day? They answered him, Because nobody has hired us. He told them, You go out into the vineyard also and you will get whatever is just and fair.*

When evening came, the owner of the vineyard said to his manager, Call the workmen and pay them their wages, beginning with the last and ending with the first. And those who had been hired at the eleventh hour (five o'clock) came and received a denarius each. Now when the first came, they supposed that they would get more, but each of them also received a denarius. And when they received it, they grumbled at the owner of the estate,

Saying, These [men] who came last worked no more than an hour, and yet you have made them rank with us who have borne the burden and the scorching heat of the day. But he answered one of them, Friend, I am doing you no injustice. Did you not agree with me for a denarius? Take what belongs to you and go. I choose to give to this man hired last the same as I give to you. Am I not permitted to do what I choose with what is mine? [Or do you begrudge my being generous?] Is your eye evil because I am good? So those who [now] are last will be first [then], and those who [now] are first will be last [then]. For many are called, but few chosen."

It is easy to read into this that it doesn't make any difference whether you work a little or a lot, because we are all going to get paid the same wages. <u>That is not what Jesus is saying</u>. The men who were standing around at the eleventh hour hadn't wasted the day by trying to stay out of work. They weren't working because nobody had hired them. They were available. If someone had hired them the first hour, they would have worked all day.

This master decided to be generous. He was <u>just</u> with the first people he hired. They got a fair day's wages which was a denarius. The other workers got <u>grace</u>. They got a whole lot more than they deserved. The men hired at the third, sixth and ninth hour did not agree on a wage. They trusted the master to be fair. It wasn't their fault that they weren't working before. The master chose to give them grace, which was more than they deserved. Don't misinterpret this parable to think that you can let somebody else carry all the responsibility, then show up at the last minute and receive the same reward.

The <u>least</u> we will ever get from God is justice, but if God chooses to give more grace to one person as opposed to another, that's his choice. You may not understand the reasons why he is making such a choice. If you are walking in agreement with God, he will do his part. Don't be concerned about what his agreement is with somebody else. That isn't your business. It is easy to get caught up in what everybody else does, because we think that God is being easier (or harder) on them. He is in charge and he is always just and gracious.

The Wedding Banquet

Matthew 22:1-14, *"And again Jesus spoke to them in parables (comparisons, stories used to illustrate and explain), saying, The kingdom of heaven is like a king who gave a wedding banquet for his son And sent his servants to summon those that had been invited to the wedding banquet, but they refused to come. Again he sent other servants, saying, Tell those who are invited, Behold, I have prepared my banquet; my bullocks and my fat calves are killed, and everything is prepared; come to the wedding feast. But they were not concerned and paid no attention [they ignored and made light of the summons, treating it with contempt] and they went away-one to his farm, another to his business, While the others seized his servants, treated them shamefully, and put them to death.*

[Hearing this] the king was infuriated; and he sent his soldiers and put those murderers to death and burned their city. Then he said to his servants, The wedding [feast] is prepared, but those invited were not worthy. So go to the thoroughfares where they leave the city [where the main roads and those from the country end] and invite to the wedding feast as many as you find. And those servants went out on the crossroads and got together as many as they found, both bad and good, so [the room in which] the wedding feast [was held] was filled with guests. But when the king came in to view the guests, he looked intently at a man there who had on no wedding garment. And he said, Friend, how did you come in here without putting on the [appropriate] wedding garment? And he was speechless (muzzled, gagged). Then the king said to the attendants, Tie him hand and foot, and throw him into the darkness outside; there will be weeping and grinding of teeth. For many are called (invited and summoned),

but few are chosen."

Jesus came to preach the kingdom. He sent the disciples to God's chosen people, not to the Gentiles or Samaritans. What did the Jews do? They rejected him and killed those he sent. The Lord then sent apostles such as Paul to the Gentiles.

Jesus must have considered the kingdom of heaven to be very important since he preached so much about it. In these numerous passages, everything Jesus talked about was related to the kingdom of heaven. These passages explain in great detail what it takes to get into the kingdom of God and stay there, as well as what will get you thrown out. They are intended to give understanding about the conditions for being in his kingdom. God doesn't want you to be cast out, and he wants to make sure you are not ignorant of the devices the devil would use to keep you out of his kingdom.

The Ten Virgins

Matthew 25:1, *"Then the kingdom of heaven shall be likened to ten virgins who took their lamps and went to meet the bridegroom."* I want to pause for a moment because most believers know the story of the five foolish virgins. They are typically thought of as being five wise virgins and five harlots, but that isn't the case. Continuing in verse 2, *"Five of them were foolish (thoughtless, without forethought) and five were wise (sensible, intelligent, and prudent)."* Ten virgins were looking for the bridegroom just as we are today. Five of them were foolish, which means they were thoughtless and without forethought, but about what? About what it took to be ready for the bridegroom to come. The other five virgins were wise, sensible, intelligent and prudent.

Matthew 25:3-9, *"For when the foolish took their lamps, they did not take any [extra] oil with them; But the wise took flasks of oil along with them [also] with their lamps. While the bridegroom lingered and was slow in coming, they all began nodding their heads, and they fell asleep. But at midnight there was a shout, Behold, the bridegroom! Go out to meet him! Then all those virgins got up and put their own lamps in order. And the foolish said to the wise, Give us some of your oil, for our lamps are going out. But the wise replied, There will not be enough for us and for you; go instead to the dealers and buy for yourselves."* The foolish virgins had plenty of time to get more oil but they procrastinated. They waited until it was time to go in and then they had to try to find more oil. Verse 10, *"But while they were going away to buy, the bridegroom came, and those who were prepared went in with him to the marriage feast; and the door was shut."*

There is a time coming when the Lord will return for his bride. No one knows the day or hour of Jesus' return except the Father. (Mark 13:32) At the appointed time, the door will open and those who are ready will go in. Those who aren't ready won't go in and the door will be shut. It will be too late at that point.

Matthew 25:11-13, *"Later the other virgins also came and said, Lord, Lord, open [the door] to us! But He replied, I solemnly declare to you, I do not know you [I am not acquainted with you]. Watch therefore [give strict attention and be cautious and active], for you know neither the day nor the hour when the Son of Man will come."* These virgins were seeking the Lord. They were all waiting for him and called him "Lord", yet he didn't <u>know</u> the foolish virgins who were unprepared for his return.

<u>The Talents</u>

Matthew 25:14-30, *"For it is like a man who was about to take a long journey, and he called his servants together and entrusted them with his property. To one he gave five talents [probably about $5,000], to another two, to another one-to each in proportion to his own personal ability. Then he departed and left the country. He who had received the five talents went at once and traded with them, and he gained five talents more. And*

likewise he who had received the two talents-he also gained two talents more. But he who had received the one talent went and dug a hole in the ground and hid his master's money. Now after a long time the master of those servants returned and settled accounts with them. And he who had received the five talents came and brought him five more, saying, Master, you entrusted to me five talents; see, here I have gained five talents more. His master said to him, Well done, you upright (honorable, admirable) and faithful servant! You have been faithful and trustworthy over a little; I will put you in charge of much. Enter into and share the joy (the delight, the blessedness) which your Master enjoys.

And he also who had the two talents came forward, saying, Master, you entrusted two talents to me; here I have gained two talents more. His master said to him, Well done, you upright (honorable, admirable) and faithful servant! You have been faithful and trustworthy over a little; I will put you in charge of much. Enter into and share the joy (the delight, the blessedness) which your master enjoys.

He who had received one talent also came forward, saying, Master, I knew you to be a harsh and hard man, reaping where you did not sow, and gathering where you had not winnowed [the grain]. So I was afraid, and I went and hid your talent in the ground. Here you have what is your own. But his master answered him, You wicked and lazy and idle servant! Did you indeed know that I reap where I have not sowed and gather [grain] where I have not winnowed? Then you should have invested my money with the bankers, and at my coming I would have received what was my own with interest. So take the talent away from him and give it to the one who has the ten talents. For to everyone who has will more be given, and he will be furnished richly so that he will have an abundance; but from the one who does not have, even what he does have will be taken away. And throw the good-for-nothing servant into the outer darkness; there will be weeping and grinding of teeth."

This is another sobering parable. God has invested his word in each one of us. It depends on what kind of ground you have allowed God to prepare in you as to the yield you will produce. When your master comes back, what kind of interest will he receive from the seed that was sown in you? What have you produced with what he has given you? Have you selfishly held on to the seed? He called such a person a good-for-nothing servant and threw him into outer darkness.

Those who had been given the most according to their abilities were required the most. Luke 12:48 says that to whom more is given, more is required. If someone else is called as an apostle and you are called into the ministry of helps, you are not required to produce the fruit the apostle is required to produce. However, **you are required to produce a <u>proportional</u> amount for what you have been given**.

The servant who had five talents produced another five. The one who had two talents produced another two. The one who had only one talent did not produce anything, because **he held on to what he'd been given**.

It doesn't matter at what level you are spiritually or what you have been given. **God didn't give you giftings and revelation for you to bury them.** He gave you revelation and giftings to be sown in good soil to bring forth thirty, sixty or a hundred fold for his glory. Every seed that has ever been sown in you by God has produced a crop. A record has been kept of the yield you produced. **You will give an account for every seed planted in you.** What have you done with them?

Today, we have diluted the standard of walking with God to the point that we think if we still have the original seed he gave us, we are doing great. If that is all you are doing, you are at the level of being "good for nothing". **If you have allowed the hardness of your heart to keep the seed from being received into your spirit and you have let the enemy steal it, you are**

less than good for nothing. You don't even have the seed originally given to you by the Lord. You see how we have missed God's standard. Most believers fit into this category. They haven't even held on to what God has given them.

Only those who are walking in humility and allowing God to prepare their ground will produce fruit. They will be considered good and faithful servants. Some of you have been given more seed than others, so you can produce more! **Every believer will stand before God to give an account of the seed that was given to them.** God has given each of his children giftings, abilities, revelation and everything that is needed in order to produce a harvest. If you have only one seed in your ground, but you keep your ground in maximum condition, you can produce a hundred fold to give to others. All that is produced by each seed is recorded and it accumulates in your heavenly account.

You need to go back over these parables and glean out everything you can. Let God do a work in your heart. The religious leaders of Jesus' time kept the letter of the law, yet they totally missed God's kingdom. Even the disciples never fully comprehended the kingdom. I encourage you to spend some time studying these parables. Don't assume you have revelation simply because you understand them with your natural reasoning. **When your spirit embraces the truth of each parable, you will begin to see major changes in your walk with God.** You will begin to notice a harvest coming forth that will change your life as well as the lives of others.

The Heart of a Child

Matthew 19:13-15, *"Then little children were brought to Jesus, that He might put His hands on them and pray; but the disciples rebuked those who brought them. But He said, Leave the children alone! Allow the little ones to come to Me, and do not forbid or restrain or hinder them, for of such [as these] is the kingdom of heaven composed. And He put His hands upon them, and then went on His way."*

We know that everything in the Word of God is truth. It does not matter if it is only said once in the whole Bible. It is important. It makes sense that if something is mentioned more than once by the Lord, it is very important. Some things have priority over others. There are greater truths that include lesser truths. This is a truth Jesus didn't want us to misunderstand, so it is recorded in three different gospels.

Mark 10:13-15, *"And they kept bringing young children to Him that He might touch them, and the disciples were reproving them [for it]. But when Jesus saw [it], He was indignant and pained and said to them, Allow the children to come to Me-do not forbid or prevent or hinder them-for to such belongs the kingdom of God. Truly I tell you, whoever does not receive and accept and welcome the kingdom of God like a little child [does] positively shall not enter it at all."*

Luke 18:15-17, *"Now they were also bringing [even] babies to Him that He might touch them, and when the disciples noticed it, they reproved them. But Jesus called them [the parents] to Him, saying, Allow the little children to come to Me, and do not hinder them, for to such [as these] belongs the kingdom of God. Truly I say to you, whoever does not accept and receive and welcome the kingdom of God like a little child [does] shall not in any way enter it [at all]."*

These three passages say basically the same thing. **Unless you become as a little child, you cannot enter the kingdom of God.** Please take a moment to ponder the enormity of this truth!

We all hope to have joyful fellowship with God and enjoy the benefits of being his child. We trust him to do what he has said he will do. Jesus said in John 14:3 that he was going to the Father but he would come and receive us to himself. **Child-like trust means that you believe all that God has promised.**

Matthew 23:13, *"But woe to you, scribes and Pharisees, pretenders (hypocrites)! For you shut the kingdom of heaven in men's faces; for you neither enter yourselves, nor do you allow those who are about to go in to do so."* The leaders in Jesus' day would not enter into God's kingdom nor would they let others enter in. We are commanded as Christian leaders to preach the kingdom of God. It is our responsibility to enter in and abide there and also to teach others how to do the same.

You may have been convicted by these parables. That is a positive thing! You can't fix something if you don't know what is wrong. You may be dealing with your own lack of child-like faith, or you may be going to a church where the leaders are shutting up the kingdom of God, just as the Pharisees did. Either way, you must deal with the reasons you are not living in the kingdom of God now. Don't let your carnality be an excuse.

We are coming closer to the time when the Lord will send his angels to separate those who qualify to be Christ's bride from those who do not. Don't take someone else's word for it. Study the Word of God yourself and find out what God requires of you. Let the Holy Spirit give you ears to hear as you repent from a pure heart. Don't make the assumption that you are a wise virgin simply because you got saved years ago. Find out if you are a foolish virgin and do what is necessary to become wise. Make sure you meet God's standard for being part of his kingdom.

Chapter 3

The Kingdom of Christ
(The Millennial Reign of Christ)

John 18 describes Jesus' trial before Pontius Pilate. Pilate asked him whether or not he was a king, and Jesus answered him in verses 36 and 37. *"...My kingdom (kingship, royal power) belongs not to this world. If My kingdom were of this world, My followers would have been fighting to keep Me from being handed over to the Jews. But as it is, My kingdom is not from here (this world); [it has no such origin or source]. Pilate said to Him, Then You are a King? Jesus answered, You say it! [You speak correctly!] For I am a King. [Certainly I am a King!] This is why I was born, and for this I have come into the world, to bear witness to the Truth. Everyone who is of the Truth [who is a friend of the Truth, who belongs to the Truth] hears and listens to My voice."*

The kingdom of God (the kingdom of heaven) is the source of Jesus' kingship. The Father established Jesus as King. The Father made him ruler over the heavens and the earth. The Father has also given him authority to return, subdue the earth and establish his kingdom here.

<u>Are You Ready</u>?
About two thousand years ago, Jesus came to earth to become the Redeemer and Saviour of the world and to establish his kingdom. In this chapter, we are going to talk about the reign of Christ when he returns to earth (the millennial reign). Many Christians have a sense that we are living during the closing of

the church age or the period of time right before Jesus returns to set up his literal kingdom on this earth. However, when you share with them what the Word of God says about preparing for that time, they don't seem to want to get ready. They act like Jesus' return is in the distant future. Even if the Lord does not come back and set up his kingdom during our lifetime, he is going to come back at some point. He is going to set up his kingdom. If he delays long enough, all of us are going to die. Once we die, the issue of qualifying to be part of his millennial reign is settled.

When you take your last breath, you will either be prepared or not. At that point, there isn't anything either you or anyone else can do about it. You have either made it or you didn't. You don't know if you have five minutes or fifty years to live. Now is the time to get ready. Each moment of every day, you need to know that you are ready. If the trumpet sounds and the Lord comes back, you need to be ready. If your life ends, you need to be ready.

It is easy to make assumptions. The devil is an expert at providing false doctrines that remove your responsibility to get ready. You can pervert the grace of God and use your liberty as an occasion for the flesh. (Galatians 5:13) You can put your faith in the "goodness" of God and believe that he's not going to let anyone miss his kingdom. If you believe that, you are sadly mistaken because the Word clearly says that the opposite is true.

Jesus gave us salvation as a free gift, and he has given each of us the opportunity to enjoy a relationship with him. God's children have the opportunity to rule with Christ, but <u>there are conditions</u> that go along with this opportunity. If we are foolish enough to ignore the conditions or reject the free gift God has given us, we cannot be in right standing with God. Jesus paid the price to remove our sins, but we have to humble ourselves, repent of our sins and receive his gift for our sins to be forgiven.

If your sin isn't forgiven, you are <u>not</u> in right standing

with God. All the promises in the Word of God are for those who are in right standing with him (in Christ). (2 Corinthians 1:20) This includes the opportunity to rule and reign with Christ in the millennial kingdom.

Suffering for Christ

2 Timothy 2:12 lists one condition that must be met for you to rule and reign with Christ. *"If we endure, we shall also reign with Him. If we deny and disown and reject Him, He will also deny and disown and reject us."* The King James Bible says, *"If we suffer, we shall also reign with him."* Regardless of the translation, it doesn't sound very comfortable! That's not exactly what we would choose as our inheritance. In fact, many seem to believe that if we have to endure or suffer anything, we must be missing God. This is a popular doctrine in America today. Yet the Word of God says **if we do not suffer (endure) with Christ, we are not going to reign with him.**

There are doctrines being taught today that indicate you don't have to suffer. In fact, you aren't supposed to endure anything negative. If you believe that doctrine, you'll refuse to suffer or endure hardship of any kind. You will also disqualify yourself from reigning with Christ.

Who do you think is the author of that doctrine? The devil! I'm not coming against any particular denomination or teaching, but I am resisting satan because he is the author of this lie! It is a way that seems right which hinders your walk with God.

Being an Overcomer

In Revelation 2:26-29, Jesus was speaking to John about being an overcomer. *"And he who overcomes (is victorious) and who obeys My commands to the [very] end [doing the works that please Me], I will give him authority and power over the nations; And he shall rule them with a sceptre (rod) of iron, as when earthen pots are broken in pieces, and [his power over them shall be] like that which I Myself have received from My Father; And I will give him the Morning Star. He who is able to hear, let him listen to and heed what the [Holy] Spirit says to the assemblies (churches)."*

The Lord clearly says that the one who overcomes will be given authority. **He who obeys God's commands to the very end and does the work that pleases him is an overcomer.** You must make sure you understand what Jesus means by "overcoming." Those who overcome will be given authority over the nations and will rule with a rod of iron just like Jesus will. Obviously, it will be in a lesser capacity, yet we will still rule over the nations with the same authority Jesus has from the Father.

In Revelation 3:20-22, Jesus was speaking to the church at Laodicea which was neither hot nor cold. *"Behold, I stand at the door and knock; if anyone hears and listens to and heeds My voice and opens the door, I will come into him and will eat with him, and he [will eat] with Me. He who overcomes (is victorious), I will grant him to sit beside Me on My throne, as I Myself overcame (was victorious) and sat down beside My Father on His throne. He who is able to hear, let him listen to and heed what the [Holy] Spirit says to the assemblies (churches)."*

This scripture lists the same prerequisite for ruling with Christ, which is that you overcome. **Being an overcomer means you <u>obey his commands to the very end</u> and <u>do what pleases him</u>.** Jesus had to meet this condition in order to sit at the right hand of his Father and we must meet the same condition to sit with Jesus on his throne.

<u>Jesus is Our Example</u>.

When Jesus was in the Garden of Gethsemene, he realized the suffering he would have to endure to carry out God's commands. He knew why he was sent to earth and what God required of him. He felt the pressure of the suffering and agony to the point that

"...His sweat became like great drops of blood falling down to the ground." (Luke 22:44b) He cried out to the Father, *"...if it be possible, let this cup pass away from me; nevertheless not as I will, but as thou wilt."* (Matthew 26:39b KJV)

God is love and he is compassionate, but there was no way to redeem man from sin without Jesus' death. **The Father didn't change his plan simply because Jesus cried out in his time of suffering.** Suppose Jesus had said, "This is not fair. I know you are God Almighty. Surely you can come up with a better way to redeem sinners than this! I am your first born Son and I should have rights." If he had talked himself out of going to the cross, would he be the King of Kings and Lord of Lords? No! **Jesus didn't resist when it came time to suffer in obedience to the Father.** He didn't refuse to endure suffering, because it was his Father's will. He obeyed, suffered and overcame, and he sat down at the right hand of the Father. The Father gave him authority over everything in heaven and in earth.

Jesus now says to us, "Those of you who have overcome and have been willing to suffer for my name's sake will reign with me, just as I rule and reign with my Father." **You may cry out in your suffering, but God isn't required to give you a way out.** Instead of making excuses, you can choose to obey what Jesus says even though you suffer for it. This will qualify you to sit down in Jesus' throne at his right hand.

Signs of Jesus' Return

There are many scriptures that explain the signs of the time before Jesus is coming back. We want to believe that we will have a major revival in the church all over the world. There will be a great falling away of the church instead. (2 Thessalonians 2:3) People's hearts will grow cold. (Matthew 24:12) People will be ever learning yet never come to the knowledge of the truth. (2 Timothy 3:7) People will say that right is wrong and wrong is right. (Isaiah 5:20) There will be great disrespect for authority and perversion of the most basic truths. (2 Timothy 3:1-5)

Getting Prepared as the Bride

I want to draw your attention to Ephesians 4:11-16. It is important for the Lord to prepare the church to be his bride. He gave the church five ministries: apostles, prophets, evangelists, pastors and teachers. He gave them to us for the *"...perfecting and the full equipping of the saints..."* (verse 12), for the work of the ministry of building up the body of Christ. The <u>body</u> is to develop to the point that we all reach a unity in the faith and a true knowledge of Jesus Christ as we seek to attain the measure of the stature of the fullness of Christ and become fitly joined together. It is his intent that we quit being like babies, tossed to and fro by every wind of doctrine, which includes the false teachings men use to draw us into error and lead us astray.

Ephesians 5:24-27 compares the relationship between Christ and his church to the marriage relationship. *"As the church is subject to Christ, so let wives also be subject in everything to their husbands. Husbands, love your wives, as Christ loved the church and gave Himself up for her, So that He might sanctify her, having cleansed her by the washing of water with the Word, That He might present the church to Himself in glorious splendor, without spot or wrinkle or any such things [that she might be holy and faultless]."*

This is the work Jesus is doing in the church! He is preparing a bride for himself and cleansing her by the washing of water with the Word. If you hear the Word of God and do not repent of the blemishes it exposed, were you cleansed? No, you were not! You can hear the word sent by God through an anointed minister to cleanse you, yet choose to stay as dirty, spotted and wrinkled as you were before. Hearing the word doesn't automatically make you clean. If you hear God speak to you and don't obey, you are only deceiving yourself.

The Lord is making sure we have access to the cleansing

water from the Bible, preaching and the Holy Spirit speaking directly to our hearts. All of this is designed to cleanse you and get you prepared as a bride ready for the Bridegroom. Matthew 25:1-13 explains that five virgins were foolish and five were wise. They all were potential brides, but when the Bridegroom came only five went into the marriage supper. Five did not go because they were foolish. **They were not ready.**

The church (synonymous with the bride) is described as being without spot, wrinkle, blemish or any such thing. (Ephesians 5:27 KJV) The question is, are you clean? Have you embraced the Word of God? Have you let his truths cleanse you of the spots, wrinkles and blemishes in your life?

Jesus didn't start getting his bride ready in our generation. He's been preparing his bride for hundreds of years. Every generation has included people who were without spot, wrinkle or blemish in their lives because they embraced the washing of water with the Word. They willingly accepted the chastening of the Lord and God dealt with them as sons. God prepared them as Jesus' bride and they did not compromise their righteousness.

There have also been people in past generations who weren't in right standing with God. They are still not in right standing with God. If they were found to be unrighteous when they died, they will be unrighteous when the resurrection comes.

At some point, the Father is going to tell Jesus that his bride is ready. We're looking forward to that event. Unfortunately, some believers are not ready. They are foolish. They are full of spots, wrinkles and blemishes. They don't seek God nor do they hunger and thirst after righteousness. They don't embrace the truth when it comes or repent of the sin it exposes. They believe the lie that it doesn't make any difference how you live your life. They think they can be in total rebellion when the Lord comes back and they will be raptured along with those who have prepared themselves (those who have oil in their lamps). In reality, they are going to end up being foolish virgins.

I don't know if you ever thought much about the number of foolish virgins, but the Bible didn't say that nine of the virgins went in and only one missed it. Half of them missed it. That is a very sobering thought. I don't know if that is a literal percentage or not, but it's important to notice that **half of them missed it even though they were all virgins**. All ten were looking for the Lord and waiting for him. They were believers, not lost people. That is a very serious parable you need to ponder on without any preconceived, denominational interpretation.

I mentioned earlier some of the signs that will take place before this age is completed. One major sign of Jesus' imminent return is that sin will abound more and more on this earth. The good news is that grace will much more abound for those of us who are seeking the Lord. (Romans 5:20) In addition, the antichrist is going to gain control of the entire earth. For a season he will enter into the temple at Jerusalem and rule over the earth. (Revelation 13:7) As he rules, great persecution will break forth on this earth. (Matthew 24:15-21) Most people are hoping that Jesus will come back to get them before the period of the antichrist's reign. Others realize it is possible that Jesus may appear halfway through the tribulation. Some scriptures give evidence that it may not occur until sometime past the middle of the tribulation. We all hope that Jesus does not wait until the end of the tribulation to return, because things will get progressively worse.

Whether Jesus comes at the beginning, middle or end of the seven year period of tribulation, the question is, "Will you be ready when he comes?" What good will it do you if the trumpet sounds <u>before</u> the tribulation begins and you aren't ready? Why would Jesus give us the parable of the foolish virgins if someone wasn't going to miss it? Why did he give that warning if it wasn't possible for someone who thought they were ready to be left behind? Jesus was speaking about people who were waiting for him, but they didn't make it. He did not listen to their excuses.

When they knocked at the door, he didn't open it. It was too late.

If you have made your robe white in the blood of the Lamb and have been confessing your sins and humbling yourself before God to receive forgiveness, Jesus continues to wash you and get out the spots and blemishes in your life. If you are in right standing with God through the blood, you are ready. If your lamp is filled with oil (symbolic of the Spirit), you can look for Jesus' return with great anticipation.

<u>Jesus' Return</u>

1 Corinthians 15:51-55, *"Take notice! I tell you a mystery (a secret truth, an event decreed by the hidden purpose or counsel of God). We shall not all fall asleep [in death], but we shall all be changed (transformed) In a moment, in the twinkling of an eye, at the [sound of the] last trumpet call. For a trumpet will sound, and the dead [in Christ] will be raised imperishable (free and immune from decay), and we shall be changed (transformed). For this perishable [part of us] must put on the imperishable [nature], and this mortal [part of us, this nature that is capable of dying] must put on immortality (freedom from death). And when this perishable puts on the imperishable and this that was capable of dying puts on freedom from death, then shall be fulfilled the Scripture that says, Death is swallowed up (utterly vanquished forever) in and unto victory. O death, where is your victory? O death, where is your sting?"*

When Jesus comes back for the bride he has prepared, she is going with him and will be with him as he returns to reign for a thousand years. It doesn't matter if you die in Christ before he returns. Your spirit remains alive. When the trumpet sounds, we will all be caught up with the Lord in the air. Our mortal bodies are going to be changed in the twinkling of an eye. We are going to put on immortal bodies that cannot die. They will have no pain and will not be limited in any way!

Let's look at 1 Thessalonians 4:15-18 which describes the

resurrection. *"For this we declare to you by the Lord's [own] word, that we who are alive and remain until the coming of the Lord shall in no way precede [into His presence] or have any advantage at all over those who have previously fallen asleep [in Him in death]. For the Lord Himself will descend from heaven with a loud cry of summons, with the shout of an archangel, and with the blast of the trumpet of God. And those who have departed this life in Christ will rise first. Then we, the living ones who remain [on the earth], shall simultaneously be caught up along with [the resurrected dead] in the clouds to meet the Lord in the air; and so always (through the eternity of the eternities) we shall be with the Lord! Therefore comfort and encourage one another with these words."*

We are going to meet the Lord in the air. For all eternity, we are going to be with him. We will see him face to face. Our family, friends and loved ones who have died in Christ will be resurrected. We will be caught up with them. We will get glorified bodies that never die, and at the same time we will come into the presence of our Lord! He will take us to the marriage supper of the Lamb that will take place in the new Jerusalem where the Father's throne dwells. He will throw a banquet for his Son and the bride, which includes all who were wise virgins. All those who have embraced the provision of the Lord to keep their robes white will be there.

The Marriage Supper of the Lamb

The marriage supper of the Lamb is described in Revelation 19:5-7. Let's look at the atmosphere of this party! *"Then from the throne there came a voice, saying, Praise our God, all you servants of His, you who reverence Him, both small and great! After that I heard what sounded like the shout of a vast throng, like the boom of many pounding waves, and like the roar of terrific and mighty peals of thunder, exclaiming, Hallelujah (praise the Lord)! For now the Lord our God the Omnipotent (the All-Ruler) reigns! Let us rejoice and shout for joy [exulting and triumphant]! Let us celebrate and ascribe to Him glory and honor, for the marriage of the Lamb [at last] has come, and His bride has prepared herself."* This is not going to be a quiet dinner. It is a celebration!

Notice that the Bride has prepared herself. She used what the Lord provided to get ready. She received the washing of water with the Word. She prepared herself by accepting the blood to keep her robe clean. Continuing in Revelation 19:8, *"She has been permitted to dress in fine (radiant) linen, dazzling and white-for the fine linen is (signifies, represents) the righteousness (the upright, just, and godly living, deeds, and conduct, and right standing with God) of the saints (God's holy people)."*

This robe is very significant. Jesus' bride is permitted to put on a robe of dazzling linen because she is holy, righteous, upright and godly in thought, word and deed. If you don't meet those conditions, will you be permitted to wear that robe? That is foolish thinking, but the devil will tell you that it doesn't make any difference if your robe is filthy. It doesn't matter because God loves you and he's going to marry you anyway. **If you believe that, you are dreaming!** Such a belief is not faith. It is a false assumption. The robe of righteousness will be given to those who qualify, which is the bride who has made herself ready.

Revelation 19:9 and 10, *"Then [the angel] said to me, Write this down: Blessed (happy, to be envied) are those who are summoned (invited, called) to the marriage supper of the Lamb. And he said to me [further], These are the true words (the genuine and exact declarations) of God. Then I fell prostrate at his feet to worship (to pay divine honors) to him, but he [restrained me] and said, Refrain! [You must not do that!] I am [only] another servant with you and your brethren who have [accepted and hold] the testimony borne by Jesus. Worship God! For the substance (essence) of the truth revealed by Jesus is the spirit of all prophecy [the vital breath, the inspiration of all inspired preaching and interpretation of the divine will and purpose, including both mine and yours]."*

At the time of the marriage supper, the earth is going to be in an uproar. Satan, through the antichrist, will be controlling this earth. He will be destroying everyone who doesn't receive the mark of the beast.

Once the bride leaves the earth, things get much worse. The Bible doesn't give a precise time as to how long the bride is with Jesus in the third heaven. At the most it is seven years, because at the end of the tribulation (which lasts for seven years), the bride comes back with Jesus as he comes to set up his kingdom on this earth. If he comes for the bride around the middle of the tribulation period, it will be about three and a half years. It could be that he won't come until even later. Whenever it is, at some point the bride will come back to earth with Jesus.

Preparing for the Millennial Reign

I am now moving forward to the time when Jesus will come back with his bride to set up his literal kingdom on this earth. Before he sets his kingdom up, he will first tear down the kingdom the antichrist has established. He will conquer those who are ruling and reigning on this earth. Let's continue in Revelation 19:11. *"After that I saw heaven opened, and behold, a white horse [appeared]! The One Who was riding it is called Faithful (Trustworthy, Loyal, Incorruptible, Steady) and True, and He passes judgment and wages war in righteousness (holiness, justice, and uprightness)."*

Is this not the Jesus who is called the Prince of Peace? He is the Prince of Peace and his peace will come upon this earth. He sent his servants to the earth for generations to try to get the people to make peace with him, but they rejected him repeatedly.

At this moment in time, Jesus will not be sitting passively on a donkey. He will be on a white horse as he declares war upon this earth. He will not be coming with peace but with a sword.

All of his ambassadors will have been withdrawn at the rapture.

Any time a nation is preparing to declare war on another nation, the first thing they do is cut diplomatic relationships and call their ambassadors back to their homeland. That is what Jesus will do first. Then he will be ready to subdue this earth and set up his kingdom.

When Jesus rode into Jerusalem on the donkey, the Bible described him as a Lamb being led to the slaughter, but at this point he will return as the Lion of the Tribe of Judah. Revelation 19:12-14, *"His eyes [blaze] like a flame of fire, and on His head are many kingly crowns (diadems); and He has a title (name) inscribed which He alone knows or can understand. He is dressed in a robe dyed by dipping in blood, and the title by which He is called is The Word of God. And the troops of heaven, clothed in fine linen, dazzling and clean, followed Him on white horses."* This is the bride I described earlier. We will follow the Lord on white horses. If these are literal white horses or if they are symbolic, I don't know. They are transportation, and they will get us from the third heaven back to the earth.

The world is not going to win this fight! There will be an invasion of the Lord and his bride upon this earth. Continuing in Revelation 19:15-17, *"From His mouth goes forth a sharp sword with which He can smite (afflict, strike) the nations; and He will shepherd and control them with a staff (scepter, rod) of iron. He will tread the winepress of the fierceness of the wrath and indignation of God the All-Ruler (the Almighty, the Omnipotent). And on His garment (robe) and on His thigh He has a name (title) inscribed, KING OF KINGS AND LORD OF LORDS. Then I saw a single angel stationed in the sun's light, and with a mighty voice he shouted to all the birds that fly across the sky, Come, gather yourselves together for the great supper of God."*

Note that only one angel cried out and all the fowls of the air around the world were brought into one place. The initial battleground is in the nation of Israel in an area called Armageddon (the valley of Megiddo). (Revelation 16:16) This is a large valley running through Israel and we know from Revelation 14:20 that once this battle starts, the destruction is so complete by the Lord that the blood of satan's army will be running to the depth of a horse's bridle.

Revelation 19:18 and 19, *"That you may feast on the flesh of rulers, the flesh of generals and captains, the flesh of powerful and mighty men, the flesh of horses and their riders, and the flesh of all humanity, both free and slave, both small and great! Then I saw the beast and the rulers and leaders of the earth with their troops mustered to go into battle and make war against Him Who is mounted on the horse and against His troops."*

This army will be led by the beast and the rulers of this earth. I think it is significant to note that typically when there is a war between nations, the high ranking officials who authorize the war rarely suffer personally. Many soldiers may die, but the rulers who start the war don't. In this battle, the rulers and all the people great and small will die.

Revelation 19:20 and 21, *"And the beast was seized and overpowered, and with him the false prophet who in his presence had worked wonders and performed miracles by which he led astray those who had accepted or permitted to be placed upon them the stamp (mark) of the beast and those who paid homage and gave divine honors to his statue. Both of them were hurled alive into the fiery lake that burns and blazes with brimstone. And the rest were killed with the sword that issues from the mouth of Him Who is mounted on the horse, and all the birds fed ravenously and glutted themselves with their flesh."*

The beast as well as the false prophet are seized and cast into the lake of fire. The rest of the army is destroyed by the sword coming out of the Lord's mouth. None of us sitting on our white horses do anything to fight. **The Lord destroys the entire army.**

Revelation 20:1-3, *"Then I saw an angel descending from heaven; he was holding the key of the Abyss (the bottomless pit) and a great chain was in his hand. And he gripped and overpowered the dragon, that old serpent [of primeval times], who is the devil and Satan, and [securely] bound him for a thousand years. Then he hurled him into the Abyss (the bottomless pit) and closed it and sealed it above him, so that he should no longer lead astray and deceive and seduce the nations until the thousand years were at an end. After that he must be liberated for a short time."*

Make sure you understand what is happening. In Israel, the false prophet will be doing all kinds of miracles and causing people to bow down to the statue of the beast who is sitting on the throne. This will be authorized and backed up by satan. These two are thrown into the lake of fire. They are not in the picture any more. Satan is not done yet, because God is not finished with his judgment. He is put in the Abyss (bottomless pit) where a seal is placed. He will be kept there for a thousand years while Jesus is ruling and reigning here on earth. The earth will be free from any satanic influence for the first time in thousands of years. Also, every military ruler or government that resisted the coming of the Lord has been removed or destroyed.

Jesus' Throne is Established

Revelation 20:4-6, *"Then I saw thrones, and sitting on them were those to whom authority to act as judges and to pass sentence was entrusted. Also I saw the souls of those who had been slain with axes [beheaded] for their witnessing to Jesus and [for preaching and testifying] for the Word of God, and who had refused to pay homage to the beast or his statue and had not accepted his mark or permitted it to be stamped on their foreheads or on their hands. And they lived again and ruled with Christ (the Messiah) a thousand years. The remainder of the dead were not restored to life again until the thousand years were completed. This is the first resurrection. Blessed (happy, to be envied) and holy (spiritually whole, of unimpaired innocence and proved virtue) is the person who takes part (shares) in the first resurrection! Over them the second death exerts no power or authority, but they shall be ministers of God and of Christ (the Messiah), and they shall rule along with Him a thousand years."*

We then move into the actual setting up of Christ's kingdom. He will set in place those who will judge the nations. 1 Corinthians 6:3 tells us that we will judge the angels. Those who qualify are going to rule with a rod of iron and they will also sit as judges over this earth under the authority of Christ. There is a lot of mystery about this and it would be nice if the Bible told us exactly what is going to take place during that time, but it doesn't. Jesus' kingdom will be set up and he will remove all resistance. He will disperse authority around the earth. Faithful saints will rule with him, but the Bible doesn't tell us exactly how this is going to work.

It doesn't matter if God's kingdom is functioning in the third heaven, in the new Jerusalem, on earth with Jesus and his throne for a thousand years or throughout eternity. It is still God's kingdom. When Jesus sets up his kingdom and establishes thrones for others to rule with him, the Father's will is going to be done on earth exactly as it is done in heaven.

There will still be human beings on this earth who don't have glorified bodies. It is significant that these people will not be influenced by satanic spirits. Satan cannot put thoughts in their minds or tempt and attack them. All the supernatural influences they had to deal with from the kingdom of darkness will not be present any longer. Every person who has been tormented, aggravated and tempted by the devil no longer has to deal with that power or influence. There won't be any false wonders or miracles performed by demonic spirits to deceive people.

It is important, with as much as we can see scripturally, to try to get a picture of what the millennium will be like. The earth will be free from any influence of satan. This is pretty unique in itself. It will also be without any corrupt government. Only the glorified saints of God will be ruling. Everyone else will have been removed from office.

Many times, we as Christians do not really understand the kingdom of God. Those of us who live in democracies have some rights that we value highly, but the democratic form of government will not exist in the kingdom of God. I'll give you an example. In America, we have separation of church and state. It is a big issue in our country that the church cannot be involved in government. When the Lord comes back, anything that is not of God will not be in the government. It will be just the opposite of the way it is now.

Matthew 13:41 and 42 was quoted previously, but I want to look at one particular thought, because I think it is very significant. It will help us get an idea of what it will be like in the kingdom of God when Jesus is ruling during his millennial reign.

"The Son of Man will send forth His angels, and they will gather out of His kingdom all causes of offense [persons by whom others are drawn into error or sin] and all who do iniquity and act wickedly, And will cast them into the furnace of fire; there will be weeping and wailing and grinding of teeth." In the King James Bible, this same verse says, *"...gather out of his kingdom all things that offend, and them which do iniquity."*

One thing we hold dear in America is the freedom of speech. We hold this so dearly, we will allow someone to blaspheme God, curse and say all kinds of profane, distasteful things to Christians. We now have the liberty to be completely offensive, but in the kingdom of God no one will have that freedom. When the Lord is in charge there will not be a vote.

For those of us who are children of God, it is going to start feeling a little more like heaven. Godly rule will be established and Jesus will set about restoring the nations. This world is going to turn around. It will go from the brink of destruction back to the original state of the Garden of Eden over a period of a thousand years. If we had honored God and yielded to his rule from the beginning, this is what the earth would have been like.

The End of the Millennial Reign

Revelation 20:7-15 describes the end of the one thousand year period when Christ's millennial reign is over. Verses 7 and 8, *"And when the thousand years are completed, Satan will be released from his place of confinement, And he will go forth to deceive and seduce and lead astray the nations which are in the four quarters of the earth-Gog and Magog-to muster them for war; their number is like the sand of the sea."*

As soon as satan is turned loose, some of the nations will immediately yield to him again. Even after having seen the difference in their lives under Christ's rule, they will still yield to satan as he leads the nations astray and gathers them for war against the Lord.

Verse 9, *"And they swarmed up over the broad plain of the earth and encircled the fortress (camp) of God's people (the saints) and the beloved city; but fire descended from heaven and consumed them."*

During the thousand year reign, Jesus has been in charge and the saints have been ruling with him. The Father is still in the new Jerusalem, but he is on his way to earth. At the end of the thousand years he arrives. He shows up with the new Jerusalem about the time satan is turned loose. As satan gathers up all the people and they come against Christ and his saints, fire comes down out of heaven and consumes them.

Revelation 20:10-15, *"Then the devil who had led them astray [deceiving and seducing them] was hurled into the fiery lake of burning brimstone, where the beast and false prophet were; and they will be tormented day and night forever and ever (through the ages of the ages). Then I saw a great white throne and the One Who was seated upon it, from Whose presence and from the sight of Whose face earth and sky fled away, and no place was found for them. I [also] saw the dead, great and small; they stood before the throne, and books were opened. Then another book was opened, which is [the Book] of Life. And the dead were judged (sentenced) by what they had done [their whole way of feeling and acting, their aims and endeavors] in accordance with what was recorded in the books. And the sea delivered up the dead who were in it, death and Hades (the state of death or disembodied existence) surrendered the dead in them, and all were tried and their cases determined by what they had done [according to their motives, aims, and works]. Then death and Hades (the state of death or disembodied existence) were thrown into the lake of fire. This is the second death, the lake of fire. And if anyone's [name] was not found recorded in the Book of Life, he was hurled into the lake of fire."*

Earlier, I talked about the beginning of the thousand year reign of Christ. The bride is called "blessed" because these particular believers are part of the first resurrection and on these the second death has no power. (Revelation 20:6) At the end of the one thousand years when the Father destroys the heavens and the earth, it is time for the white throne judgment. Everyone whose names are not found written in the Lamb's Book of Life will be thrown into the lake of fire. This is the second death. It is appointed for all of us to die once and after that there is the judgment. (Hebrews 9:27) Those who take part in the first resurrection will not experience the second death, because their names are written in the Lamb's Book of Life.

I want to close this chapter by looking at 1 Corinthians 15:20-24. *"But the fact is that Christ (the Messiah) has been raised from the dead, and He became the firstfruits of those who have fallen asleep [in death]. For since [it was] through a man that death [came into the world, it is] also through a Man that the resurrection of the dead [has come]. For just as [because of their union of nature] in Adam all people die, so also [by virtue of their union of nature] shall all in Christ be made alive. But each in his own rank and turn: Christ (the Messiah) [is] the firstfruits, then those who are Christ's [own will be resurrected] at His coming. After that comes the end (the completion), when He delivers over the kingdom to God the Father after rendering inoperative and abolishing every [other] rule and every authority and power."*

First, Christ was resurrected. Then all those who are part of Christ's bride are resurrected at his coming, which is the first resurrection. Jesus rules during the thousand year reign. Then comes the end as he delivers over his kingdom to God the Father. 1 Corinthians 15:25 and 26, *"For [Christ] must be King and reign until He has put all [His] enemies under His feet. The last enemy to be subdued and abolished is death."*

At the final white throne judgment, death, hell and the grave will be cast along with satan into the lake of fire. 1 Corinthians 15:27 and 28, *"For He [the Father] has put all things in subjection under His [Christ's] feet. But when it says, All things are put in subjection [under Him], it is evident that He [Himself] is excepted Who does the subjecting of all things to Him. However, when every thing is subjected to Him, then the Son Himself will also subject Himself to [the Father] Who put all things under Him, so that God may be all in all [be everything to everyone, supreme, the indwelling and controlling factor of life].*

The millennial reign of Christ will be a glorious time on the earth. I have only given a brief outline of that period of time. The joy of watching the earth flourish under the righteous rule of Christ and his bride will be awesome. If you are a child of God, don't miss the opportunity you have been given. Seek the kingdom above all else!

Chapter 4

The Final <u>Recorded</u> Stage of the Kingdom of God

It is obvious that we are living in the time when the kingdom of God operates in the spiritual realm. We have not yet reached the time for the establishment of Jesus' literal kingdom on the earth. At the end of the one thousand year reign, the Father will come to earth with the new Jerusalem. This will begin the final <u>recorded</u> stage of the kingdom of God.

1 Corinthians 15:24 says Jesus will deliver the kingdom to God the Father after all is subdued. Remember, Jesus was given the authority to reign until everything was brought into subjection to him, including the last enemy which is death.

Everything I am sharing about the kingdom of God is gleaned from various passages in the Word of God. The Bible doesn't give us all of the answers we would like to have about God's kingdom. It is a great mystery, but we can get some insight into what God does reveal. It is very important that we don't allow ourselves to come to conclusions that are not biblical. We must find clear statements from God's Word and let that settle it. There is nothing wrong with having a theory about what we think <u>may</u> happen, but we must be very careful we don't let theory replace what the Word actually says. We especially want to be very careful that we don't <u>change</u> anything the Bible says simply because it doesn't line up with our theory. If God had wanted us to know every detail, he would have explained it thoroughly.

<u>Final Recorded Events</u>

This particular chapter is about the final <u>recorded</u> stage of the kingdom of God, but it is not the final stage of the kingdom. As the millennial reign ends and the Father shows up in the new Jerusalem, the next scene in history is the white throne judgment. Revelation 20:11, "*Then I saw a great white throne and the One Who was seated upon it, from Whose presence and from the sight of Whose face earth and sky fled away, and no place was found for them.*"

Revelation 21:1, "*Then I saw a new sky (heaven) and a new earth, for the former sky and the former earth had passed away (vanished), and there no longer existed any sea.*" Isaiah 65:17 describes the same event. "*For behold, I create new heavens and a new earth. And the former things shall not be remembered or come into mind.*" In my Bible there is a footnote that says "a new heaven and new earth" actually means the entire universe. The Hebrew language has no single word to express the concept of the cosmos or universe, so heaven and earth are substituted. God is going to create a new universe and the former one will no longer be remembered.

As we move into this final recorded stage of the kingdom, only the saints will remain of those who inhabited the former earth. Satan and all demonic spirits will be gone. Everyone who was not a child of God will be gone. The children of God will have their glorified bodies at this point, and they will also have the mind of Christ.

2 Peter 3:10-14, "*But the day of the Lord will come like a thief, and then the heavens will vanish (pass away) with a thunderous crash, and the [material] elements [of the universe] will be dissolved with fire, and the earth and the works that are upon it will be burned up. Since all these things are thus in the process of being dissolved, what kind of person ought [each of] you to be [in the meanwhile] in consecrated and holy behavior and devout and godly qualities, While you wait and earnestly long for (expect and hasten) the coming of the day of God by reason of which the flaming heavens will be dissolved, and the [material] elements*

[of the universe] will flare and melt with fire? But we look for new heavens and a new earth according to His promise, in which righteousness (uprightness, freedom from sin, and right standing with God) is to abide. So, beloved, since you are expecting these things, be eager to be found by Him [at His coming] without spot or blemish and at peace [in serene confidence, free from fears and agitating passions and moral conflicts]."

If the manifestation of the kingdom of God is your hope, you ought to be living in such a way that you are without spot or blemish. You should have peace and be free from fears, agitating passions and moral conflicts because you are looking for the new heaven and new earth.

At this point, we are on the very threshold of moving into eternity where time as we know it ceases to exist. This is the conclusion of the ages where time has been marked. We will be living with our Father, and we need to get a picture of where we are at that time.

The New Jerusalem

I have already relayed the description of the new Jerusalem from Revelation. At the point when it arrives and is set down on the new earth, we will enter into a glorious era. The white throne judgment will be over. Nothing of the previous universe will remain except the children of God. We won't even remember what had existed previously.

Revelation 21:2-8, *"And I saw the holy city, the new Jerusalem, descending out of heaven from God, all arrayed like a bride beautified and adorned for her husband; Then I heard a mighty voice from the throne and I perceived its distinct words, saying, See! The abode of God is with men, and He will live (encamp, tent) among them; and they shall be His people, and God shall personally be with them and be their God. God will wipe away every tear from their eyes; and death shall be no more, neither shall there be anguish, (sorrow and mourning) nor grief nor pain any more, for the old conditions and the former order of things have passed away.*

And He Who is seated on the throne said, See! I make all things new. Also He said, Record this, for these sayings are faithful (accurate, incorruptible, and trustworthy) and true (genuine). And He [further] said to me, It is done! I am the Alpha and the Omega, the Beginning and the End. To the thirsty I [Myself] will give water without price from the fountain (springs) of the water of Life. He who is victorious shall inherit all these things, and I will be God to him and he shall be My son. But as for the cowards and the ignoble and the contemptible and the cravenly lacking in courage and the cowardly submissive, and as for the unbelieving and faithless, and as for the depraved and defiled with abominations, and as for murderers and the lewd and adulterous and the practicers of magic arts and the idolaters (those who give supreme devotion to anyone or anything other than God) and all liars (those who knowingly convey untruth by word or deed)–[all of these shall have] their part in the lake that blazes with fire and brimstone. This is the second death."

God makes it very clear as to who will be cast into the lake of fire and who will remain with him. The ones who overcome by the blood of the Lamb and the word of their testimony will inherit God's new creation. The cowards and those who will not overcome will have their place in the lake of fire, which is the second death.

The abode of God is going to be with men. He is going to wipe every tear away from our eyes. We will never die again and there will be no more sorrow or pain. Jesus says in John 14:2 that he is preparing a place for us in this glorious city.

Revelation 22:1-7 gives a further description of the new Jerusalem. *"Then he showed me the river whose waters give life, sparkling like crystal, flowing out from the throne of God and of the Lamb Through the middle of the broadway of the city; also, on either side of the river was the tree of life with its twelve varieties of fruit, yielding each month its fresh crop; and the leaves of the tree were for the healing and the restoration of the nations. There shall no longer exist there anything that is accursed (detestable, foul, offensive, impure, hateful, or horrible).*

But the throne of God and of the Lamb shall be in it, and His servants shall worship Him [pay divine honors to Him and do Him holy service]. They shall see His face, and His name shall be on their foreheads. And there shall be no more night; they have no need for lamplight or sunlight, for the Lord God will illuminate them and be their light, and they shall reign [as kings] forever and ever (through the eternities of the eternities). And he [of the seven angels further] said to me, These statements are reliable (worthy of confidence) and genuine (true). And the Lord, the God of the spirits of the prophets, has sent His messenger (angel) to make known and exhibit to His servants what must soon come to pass. And behold, I am coming speedily. Blessed (happy and to be envied) is he who observes and lays to heart and keeps the truths of the prophecy (the predictions, consolations, and warnings) contained in this [little] book."

Revelation 22:2 describes the tree that is on either side of the river coming out from the throne of God in the new Jerusalem. The leaves of this tree are for the healing of the nations, but what nations is God talking about? The former earth had many nations but it no longer exists. This healing is not for us, because we will not have any sickness or death in our glorified bodies. The impression is given that there are going to be some kind of beings who are susceptible to problems just as we are now. Apparently, they can come to the city and receive healing.

Nothing offensive will be allowed in the new Jerusalem. Why would God make this statement when everything offensive has already been cast into the lake of fire? It appears that there will be some people who will come to receive healing, yet any who are offensive won't be allowed into the city. This implies that there could be offensive things outside of the city.

Revelation 22:4 says that we can actually see God's face. In John 6:46, we are told that no man has ever seen the face of God the Father, but we are going to see him! The new Jerusalem has no night nor does it have any sun or moon, because the Lord is the light of the city. (Revelation 21:23)

God is the Creator

When I teach on any particular subject, I try to stay very close to what clear scriptures say. I don't theorize or guess at what might or might not happen, but I'm not ignorant of what God says. God is the Creator and he is going to create for us a whole new universe. He is going to live among us. 1 Corinthians 2:9 says that what God has prepared for those who love him has never even entered the heart of man. He has things prepared for us that we don't even know exist. There is a whole realm of the unknown that he is preparing.

The Lord is going to establish us as kings. Once he establishes us as kings, we will reign for eternity. There are going to be nations for us to rule and reign over. Since he is the Creator, what would hinder him from creating life on the new planets he has made? I don't know what size the new earth will be, but it might not be large enough for us to divide into enough individual kingdoms to rule over. Of course, God could decide to make the new earth a million times larger than the present one. The Bible simply doesn't say. He could also create a million other planets and establish life on each one.

Please hear what I am saying. I'm not saying that this is what God is going to do. I'm just saying **we shouldn't limit our faith about what God can do**. The Bible doesn't give details about all the things God will do or create when he makes new heavens and a new earth. The Bible does say that he is going to make us kings, and we are going to rule and reign for eternity. I don't believe we even have a glimpse of the magnitude of what God is going to do. As we move into the final recorded stage of the kingdom of God, we won't be governed by time as we know it today. That is hard to comprehend, but it is very exciting.

We have a glimpse of what is coming when Jesus comes back and what will happen after the thousand year reign, but what about now? We're here now. Jesus hasn't come back to set up his literal kingdom on this earth, but what does God have for us now? **He is God.** His kingdom is in effect now. I am his child now. If you are born again, you're his child now, so you are already a joint-heir with Jesus. We are citizens of the kingdom of God. Doesn't it make sense that there ought to be some benefits for us now? In the remainder of the book, we are going to look at what is available to us as children of God now and see how that relates to the kingdom of God.

Chapter 5

The Kingdom of God Now

I have touched on different aspects of the kingdom of God. In this chapter I am going to get into the kingdom of God <u>now</u>, which is the very essence of this book. We need an understanding of the kingdom of God as a whole. Regardless of which stage we are talking about, it is still God's kingdom. The kingdom of God, the kingdom of Christ, the kingdom of heaven, and the millennial kingdom are part of God's kingdom, and the rules are basically the same.

<u>God Doesn't Change</u>
This is an important point we need to remember at all times. **God is not man and he doesn't change.** The standards for his kingdom in the earth are the same as they are in heaven. In Matthew 6:9 and 10 (KJV), Jesus said to pray, *"...Our Father which art in heaven, Hallowed be thy name. Thy kingdom come. Thy will be done in earth, as it is in heaven."* The Lord made no distinction between the way the kingdom is operated in heaven and the way it is to be on earth. Most of us think of the millennial reign as when the Lord's kingdom will be here on earth, but what about the kingdom of God that is functioning on the earth now?

There are many promises in the Bible for God's children. Most people either believe the blessings are for the past or for the future, but they never seem to receive God's blessings <u>now</u>. Whenever revival has broken out in history, it was because somebody found out God has something for his people <u>now</u>. The Word of God is clear as to what is available to us as children of

God in his kingdom now. Every child of God has the Spirit of God living in them. Ephesians 1:13 and 14 say that when we are sealed by the Spirit, we receive the earnest of our inheritance. It is only a portion of what we will inherit. It is not the fullness of the Spirit that we are going to have in eternity, but it is much better than anything we had before.

The degree to which individual Christians are enjoying the Spirit who dwells in them varies greatly. You experienced the Holy Spirit coming into your heart when you were born into the kingdom of God. The fact that the Spirit came into you is proof that you are a child of God, but some of you stopped there and never went any farther. Others realized that the Spirit in you is the power of God. You accepted that power when the Holy Spirit came upon you. (Acts 1:8) Some of you have read 1 Corinthians 12 and realized the gifts of the Holy Spirit could manifest in you and you began to enjoy his presence in new ways.

Eternal Life

I share in the book, *My Sheep Hear My Voice*, that one of the first gifts you received when you were born into God's family was the gift of eternal life. (John 17:1-3) This gift means **you can actually know God in a personal, intimate way.** You can spend quality time with God in his presence, learn to communicate with him, and hear his voice so that you can actually get to know him. That is another level of flowing in the Spirit.

You can continually search the Bible for the promises that are available now. It is imperative that you meet the conditions to receive those promises in order to get them off the pages and into your life.

A Reminder

This is the approach I want you to take as we review the kingdom of God now. Don't lock yourself into what you "know" and refuse to be open to learn something new. Christians should always be open to go to another realm in the Spirit! We are never going to exhaust our inheritance in this life. We should never try to limit the blessings of God and the opportunities to know him better. We should always be hungering and thirsting after righteousness, yet rejoicing with contentment because we are already blessed! God promises that to those who have, more will be given. Never allow yourself to think you have arrived. No one has arrived. We are all seeking to come to the fullness of the measure of the stature of Christ. Even when we become teachers, we are still students.

The Manifestation of God's Kingdom by the Holy Spirit

The kingdom of God has always been with God. We know a little bit of what it is going to be like when Jesus comes back. We are looking forward to the time when the Father comes with the new Jerusalem. The disciples believed that Jesus was going to set up his kingdom when he lived on the earth two thousand years ago. Even though he tried to tell them he came to die, they could not hear it.

Jesus came to pay the price so that everyone past, present and future could have the gift of eternal life. He wants each of his children to know him in a very personal, intimate way and spend eternity with him.

Luke 17:20 and 21, *"Asked by the Pharisees when the kingdom of God would come, He replied to them by saying, The kingdom of God does not come with signs to be observed or with visible display, Nor will people say, Look! Here [it is]! or, See, [it is] there! For behold, the kingdom of God is within you [in your hearts] and among you [surrounding you]."*

Jesus' basic message was the kingdom of God. That is why on this occasion the Pharisees asked him, "When is the kingdom of God going to come?" Jesus said his kingdom was not coming with outward signs.

Think about this. When Jesus comes to set up his millennial

kingdom, are there going to be visible signs that appear at that time? Of course there are! He is going to come in the clouds on a white horse with his bride. (Revelation 19:11-14) There <u>are</u> going to be clear signs when he sets up the millennial reign, so in this passage he is obviously talking about what is available <u>now</u> in the spiritual realm. The kingdom is here <u>now</u>.

It was hard for the disciples to understand that Jesus had to leave them, but he said it was more expedient for him to do so. (John 16:7) They had the Saviour with them. How could it be better for him to leave? The Lord explained to them that the Father would send the Comforter (the Holy Spirit) to dwell in them. (John 14:16 and 17) They didn't understand why that would be better than having Jesus, but he wanted to have personal fellowship with each individual person. He couldn't do that with the constraints of a human body. While he was on earth, he was limited by his humanity. He had to return to the Father and send the Holy Spirit. Through the Spirit, he can personally come into every one of our hearts. He can live within us, fellowship with us intimately on a one-to-one basis, and be the literal Lord of our lives.

Again, I am talking about the move of the Holy Spirit. You will never fully understand the work of the Spirit in this life, but you can enjoy what you have received from him. It's wonderful to fellowship with God through his Spirit. Physically, the Father and the Son are in the third heaven. Jesus is sitting at the Father's right hand. It is the Spirit, the third part of the Trinity, who is here on earth. In John 14:23, Jesus said **if you love him and keep his commandments, he and the Father would come to fellowship with you**. They will set up their throne of authority within you. The Holy Spirit can manifest himself, the Father and the Son in your heart.

Every born again Christian receives the Holy Spirit to seal their salvation, but they don't automatically get fellowship with the Father and the Son. There are conditions for having that relationship. The gift of eternal life is your privilege to have the Godhead manifesting and ruling in your heart, but Jesus must be the Lord of your life for this to happen. **You must obey him because you love him.** That is the only condition for having an intimate relationship with the Lord. When you yield to his Lordship, the Spirit of God manifests within you and also surrounds you.

The Spirit in You Versus You being in the Spirit

The Bible talks about the Spirit being in you and you being in the Spirit. Many believers think these terms are synonymous, but they are not. When you have the Spirit of God in you, he gives you the power to bring your body under subjection and meet the conditions to be in him. **Getting in him is the key!**

This illustration about the difference between the Spirit being in you and you being in the Spirit may help you. Suppose a glass full of water represents me, and the water in the glass represents the Holy Spirit. I am filled with the Spirit (filled with water). He is in me. I can try to do what God says, but the enemy can attack my vessel (the glass). I can splash out a little of the Spirit and run satan off, but he always seems to be aggravating me. However, being in the Spirit is like being in an entire room filled with water. I can set my glass of water inside the room filled with water, and then the water is in me and also around me. Anyone outside the room can only see the water (the Holy Spirit). They can't get access to my "glass" without coming through the Spirit.

This is what living in the kingdom of God is all about. Not only is the Spirit within, he is also surrounding you. Satan can't get any access to your "glass" because you are in Christ. The Spirit in you and around you makes you "devil proof".

In that place of security, no weapon that is formed against you can prosper. (Isaiah 54:17) When you are in right standing with God, you are in the center of his will. That is the basic description of being in the kingdom of God now. Being in the Spirit, in

Christ or in the Vine are all synonymous with kingdom living. When you abide in the Vine, the fruit of the Spirit which includes love, joy, peace, patience, kindness, goodness, faithfulness, gentleness and self-control will manifest in you. (Galatians 5:22)

Every child of God has experienced living in his kingdom on occasion and we all loved it! I have never met a Christian who didn't love being in God's presence. The problem is, it seems to be a very fragile thing for most believers. Many times we aren't sure how we got in the Spirit, and we are less sure of what got us out. We spend our lives moving in and out of the kingdom, and we end up spending only a small portion of our lives actually abiding in God's presence.

Most Christians believe close fellowship with God is just a "honeymoon" period you get to enjoy when you are first saved. Then you get on with the reality of life and hang in there until the Lord comes back. During the millennial reign, you'll get to enjoy that fellowship again. **That is a lie from satan!** We have been given the opportunity to enjoy God's presence <u>now</u>.

One of the things that will happen during the close of the church age is the manifestation of the sons of God. God is getting his bride ready. She is going to be without spot, wrinkle or blemish. God's cleansing and preparation for fellowship with him are available now, but if you do not meet his conditions, you are going to be waving good-bye to those who are prepared to leave when the trumpet sounds. You are going to be one of the foolish virgins.

You have time to become wise! That is why this book was written. If you do not start understanding and walking in the principles of God now, you certainly will not be qualified to walk in them when the millennial reign comes. This is your training time, and now is the time to prepare to rule and reign with Christ for eternity.

Living in the Kingdom Now

Romans 14:17 gives a description of the kingdom of God now. *"[After all] the kingdom of God is not a matter of [getting the] food and drink [one likes], but instead it is righteousness (that state which makes a person acceptable to God) and [heart] peace and joy in the Holy Spirit."* The King James Bible puts it this way. *"For the kingdom of God is not meat and drink; but righteousness, and peace, and joy in the Holy Ghost."* In the natural, we are concerned about our basic needs, but that isn't what the kingdom of God is all about. The kingdom is right standing with God. It is having God's peace that passes all understanding and having the joy of the Lord, full and running over. If you are not in right standing with God and you don't have his peace and joy in your life, then **you are not living in the kingdom of God**. When you abide with God, you will feel his presence. **If you are obeying him because you love him and your life is filled with joy that is not affected by your external circumstances, you are living in God's kingdom now.**

Many of you studying this book have spent time living in the kingdom but you didn't even realize it. If you don't understand what you have already experienced, you are not likely to explore the other benefits God has made available to you. It is imperative that you realize that the kingdom of God is available to you now as a child of God. I also want you to understand what it takes to get into the kingdom and stay there, as well as what some of the benefits are. Many believers don't realize the basic benefits of living in God's kingdom. You have the right to abide there, but you must obey God's laws which control his kingdom.

Righteousness

There are conditions to living in the kingdom of God, so let's take some time to explore this further. Matthew 6:33 explains God's priorities. *"But seek (aim at and strive after) first of all His kingdom and His righteousness (His way of doing and being right), and then all these things taken together will be given you besides."*

One reason we never qualify to walk in the kingdom is that we really don't understand righteousness. Romans 3:10 says that no one is righteous. No person, in their own strength or abilities, can do anything to be in right standing with God. Only Jesus lived a righteous life. Only his blood can cleanse you from unrighteousness. It is available to cleanse the sins of the Adam nature so there is nothing to contaminate the Christ nature within. Right standing with God is simply "his way of doing and being right". (Matthew 6:33b) **Righteousness is not your opinion or my opinion of what is right, but what God says is right.** It is not what we think should be done, but what God says should be done. God says to make his ways and his righteousness our priority. When you seek God's kingdom and his righteousness above all else, everything else will be added to you.

The Earnest of Our Inheritance

What we have available now is an earnest of God's eternal kingdom. It is time to get prepared as Christ's bride. God is preparing his people to reign with him, but even though we do not yet have the fullness of what God has planned for us, the earnest that is available to us now is glorious! God's principles and standards are the same now as they will be for eternity.

Luke 7:28 says, *"I tell you, among those born of women there is no one greater than John; but he that is inferior [to the other citizens] in the kingdom of God is greater [in comparable privilege] than he."* Jesus, speaking of John the Baptist, is saying here that there is no one greater than John was. At the same time, the privileges of the least one in the kingdom of God are greater than the privileges John the Baptist had. There is no comparison between the privileges we have as believers with the Spirit of God living within us versus the time when Jesus' followers didn't have the Spirit resident within them.

What have you done with this great heritage? You have the Spirit of the living God residing in you at all times, yet most of you can't even imagine having a close relationship with him. The men and women of faith who believed God and looked for this promise never received it, but God has given it to us! (Hebrews 11:39 and 40) Yet we often act like God is trying to take something away from us. We let the devil rob us of our inheritance daily because we won't trust the One who saved us. We proclaim the omnipotence of God yet we won't trust him. **We think we are more wise than he is, so we continue to run our own lives and live without God's fellowship that is only available in his kingdom.**

The Fundamentals of Lordship

The reason most people have trouble with God's kingdom is that Jesus Christ is the literal, functional Lord of that kingdom. If you want to reduce the size of your congregation, start preaching Lordship. The hypocrites don't want anything to do with Lordship. When it comes down to allowing Jesus to function as Lord and make all the decisions in your life, most people don't begin to comprehend what that means. Asking Jesus to run your life doesn't even enter their minds, let alone choosing to take every thought captive to Christ for him to make the "call" as to whether it is from God, satan or self.

Kept From the Evil One by Abiding in the Spirit

In John 17:1-3, Jesus began his intercessory prayer by sharing about the gift of eternal life, which is that we can know the Father and the Son personally. Let's look at verses 15-21 of chapter 17 as Jesus is praying to the Father on our behalf. *"I do not ask that You will take them out of the world, but that You will keep and protect them from the evil one. They are not of the world (worldly, belonging to the world), [just] as I am not of the world. Sanctify them [purify, consecrate, separate them for Yourself, make them holy] by the Truth; Your Word is Truth. Just as You sent Me into the world, I also have sent them into the world. And so for their sake and on their behalf I sanctify (dedicate, consecrate) Myself, that they also may be sanctified (dedicated, consecrated, made holy) in the Truth.*

Neither for these alone do I pray [it is not for their sake only that I make this request], but also for all those who will ever come to believe in (trust in, cling to, rely on) Me through their word and teaching, That they all may be one, [just] as You, Father, are in Me and I in You, that they also may be one in Us, so that the world may believe and be convinced that You have sent Me."

The Lord did not pray that God would take us out of this world, but that the Father would keep us from the evil one. He also prayed that the Father would sanctify us, which means to set us apart or separate us unto God. Jesus brought the good news that we can live in the world without being contaminated by it.

When Jesus returned to the Father, he sent back the Holy Spirit as our Comforter, so that they could be <u>in you and around you</u>. Acts 17:28a (KJV) says, *"For in him we live, and move, and have our being..."* Kingdom living <u>now</u> is about <u>being in God</u> so he is around you as well as within you. It is in that place of security that you can have the peace that passes all understanding. How can anything threaten you when you are in God?

<u>How to Walk in the Spirit</u>

Most Christians aren't sure if God is on their side. They don't know if God is pleased with them or not. However, if you are dwelling in the presence of God and you know you are in right standing with him, you can boldly say, "If God be for me, who can be against me?" The only condition for enjoying this promise is remaining uncompromisingly righteous.

You move into right standing with God by humbling yourself and accepting what Jesus did on the cross to pay for your sins.

From that point, all you have to do is walk with God and stop submitting to your sinful nature. If you do make a mistake and sin, immediately confess your sin and repent. Jesus is faithful and just to forgive your sin and cleanse you from all unrighteousness.

In Galatians 5:16, Paul shares a critical key to walking in the Spirit. If you walk in the Spirit, you cannot walk in the flesh at the same time. Paul had to learn how to abide in God's presence just as we must learn. In Paul's early years of ministry he had a heart after God, but sometimes he did things he didn't want to do. There was a war going on between his flesh and the Spirit. His flesh was still alive and it continued to hinder him, even though in his heart he really wanted to obey God. (Romans 7) Paul also shared in Colossians 3:5 that we are to mortify (kill) our flesh by refusing to submit to it. God helped Paul overcome his flesh by supplying the sufficient grace needed to get the job done.

It doesn't make any difference how many flaws you may have. If you will humble yourself and move into God's kingdom, yield to his Lordship and learn to stay in the Spirit, he will give you enough grace to cover your sins. **God does not try us beyond what we are able to endure, but with every temptation he will make a way of escape.** (1 Corinthians 10:13) He will deal in our lives at the level we are able to handle. He will cover the things that are not to be dealt with at the current time. His grace will keep us in right standing with him.

Paul stated in Romans 8:1 that there is no condemnation for those who are in Christ Jesus and do not walk after the flesh but after the Spirit. **All sin is condemned in the flesh.** (Romans 8:3) When you get into the Spirit, there is no condemnation! Every time Paul got in the flesh, there was nothing but condemnation. He was wise enough to give us some insight into what it is to really be in the Spirit. Today, many believers say, "I am in the Spirit," but there isn't any fruit to prove it. Those who are truly in the Spirit do not walk after the flesh!

How can you be walking in the Spirit if you are not in fellowship with God and hearing his voice? You must be able to communicate with him and also obey what he is speaking to you. That is the true evidence of walking in the Spirit. You can't be in the flesh and in the Spirit at the same time. Again, look at what Galatians 5:16 says. *"But I say, walk and live [habitually] in the [Holy] Spirit [responsive to and controlled and guided by the Spirit]; then you will certainly not gratify the cravings and desires of the flesh (of human nature without God)."* This is a very clear and simple statement. If you walk and live habitually in the Spirit by letting him control and guide you, you will <u>certainly not</u> satisfy the cravings and desires of the flesh.

If you haven't read my first book, *My Sheep Hear My Voice*, you should plan to read it very soon. It teaches the basics of how to walk in the Spirit. It gives detailed, clear instructions on how to yield to and be controlled by the Spirit of God and how to abide in Christ. It explains how to habitually walk with God and stop yielding to the desires of the flesh. You must do this if you want to enjoy consistent kingdom living. God tells us how to walk in habitual obedience in Proverbs 3:5 and 6. *"Lean on, trust in, and be confident in the Lord with all your heart and mind and do not rely on your own insight or understanding. In all your ways know, recognize, and acknowledge Him, and He will direct and make straight and plain your paths."*

You begin by deciding to trust the Lord with all your heart. You discipline yourself to quit leaning to your own understanding, which is your carnality and your way of doing things. You must stop being lord of your life and instead acknowledge the Lord in all your ways. Then he will direct your paths. If you obey God's directions for the simple reason that you love him, you are sowing love into God. You will reap love back from him and start building a love relationship with him. You will learn how to stay in the Spirit, which means you will be living consistently in the kingdom of God.

Once Jesus is the literal, functional Lord of your life, this will become a way of life. Then you can start enjoying all the other benefits of kingdom living that will be described later on in this book. If you don't believe and receive this as part of the earnest of your inheritance, you have already been robbed by satan. 2 Corinthians 1:20 says that all the promises of God are "yes" but they are conditional on you being in Christ (in the kingdom).

You can't live in the world God has already condemned and enjoy the benefits of kingdom living. You have to come out of the world and move into God's kingdom. God's kingdom covers the entire earth. No matter where you go, you can reside in God's kingdom and enjoy its benefits.

Set your heart to believe that the kingdom is available to you now. As we continue through this book, we will start looking at what is available to you in the kingdom of God.

Chapter 6

Why Do We Need the Kingdom Now?

In John 17:15, Jesus prayed that the Father would not take us out of the world, but that he would keep us from the evil one. The only way we can be protected from the enemy and his kingdom (which is in this world) is to be in a kingdom he cannot access. There are many nations in the world, and satan has access to every one of them. In fact, he has access to everything <u>natural</u> on the face of this earth.

In the spiritual realm, there are only two kingdoms: the kingdom of darkness and the kingdom of light. The devil has access to the kingdom of darkness everywhere it operates in the earth. The only place he does not have access is the kingdom of God. God's kingdom, which functions throughout the earth, is the only place of security for a Christian. This security is one of the many reasons we need to abide in the kingdom of God now. When Jesus prayed for God's children in John 17, he asked for their protection from the evil one. We are here now and so is the devil. He is trying to destroy you and me <u>now</u>. His goal has always been to destroy God's children who are living on this earth. We can only be protected from the enemy by abiding in the kingdom of God which is available <u>now</u>.

There was a time when Lucifer lived in the kingdom of God in the third heaven, but he was removed because he wouldn't stay yielded to God. He tried to usurp authority over God. (Isaiah 14:12 and 13) If you do the same thing the devil did, you will also be removed from the kingdom of God. As soon as you decide to exalt yourself above God and take over the lordship of your life, you will no longer feel God's peace and joy or the Holy Ghost around you. You will, however, sense the devil attacking you because he has gotten access to you. When you move into the flesh, you are "of the world". It doesn't matter to what level you are yielding to the devil or your flesh. If Jesus is not lord of your life, satan has access to you because you are in his kingdom. The only way to get back into the kingdom of God is to repent and yield yourself to God again.

"Work Out" Your Salvation

In Philippians 2:12b, Paul talks about working out our salvation with fear and trembling. It is important that this verse not be taken out of context, so let's look at what this really means by examining the whole passage. Paul is elaborating on Jesus' humility before God. Because Jesus obeyed unto death, God highly exalted him by making him King of Kings and Lord of Lords. God has commanded that every knee will bow and every tongue will confess that Jesus is Lord.

Philippians 2:9-16, *"Therefore [because He stooped so low] God has highly exalted Him and has freely bestowed on Him the name that is above every name. That in (at) the name of Jesus every knee should (must) bow, in heaven and on earth and under the earth, And every tongue [frankly and openly] confess and acknowledge that Jesus Christ is Lord, to the glory of God the Father. Therefore, my dear ones, as you have always obeyed [my suggestions], so now, not only [with the enthusiasm you would show] in my presence but much more because I am absent, work out (cultivate, carry out to the goal, and fully complete) your own salvation with reverence and awe and trembling (self-distrust, with serious caution, tenderness of conscience, watchfulness against temptation, timidly shrinking from whatever might offend God and discredit the name of Christ). [Not in your own strength] for it is God Who is all the while effectually at work in you [energizing and creating in you the power and desire], both to will and to work for His good pleasure and satisfaction and delight.*

Do all things without grumbling and faultfinding and complaining [against God] and questioning and doubting [among yourselves], That you may show yourselves to be blameless and guileless, innocent and uncontaminated, children of God without blemish (faultless, unrebukable) in the midst of a crooked and wicked generation [spiritually perverted and perverse], among whom you are seen as bright lights (stars or beacons shining out clearly) in the [dark] world, Holding out [to it] and offering [to all men] the Word of Life, so that in the day of Christ I may have something of which exultantly to rejoice and glory in that I did not run my race in vain or spend my labor to no purpose."

This godly standard is in effect <u>now</u>. Many times God gives us a standard we are supposed to obey, but we would like it to be in effect in the past or believe it applies to the future. We try to make some excuse as to why we cannot do it now. Paul is instructing us to live in such a way that we are lights to the nations because we are blameless <u>now</u>. We are to be blameless, guileless, innocent and uncontaminated children of God without blemish and faultless in the midst of a wicked, spiritually perverted generation. This is not a description of believers who have been raptured. We are to be in this condition **<u>now</u>**. Verse 14 says we are to do everything without grumbling, faultfinding and complaining against God. Quit questioning and doubting God and get busy walking in his righteousness!

Philippians 2:12 says to work out, cultivate, carry out to the goal and truly complete your own salvation. That seems a bit puzzling at first glance. The King James Bible says, *"Work out your own salvation with fear and trembling."* I thought Jesus <u>gave</u> us salvation. How can we <u>work out</u> our salvation? This seems to be confusing because we know we are saved by grace through faith, not of works lest any man should boast. (Ephesians 2:8 and 9) Salvation is a gift of God, so why is he telling us to work it out? If we're going to work out our salvation daily, then it would seem that we might have something to boast about. It seems confusing, so most of us simply read over this and go on.

It becomes clear when you realize that the word *work* used in Philippians 2:12 differs from all the other Greek words that are translated into *work* in the New Testament. This is the only place this particular meaning is used. It has a different definition than what we would typically define as *work*. It means "to do work fully, i.e. accomplish; by implication to finish, fashion:-cause, do (deed), perform, work(out)". (Strong's #2716) The ultimate end of our salvation is that we are rescued and delivered from sin. The word *salvation* means "rescue or safety (physically or morally);-deliver, health, salvation, save, saving". (Strong's #4991)

Being Rescued and Kept Safe

I want to focus on the terms, "rescuing ourselves" and "safety", since these are two basic meanings of salvation. From whom do we need to be rescued and kept safe? The devil. The devil wants to destroy us. He wants to take us to hell with him, and he wants us to spend eternity in the lake of fire. That is where each one of us was destined to go, because we have all sinned and come short of the glory of God. However, when we accepted what Jesus did on the cross, he rescued us. When we go back to the Father and get our glorified bodies, that is the culmination of our salvation. From that point on, the devil has no more access to us. The Father is going to cast him into the lake of fire and we will not have to deal with him anymore.

But what about now? When you were born again, Jesus forgave all your sins. Did you not get rescued at that point? Yes, we were all prisoners of satan and God rescued us! The problem is that many of us have been kidnapped repeatedly since then. The devil tricks us and binds us up time and time again. When we cry out to God, he rescues us once again. How many times have you been rescued? You need to work out and walk out your salvation daily! **You need to stay rescued!**

The second part of salvation is "safety". The Father transferred you out of the kingdom of darkness and into the kingdom of his Son. (Colossians 1:13) It is in the kingdom of light (the kingdom of God now) that you have the safety of your salvation.

The problem is, many believers aren't smart enough to burn their passports to the old kingdom. They keep crossing the border and going back into darkness again. The first thing you know, they are entangled again with sins and weights until they are miserable. They have to be rescued again.

This scripture is telling us to cultivate the safety we have received. God wants us to move into his kingdom and then live and move and have our being in him. God intends for us to grow up in his kingdom and become instruments of righteousness and vessels of honor that he can use for his glory. It is in the kingdom that we develop our salvation and learn to quit grumbling all the time. As a result, we become blameless, guileless, innocent and uncontaminated.

How can you be uncontaminated when you live in a contaminated world? The only place of safety is the kingdom of God. This is part of your salvation. You would have to wait until death or the rapture to be rescued if the kingdom of God wasn't here now.

What about every believer who has lived for the last two thousand years? How did they survive? Think about all the precious saints of God who never denied Christ. Some were martyrs. They submitted to every kind of abominable torture you can imagine, yet they never denied Christ. Where did they ever get enough power to do that? From the kingdom of God within them. No matter what was done to them, their souls could not be destroyed. (Hebrews 11)

God gives his children power! If he calls you to be a martyr, he will give you the power to lay down your life. He also gives you the power to keep your life so that no one can take it. All these provisions are in the kingdom of God.

Fellowship with God Now

There is nothing more precious about God's kingdom now than the fact that we can fellowship with our Father and get to know him. We don't have to wait until we die and go to heaven to have fellowship with him. There is much available to us in the earnest of our inheritance. We need it <u>now</u>. We need our Father <u>now</u>. We need his love <u>now</u>. We need to be protected <u>now</u>. We need to be empowered <u>now</u>, and we need the earnest of our inheritance to survive <u>now</u>. **All of God's promises for us are in his kingdom <u>now</u>.**

Chapter 7

What Are the Conditions for Living in the Kingdom Now?

<u>You Must Be Born Again</u>
John 3:3-5 lists the first condition for living in the kingdom of God <u>now</u>. *"Jesus answered him, I assure you, most solemnly I tell you, that unless a person is born again (anew, from above), he cannot ever see (know, be acquainted with, and experience) the kingdom of God. Nicodemus said to Him, How can a man be born when he is old? Can he enter his mother's womb again and be born? Jesus answered, I assure you, most solemnly I tell you, unless a man is born of water and [even] the Spirit, he cannot [ever] enter the Kingdom of God."*

Jesus is telling Nicodemus that unless a man is born again, he will <u>never</u> enter the kingdom of God. The most basic qualification for living in God's kingdom is being born into the family of God. Some day we are going to enter into the new Jerusalem where we will spend eternity. The only people living there will be God's children. Many people haven't thought about that. The first condition for ruling and reigning with Christ throughout eternity is becoming one of God's children. God created his kingdom for his family. The Lord said in John 14:2 that he was going to prepare a place for God's children. The basic requirement to live in the kingdom of God now (or at any time in the future) is that you be born again.

In our day and time, there are millions of "professing Christians" around the world who have never been born again. There are entire denominations that don't even preach salvation.

Many of those groups would scoff at someone who says they are born again. Yet Jesus told Nicodemus that unless you are born again, you will never enter into his kingdom. It would be foolish to ignore such an explicit warning from the Son of God himself.

Many people reject the whole concept of being born again because it is foolishness to their minds. They can't understand the concept. Nicodemus was a very educated man yet he immediately asked the question, "How can I be born again? Can an old man enter into his mother's womb and be born again?" He had no understanding of the spiritual realm.

Every person who is a child of God knows the change they experienced when they were born again. If you really want to walk with God in his kingdom, you cannot afford to ignore this step. Study the Word and find out what it takes to become a child of God. Unless you meet God's conditions for being born again, you will never be able to enjoy the other blessings from God.

You can <u>never</u> enter God's kingdom if you are not born again, but **being born again does not automatically guarantee that you will abide in God's kingdom now**. This is where many believers get into error, because they assume that a salvation experience automatically gives them the ability to <u>live</u> in God's kingdom.

<u>Come As a Child</u>

In Luke 18:16b and 17, the people were bringing their children to Jesus. The disciples rebuked some of the parents for bringing them, but the Lord replied, *"...Allow the little children to come to Me, and do not hinder them, for to such [as these] belongs the kingdom of God. Truly I say to you, whoever does not accept and receive and welcome the kingdom of God like a little child [does] shall not in any way enter it [at all]."* Unless your attitude toward the kingdom is the same as a little child's, you will never enter into it.

This is a very important point. Little children have the ability to trust their parents without having proof that the parents are trustworthy. **A small child will trust his or her parents without question.**

Jesus is saying in these scriptures that this is the attitude you should have toward him. **You must have a child-like attitude toward God and his kingdom by totally trusting him with all your heart.** Many times we release our faith into everything but God. We also distrust God because of all the people in our lives who haven't been trustworthy. There is only one problem with that. **God is trustworthy**. He's been proving his faithfulness for thousands of years.

Trust the Lord with All Your Heart

The first part of Proverbs 3:5 and 6 say to trust in the Lord with all your heart. That is another basic condition for living in the kingdom of God. You can humble yourself at any given moment and trust God with all of your heart. If you trust him, seek his kingdom and repent of any sin in your life, you can come into the kingdom of God. You can be in the presence of God, and it is wonderful.

Every real child of God has been in the kingdom of God on certain occasions. The question is, where do you live? Is the kingdom a place you visit occasionally? Do you look forward to Jesus coming back so you can live in his kingdom all the time? **The kingdom of God is here now, and you can live in it all the time now if you meet the conditions.** You have to be born again and you have to come as a little child. You must trust the Lord with all your heart.

You may wonder what it means to trust the Lord with all your heart. The opposite of trusting God with all of your heart is trusting yourself. You have to do the second part of Proverbs 3:5 (KJV), which says, *"...lean not unto your own understanding."* Leaning to your own understanding is trusting yourself. It's having faith in you. It is being lord of your life and directing your life, rather than trusting God with all your heart, acknowledging him and letting him direct you. If you are being lord of your life, leaning to your reasoning and directing your life, you disqualify yourself from living in the kingdom of God now. Even though you may be born again, you still cannot <u>live</u> in God's kingdom. You may humble yourself from time to time and come like a little child when you are desperate. God will grab you up in his arms, but too often you move right back out on your own again.

<u>Jesus is Lord</u>

One of the primary conditions for living in the kingdom of God now is recognizing Jesus Christ's right to be Lord of that kingdom. Everyone is commanded to bow the knee and recognize Jesus Christ as Lord. All real Christians know this truth in their hearts. You cannot be born again without instinctively knowing that he is your Lord.

The Word of God says every knee will bow and every tongue will confess that he is Lord. (Romans 14:11) When Jesus returns, he is going to rule with a rod of iron. People will have no choice but to bow before him. He will set up his literal kingdom and eliminate anyone who resists his authority. All people will bow the knee at that time, but now you have a choice.

We as Christians call Jesus "Lord" and say we want to live in his kingdom. Yet when he says to bow our knees to him and submit, we resist him. We profess that we want to spend eternity with the Lord. **We praise him and tell lost people that Jesus is Lord, yet when it's time for <u>us</u> to submit, we resist him.** We look for excuses and try to justify our rebellion, but there is no getting around it.

If you aren't bowing your knee on a daily basis to his Lordship and acknowledging him in all your ways, you are in rebellion. It is as simple as that. You can cover it up and lie to yourself, but on the day of judgment, the hidden things of darkness will be brought to light. (1 Corinthians 4:5) You are resisting the Lord if you refuse to bow your knee to him. You can't plead ignorance because your pastor doesn't teach this. You are commanded by God to study to show yourself approved a workman that need not be ashamed, rightly dividing the word of truth. You are commanded to seek God with all your heart. You are called to hunger and thirst so that you will be filled. (Matthew 5:6)

If I can choose to bow my knee to God, I can also choose to stand back up again. I have a free will and I can choose to bow my knee or not. I can rebel against God like I did for years or I can humble myself before God and accept him as Lord in my life. Anyone who has really submitted to the Lord will tell you that life is much better when he is Lord.

1 Peter 5:5b tells us that God resists the proud but he gives grace to the humble. In verse 6, Peter goes on to say, *"Therefore humble yourselves [demote, lower yourselves in your own estimation] under the mighty hand of God, that in due time He may exalt you."* The proud are those who refuse to humble themselves before God. They think they are smarter than God, so they direct their own lives through their reasoning and understanding. The humble are those who recognize that Jesus is Lord. He is the one who has the authority and power to make us what God wants us to be. He's the one who has access to release all the promises that are our heritage. He has the plan for our lives.

These are powerful scriptures and you would be wise to study the whole fifth chapter of 1 Peter. God's motive for wanting you to humble yourself and yield to his Lordship is very simple. In due season, he wants to exalt you. Everywhere I go in the world, I find believers who resist God. They don't trust God, because they are afraid he will take something good away from them and give them something bad. Most would not admit that if you ask them face to face, but their lives say it.

Many of you don't trust God and you won't believe his word, but you will trust the devil and believe what he says. The devil will tell you that what is good is bad and you believe him. He will tell you that what is bad is good and you believe him. God will tell you what is good and you won't believe him. He'll tell you what is bad and you won't believe him. We have all done foolish things in our lives, including myself, but that is the wonderful thing about repentance. **You can quit believing the devil and start trusting God with all your heart.**

Being a Disciple

Matthew 16:24-26 explains the basics of what it takes to be Jesus' disciple. *"Then Jesus said to His disciples, If anyone desires to be My disciple, let him deny himself [disregard, lose sight of, and forget himself and his own interests] and take up his cross and follow Me [cleave steadfastly to Me, conform wholly to My example in living and, if need be, in dying, also]. For whoever is bent on saving his [temporal] life [his comfort and security here] shall lose it [eternal life]; and whoever loses his life [his comfort and security here] for My sake shall find it [life everlasting]. For what will it profit a man if he gains the whole world and forfeits his life [his blessed life in the kingdom of God]? Or what would a man give in exchange for his [blessed] life [in the kingdom of God]?"*

Your soul was created to spend eternity with God. If you refuse to trust him, you are giving up the opportunity to abide in his kingdom now as well as in the future.

Continuing in Matthew 16:27 and 28, *"For the Son of Man is going to come in the glory (majesty, splendor) of His Father with His angels, and then He will render account and reward every man in accordance with what he has done. Truly I tell you, there are some standing here who will not taste death before they see the Son of Man coming in (into) His kingdom."* Every disciple who was with Jesus at that time is dead, yet the Lord said that some of those standing with him would not die until they saw the Son of Man coming in his kingdom. That happened on the day of Pentecost. That's why it was more expedient for Jesus to go back to the Father. He sent the Comforter to dwell with us and be in us.

Take Up Your Cross

God has laid out the conditions for living in his kingdom now. You must take up your cross and follow the Lord, which simply means you acknowledge him in all your ways. He will direct your paths as you obey because you love him and recognize his right to be Lord. Anything you may give up for his sake, you will receive a hundred fold in this life (with persecutions) and in the world to come, eternal life. (Mark 10:29 and 30) Do you remember why God wants you to humble yourself? So that he can exalt you. God wants to make you the head and not the tail. (Deuteronomy 28:13) He wants to make you more than a conqueror. (Romans 8:37) He wants to make you a king and priest according to Revelation 1:6. He wants to make you a vessel of honor in his house. (2 Timothy 2:20 and 21)

There are conditions for receiving these promises and the Lord knows all the conditions. He alone has the power and wisdom to bring those promises into being. He wants to be in charge so he can bless his children. **The simplicity of walking with God is denying yourself, taking up your cross and following him.** Humble yourself as a little child, recognize his right to be Lord, get off the throne and start acknowledging God in all your ways. Let him direct your paths.

Bearing Good Fruit

Matthew 6:33 (KJV) says, *"But seek ye first the kingdom of God, and his righteousness, and all these things shall be added unto you."* We need food and shelter, but the Lord is saying to get our priorities in the right order. The number one priority is seeking the kingdom of God and his righteousness, which is being in right standing with God. This righteousness is only found in Christ. God promises that if we make him our first priority, all of our needs will be added to us.

In God's kingdom, you are known by your fruit. **Not everyone who says "Lord, Lord" will enter the kingdom of heaven, but rather <u>he who does the will of the Father</u>**. (Matthew 7:21) Every child of God wants to be part of God's kingdom, but Jesus himself placed this condition on those who would enter the kingdom of heaven.

It is very important for us to be able to communicate with our Father, and it is crucial for us to develop a life of obedience to him. Like Jesus, we are not to seek or consult our own will but only seek to do the good pleasure of our Father in heaven.

Very few Christians examine themselves and admit that they are acting wickedly when they disregard God's commands. You can get into the habit of hearing the Word of God and being convicted by the Holy Spirit yet disregarding the word and continuing in sin. You know that you ought to repent and obey, but you disregard the Word of God that applies to your daily life because it isn't what you want to do. You may have been taught that there is no consequence as long as you say, "Lord, I'm sorry for all the bad things I did all week." You continue to disregard what God has said in your life and refuse to acknowledge your wickedness.

The Lord says in Galatians 6:7 (KJV), *"Be not deceived; God is not mocked: for whatsoever a man soweth, that shall he also reap."* God is looking at your fruit. What you do on a daily basis produces fruit, and it's either good or bad fruit in the eyes of God. **If you want to enter into and live in the kingdom, you are required to do the will of the Father.** You must also have a relationship with God and get to know him on a personal basis. The great apostle Paul even said, *"But I keep under my body, and bring it into subjection: lest that by any means, when I have preached to others, I myself should be a castaway."* (1

Corinthians 9:27 KJV) God continued to approve Paul on the condition that he kept doing the will of the Father.

Does the Lord <u>know</u> you? Do you have a personal relationship with him? If not, he will reject you. Matthew 7:24-27, *"So everyone who hears these words of Mine and acts upon them [obeying them] will be like a sensible (prudent, practical, wise) man who built his house upon the rock. And the rain fell and the floods came and the winds blew and beat against that house; yet it did not fall, because it had been founded on the rock. And everyone who hears these words of Mine and does not do them will be like a stupid (foolish) man who built his house upon the sand. And the rain fell and the floods came and the winds blew and beat against that house, and it fell-and great and complete was the fall of it."*

The Word has a way of making things pretty clear. That's why a lot of people don't read their Bibles. It is too plain. I hear a lot of people say, "I can't understand the Bible." All you need to do is find a scripture in which Jesus is giving clear, practical instructions on how to walk with him. Those verses are not hard to understand. Many believers prefer to find a "mystery" that is confusing enough that they have an excuse for not obeying it.

The Lord will examine your fruit to determine what kind of tree you are, whether good or bad. He isn't interested in what kind of works you have done. All miraculous works are done by God anyway. If he chooses to do them through one of us, he does it for his glory. If we take the glory for it, that is all the reward we are ever going to receive.

When you obey because you love the Father, good fruit is produced. **Good fruit is doing the will of the Father and getting to know the Lord.** This "knowing" means a personal, intimate relationship that comes through experience and spending quality time together. You must have a personal relationship with Jesus and the Father.

Many believers accepted Jesus simply because they do not

want to go to hell. They have no real understanding of the kingdom of God, and they do not pursue a personal relationship with him. They are completely unaware that God desires for us to abide in his presence and qualify to reign with Christ. They assume that their salvation experience qualifies them for everything God has planned for the future yet they have never sought to know God in their hearts. They have no comprehension of what God requires of them.

Why is it important that Jesus came to die for us? Is his death merely a provision to keep us out of hell? No! If he had not died for us so that our sins could be removed, we would never have been able to enter God's kingdom. **Jesus gave his life because he wants us to spend eternity with him in his kingdom.** You have to be forgiven of your sins, because no sin can come into the presence of God who abides in the midst of his kingdom. Forgiveness gives you access to the kingdom of God.

Sin Will Move You Out of the Kingdom

The only thing that will pull you out of God's kingdom is sin. Sin cannot live in the kingdom of God. That's why God said to mortify your flesh. (Colossians 3:5) You need to kill it! God has condemned all sin in the flesh. (Romans 8:3) When you die to self and kill the flesh, you cannot live in sin any longer. The only other option is to live in the Spirit. In Galatians 5:16, Paul said if you walk in the Spirit, you shall not fulfill the lust of the flesh. As you walk in the Spirit and in humility before God, you will also be walking and living in the kingdom of God without sin. Satan will have no access to you. **You have to rise up in rebellion, take over the lordship, and move back into the flesh before you can sin.** Sin moves you out of the kingdom. You can't be in the flesh and the Spirit at the same time. **Because sin pulls you out of fellowship with God, he wants you to keep it out of your life.**

I'm not perfect and I'm sure each of you reading this book is not perfect. I've traveled to over eighty nations around the world and I've never met a perfect person yet. We all have sinned and come short of the glory of God. (Romans 3:23) However, if we confess our sins, he will forgive our unrighteousness. (1 John 1:9) Repentance puts us back in right standing with God. The wonderful thing about Jesus' blood is that it doesn't just cover our sins. It washes them away. Because of the blood, we can boldly come before the throne of grace which is in the kingdom of God. (Hebrews 4:16)

Making Progress

If you will deal with the basic conditions of living in the kingdom of God, everything will start falling into place. Weaknesses you have, as well as accesses the devil may have, will begin to dwindle away. Old things will start passing away and all things will become new. (2 Corinthians 5:17b) Learn to repent quickly and get right back in the kingdom if you sin. Find out what got you out of the kingdom, repent and let God show you the root of your sin. Then the devil can't use that same trick on you again. Sooner or later, he will run out of tricks.

When you first begin walking with God, he is going to deal primarily with the accesses the devil has in your life, because he doesn't want sin to keep separating you from him. Hebrews 12:6 says, *"For the Lord corrects and disciplines everyone whom He loves, and He punishes, even scourges, every son whom He accepts and welcomes to His heart and cherishes."* He is trying to get rid of every satanic access in your life, because the devil is the reason that you can't be blessed and exalted. Satan is trying to destroy you. God wants to separate you from the devil and his kingdom of darkness. God wants you to abide in his kingdom so you can be blessed abundantly.

Chapter 8

What Are Some of the Benefits Now?

<u>What is Righteousness?</u>
Romans 14:17 says the kingdom of God is not meat or drink but righteousness, peace and joy in the Holy Ghost. The word ***righteousness*** means "equity (of character or actions); specifically (Christian) justification:-righteousness." (Strong's #1343) It is the right way of <u>doing</u> and <u>being</u>. It is the right thing to do, say and be when you are in fellowship with God. **You are in right standing with God when there is <u>nothing</u> separating you from him.** Sin is the only thing that can separate you from God. When you are righteous, it's not because of your own works but because of Jesus' righteousness and what he did on the cross. When you accept the blood of Jesus and apply it to your sin, you are put in right standing with God. You can't do anything to become righteous except to receive the gift. Your responsibility is to not compromise the righteousness God has given you.

When I was a child, my mother would wash my filthy clothes. She would put clean clothes on me and give me these instructions. "Don't get your clothes dirty. We are going to town after a while." In my mind, that meant I couldn't have any fun. I lived on a farm and if I did anything fun, my clothes were going to get dirty again. I had to behave myself if I was going to keep my clothes clean.

We have that same attitude toward walking with God. We sometimes get so filthy we can't stand ourselves, so we ask God to run us through the spiritual washing machine. He washes our garments and we act nice <u>for a while</u> because he has forgiven us, but he wants us to <u>sin no more</u>. That means we aren't to get dirty again. We try to talk with him for a while and have fellowship with him, but most people can't hear him talking to them, so they lose interest. They try to think of something to do, but everything they can think of is something he said not to do.

Something is wrong if believers are excited about going to heaven but miserable about walking with God now. The Bible says there is fullness of joy in God's presence. (Psalm 16:11) Many people seem to think God is a grouchy old man with a big stick who is ready to hit them over the head when they do something wrong. How could anybody have fun with somebody like that? Most believers have the wrong idea about what God is like. Do you think man invented fun or did God put the ability to laugh in us? Do you think our sense of humor came from the devil? No, it came from our Father!

My dad was a minister for nearly sixty years. He once told a congregation that he knew God had to have a sense of humor or he would not have created the "monkeys" in some of the members in the church. That might hurt some people's feelings, but we can look at each other or ourselves and realize God does have a sense of humor. Proverbs 17:22 says a merry heart does good like a medicine. It's good for you to be merry! In the medical field, they are finding that a positive attitude and a joyful spirit are major contributors to recovery from illness. You can visit someone who is sad and depressed and cheer them up with a joyful spirit. The first thing you know, they start feeling better.

We are serving a God who wants to give us <u>fullness</u> of joy, so being in right standing with him cannot be a negative thing. There is nothing in this world that should make you happier than knowing you are in right standing with God. Most of us were never taught how to be righteous, much less how to <u>enjoy</u> being in right standing with God. Many believes don't realize the benefits of having nothing separating them from God and his grace.

No Weapon Shall Prosper

God has called us to do the same works that Jesus did, which is to destroy the works of the devil. (John 3:8 and 14:12) Satan is going to retaliate when you start messing up his works. You may have done the work of the Lord and destroyed some work of the devil, but he counter-attacked. Look at what Isaiah 54:17 says. *"But no weapon that is formed against you shall prosper, and every tongue that shall rise against you in judgment you shall show to be in the wrong. This [peace, righteousness, security, triumph over opposition] is the heritage of the servants of the Lord [those in whom the ideal Servant of the Lord is reproduced]; this is the righteousness or the vindication which they obtained from Me [this is that which I impart to them as their justification], says the Lord."*

In this verse, God is referring to his servants who are in right standing with him. The promise is that no weapon which is formed against you shall prosper. It will not accomplish what it was sent forth to do. It doesn't say that there wouldn't be any weapons formed against you. Many Christians assume that being right with God means they will never have another problem in their lives again. They believe that the devil is not allowed to come against them in any way whatsoever, but that isn't what God promised. He said the devil's weapons wouldn't prosper if you stay in right standing with God.

Servants of the Lord

Notice how God refers to us as "servants of the Lord" in this verse. This is where many people have problems today. They want to be lords instead of servants of the Lord. Even Jesus' disciples wanted to know who would be the greatest in God's kingdom. If you want to be the greatest, learn to be the servant of all. (Mark 9:35) **The key to greatness in God's kingdom is being a servant.** Humble yourself under the mighty hand of God and take on the form of servant, just like Jesus did. In due season

God will exalt you in this life, and you will also rule and reign with Christ in his kingdom in the life to come.

One thing you need to know about authority is that all leadership comes out of subjection. **If you are too big to serve, you are too small to lead.** God is never going to put someone in authority who has not first learned to be under authority. You learn how to be under authority by serving. Even if you are given a high ranking position in the kingdom of God, you will still be serving him.

The only reason we have problems is because the enemy has access to us when we are in the flesh. Weapons he has formed against us are prospering to some measure. However, the more consistently we stay in God's kingdom, the less successful the enemy's weapons will be. **When we are consistently righteous, we can access the benefits of God in his kingdom.** The benefits are far beyond anything the kingdoms of this world have to offer, but there is a qualifying for those benefits. You will never qualify for the benefits if you don't first learn how to get in God's kingdom and live there. As you start functioning within his kingdom, you begin to grow up and learn how to meet the conditions for all the other blessings God has for you.

We will always be servants, but we are children serving our Father, not slaves serving a master. We have problems with the word "servant" because we see it in the sense of someone using us and taking away our rights. God doesn't have that motive for wanting us to serve him. He wants us to serve him so he can bless us and take us to a realm beyond anything we could imagine in the natural.

Be Steadfast in Righteousness

I encourage you to get your concordance and look up all the verses that relate to righteousness. Look at how much of our inheritance is tied to us being righteous. The Amplified Bible refers to those who are "uncompromisingly righteous" as the recipients of God's blessings. It's not enough to humble yourself and ask God to forgive you. It's important that you have <u>steadfastness</u>. 1 Peter 5:6 says to humble yourself under the mighty hand of God so that in due season he may exalt you. You must be consistently humble <u>for a season</u>. Many believers won't stay humble for a season, and they wonder why God doesn't exalt them. They expect him to exalt them tomorrow. The season is needed to test your heart to see if you really trust God so that when he does exalt you, you won't get puffed up in pride.

<u>God's Peace</u>

Another part of the kingdom of God now is his **peace.** This is the peace of God that passes all understanding as described in Philippians 4:6-8. *"Do not fret or have any anxiety about anything, but in every circumstance and in everything, by prayer and petition (definite requests), with thanksgiving, continue to make your wants known to God. And God's peace [shall be yours, that tranquil state of a soul assured of its salvation through Christ, and so fearing nothing from God and being content with its earthly lot of whatever sort that is, that peace] which transcends all understanding shall garrison and mount guard over your hearts and minds in Christ Jesus. For the rest, brethren, whatever is true, whatever is worthy of reverence and is honorable and seemly, whatever is just, whatever is pure, whatever is lovely and lovable, whatever is kind and winsome and gracious, if there is any virtue and excellence, if there is anything worthy of praise, think on and weigh and take account of these things [fix your minds on them]."*

One sign of the last days is that hearts will be failing for fear of the things that are coming on the earth. (Luke 21:26) This is happening now. Because of advances in communication, we immediately know every evil thing that is happening around the world. Every abomination that takes place anywhere on the earth can be seen through our televisions. People have reason to be anxious if they have their security in anything but the Lord. If you have built your house on anything other than the rock (which is Christ), you have reason to be nervous about the coming storms because they will cause your house to fall.

If your faith is in Christ and you are obeying him, you are anchored on the rock. (Luke 6:47 and 48) You can have the peace of God that passes all understanding. **God doesn't want you to be anxious about anything.** God's peace will keep your hearts and minds through Christ. Philippians 4:8 lists several things to be meditating on while he is taking care of your problems. 1 Peter 5:7 says to cast all your cares on the Lord because he cares for you. You can't cast everything on him and trust him if you haven't bowed your knee to him as your Lord. If he's not the functional Lord of your life, you'll keep picking up your problems again.

The fruit of your lordship is that you keep trying to fix everything. The fruit of his Lordship is that you cast everything on him. You simply get your orders, do what you are told to do and leave the rest to him. Subsequently, you can enjoy the peace that passes all understanding when the storm is raging around you.

Many Christians have peace because they will only stay where things are peaceful. They can't handle real life. God's peace doesn't go away just because things get disturbed around you. There is a shield around the kingdom of God, and the weapons of the enemy cannot penetrate that shield and come into God's kingdom. The devil has to entice you to leave God's kingdom so he can fire at you effectively. We need to learn how to stay in God's presence and refuse to leave.

Fullness of Joy

The third part of the description of the kingdom of God in Romans 14:17 is **joy**. Psalm 16:11 says that in the presence of the Lord there is fullness of joy. John 15:10 and 11 tell a little more about how the Lord sees this joy. *"If you keep my commandments [if you continue to obey My instructions], you will abide in My love and live on in it, just as I have obeyed My Father's commandments and live on in His love. I have told you these things, that My joy and delight may be in you, and that your joy and gladness may be of full measure and complete and overflowing."*

God wants your blessings to be pressed down, shaken together and running over. That's why God is revealing these truths to you. You may think these are hard sayings, but God isn't trying to make you unhappy. He is trying to expose the lies the devil has been telling you. If you want to be in right standing with God and live in his kingdom, you must walk in obedience to him and live by his principles. He is telling you these things so that his joy and delight may be complete in you.

God's Kingdom is in the Holy Ghost.

Another thing you need to know about the kingdom of God is that it is positional. **The kingdom of God is in the Holy Ghost.** The terms "in the Holy Ghost", "in Christ" and "in the kingdom" are interchangeable. You can't be in the kingdom of God now and not be in the Spirit. The Holy Spirit and Jesus dwell within the kingdom of God.

Acts 17:28a (KJV) says, *"For in him we live, and move, and have our being."* **You can't do your own thing all day and then get in Christ every once in a while.** You need to live in him, move in him and have your being in him. That is the essence of living in the kingdom of God now. Whether you are at home relaxing, working or whatever you are doing, you are supposed to be in him. The Spirit goes with you wherever you are and abiding in him should become a way of life. You can live in the kingdom consistently. When you do, eternal life will start to manifest in you.

Enjoying Eternal Life

Eternal life is mentioned in John 10:27 and 28a (KJV). *"My sheep hear my voice, and I know them, and they follow me: And I give unto them eternal life."* Each one of us who has been born into the family of God has been given the gift of eternal life. Most Christians don't even know the Biblical definition of eternal life. Jesus describes eternal life in John 17:2 and 3. *"[Just as] You have granted Him power and authority over all flesh (all humankind), [now glorify Him] so that He may give eternal life to all whom You have given Him. And this is eternal life: [it means] to know (to perceive, recognize, become acquainted with, and understand) You, the only true and real God, and [likewise] to know Him, Jesus [as the] Christ (the Anointed One, the Messiah), Whom You have sent."*

This word <u>know</u> is talking about knowing someone in an experiential way, with an intimacy such as the way a husband knows his wife. The children of God have been given the privilege to know our Father and our Lord in a very personal, intimate way. You can't know anyone that intimately without spending quality time together and both parties sharing from the heart and not the head.

When you start living in the kingdom and experiencing God's peace and joy, you will also start enjoying his company. **God is going to reveal himself to you and fellowship with you.** Jesus will direct your life by speaking to you. You will learn how to recognize his voice. You will begin to bring your body under subjection and obey his voice so that you can stay in his kingdom.

John 14:15 says, *"If you [really] love Me, you will keep (obey) My commands."* Obedience from a pure heart produces kingdom living, and John 14:21 and 23 tell some benefits of this relationship. *"The person who has My commands and keeps them is the one who [really] loves Me: and whoever [really] loves Me will be loved by My Father, and I [too] will love him and will show (reveal, manifest) Myself to him. [I will let Myself be clearly seen by him and make Myself real to him.] If a person [really] loves Me, he will keep My word [obey My teaching]; and My Father will love him, and We will come to him and make Our home (abode, special dwelling place) with him."*

When you accept Jesus as the Lord of your life and start obeying him because you love him, both he and the Father will set up their throne in you. That is eternal life being <u>manifested in you</u>. That is kingdom living <u>now</u>. **Jesus is talking about having <u>continual fellowship</u> with God <u>now</u>.** You are <u>not</u> living in the kingdom if the Father and the Son are not ruling in your heart. They are not ruling in your life if you are not loving God through your obedience.

James 2:5 says, *"Listen, my beloved brethren: Has not God chosen those who are poor in the eyes of the world to be rich in faith and in their position as believers and to inherit the kingdom which He has promised to those who love Him?"* God wants those who love him (through obedience) to inherit his kingdom.

<u>Jesus is the Vine</u>.

In John 15:1 and 2, Jesus said, *"I am the True Vine, and My Father is the Vinedresser. Any branch in Me that does not bear fruit [that stops bearing] He cuts away (trims off, takes away); and He cleanses and repeatedly prunes every branch that continues to bear fruit, to make it bear more and richer and more excellent fruit."* Why does the Father do the work of the Vinedresser when you are abiding in Jesus? If you are in Christ and you are bearing fruit, the Father is going to cleanse and prune you so that you continue to bear richer and more excellent fruit. He will also cut off any dead branches. His reason for doing this is found in John 15:8. *"When you bear (produce) much fruit, My Father is honored and glorified, and you show and prove yourselves to be true followers of Mine."*

Jesus wants you to live a life that honors God our Father. **You have the ability to do something that honors and glorifies**

Almighty God! You glorify the Father by doing nothing more than abiding in the Vine. Live in the kingdom by staying humble before God. Let the Father do what he wants to do in your life by proving yourself to be a true follower of the Lord.

Matthew 13:12 says that those who have will be given more. When you're bearing fruit, God blesses you with his expert gardening skills. You will produce more and more until you prove to everyone that you are a true follower of Jesus because of your fruit. **The world will know you by your fruit, because what you do speaks louder than what you say.** The Father is trying to get us to consistently stay in his kingdom until he can get us to a level of maturity that we are bearing abundant fruit, both in quality and quantity, so that everyone can taste and see that God is good. This will rebound to God's praise and glory.

This is only a limited explanation of what God is offering you in his kingdom. These are only a few of the benefits available to those who remain consistently righteous. God has so much for you to enjoy!

Chapter 9

What Are Some of the Benefits in the Future?

In this chapter we are going to address how our future will be affected if we live in the kingdom of God now. Let's look at John 1:11-13. *"He came to that which belonged to Him [to His own-His domain, creation, things, world], and they who were His own did not receive Him and did not welcome Him. But to as many as did receive and welcome Him, He gave the authority (power, privilege, right) to become the children of God, that is, to those who believe in (adhere to, trust in, and rely on) His name-Who owe their birth neither to bloods nor to the will of the flesh [that of physical impulse] nor to the will of man [that of a natural father], but to God. [They are born of God!]"*

<u>Becoming a Son of God</u>
Each one of us who is born of God has been given the <u>power</u> and <u>privilege</u> to become a son of God. Romans 8:14 makes a very profound statement. *"For all who are led by the Spirit of God are the sons of God."* It is easy to assume that being born into the family of God automatically makes you a son of God, but it doesn't. Being born into God's family gives you the privilege to <u>become</u> a son of God. Romans 8:14 gives the condition for becoming a son. **All who are <u>led by the Spirit</u> are the sons of God.** Just because a person is born of God doesn't mean they are being led by the Spirit.

Paul refers to carnal Christians in 1 Corinthians 3:1-3. These Christians should have been mature, but they were still babies because they never grew up. They were not being led by the

Spirit of God. The Bible gives many warnings to those who do not walk in the Spirit. When we choose to walk in the flesh rather than in the Spirit, there are consequences. However, if we will walk in the Spirit, there are great benefits to be reaped. One of the greatest benefits is becoming sons of God.

It is easy to get confused about the difference between being born again and being a son of God. In Romans 8:14, God is referring to his children who are led by the Spirit, which allows them to be manifested as his sons. Every child of God has been given the <u>power</u> to become a son. Like many other promises of God, you can live your entire life and never enjoy the privilege of your inheritance because you never meet the conditions for it. **If you do not understand God's conditions for becoming a son of God, satan will steal this part of your inheritance from you.** He will lead you in a way that seems right and cause you to miss the mark God has set before you.

You cannot consistently walk and live in the kingdom of God without being led by the Spirit. That is the basic foundation of living in God's kingdom now. Galatians 5:16 says if you walk in the Spirit, you cannot fulfill the lusts of the flesh. **Every person on this earth is either walking in the flesh or walking in the Spirit.**

Those who are not born again have only one option. They are in the flesh. They are lords of their own lives, and they can be good or evil lords. It doesn't matter which they are because they are still in the flesh.

When you were born into the family of God, you were given another option. You were given the <u>power</u> to become a son of God when you got saved. **The Spirit of God is living within you and you have the power of the Spirit to bring your carnality (Adam nature) under subjection and kill it.** You can turn from the old way of walking in the flesh to newness of life in Christ. **You can walk in the Spirit.** You can live and move and have your being in the Spirit. You have the option to live in the kingdom, but that doesn't mean you are going to do it. It's your choice.

Even if you <u>choose</u> to be in the Spirit, that doesn't mean you are capable of doing it at this time. If your flesh is alive, it will war against the Spirit in you and try to hinder you from doing the righteous things you want to do. Paul found out in Romans 7 that his flesh was still very much alive. Paul had to mortify his flesh. Otherwise, it would have always hindered him from walking with God. The same is true for us.

<u>Nothing of Your Flesh is Good</u>.

In Romans 7:18a, Paul says, *"For I know that nothing good dwells within me, that is, in my flesh."* I am going to expound on this, because it is very important. As I teach people how to walk in the Spirit, it is continually apparent that one of the hardest things to deal with is accepting the fact that **there is <u>nothing</u> good in <u>any</u> person's flesh**. Everyone seems determined to prove they can do something righteous in their flesh. Consequently, people waste many years before they do what God says is required to walk in the Spirit, which is to deny their flesh and mortify it. Satan robs them of all that time because they still try to justify being lord and walking in the flesh. **You must come to the point that you <u>know</u> that nothing of your flesh is good.** When you are walking in the flesh, you are yielding to the dictates (control) of the flesh. Adam, not Christ, is the lord of your life!

However, when you deny your flesh, yield to Christ and bring your flesh under subjection to do what he says, then you are <u>walking</u> in the Spirit and <u>being led</u> by the Spirit. Christ is the Lord of your life, which means you are no longer in the flesh.

Continuing in Romans 7:18b-19, *"...I can will what is right, but I cannot perform it. [I have the intention and urge to do what is right, but no power to carry it out.] For I fail to practice the good deeds I desire to do, but the evil deeds that I do not desire to do are what I am [ever] doing."* Everyone can relate to having been through this. We have all struggled with the power of the flesh manifesting within us, but we shouldn't remain in that position. When we were born again, we were given the Spirit of God and the power to become the sons of God.

Romans 7:20-25, *"Now if I do what I do not desire to do, it is no longer I doing it [it is not myself that acts], but the sin [principle] which dwells within me [fixed and operating in my soul]. So I find it to be a law (rule of action of my being) that when I want to do what is right and good, evil is ever present with me and I am subject to its insistent demands. For I endorse and delight in the Law of God in my inmost self [with my new nature]. But I discern in my bodily members [in the sensitive appetites and wills of the flesh] a different law (rule of action) at war against the law of my mind (my reason) and making me a prisoner to the law of sin that dwells in my bodily organs [in the sensitive appetites and wills of the flesh]. O unhappy and pitiable and wretched man that I am! Who will release and deliver me from [the shackles of] this body of death? O thank God! [He will!] through Jesus Christ (the Anointed One) our Lord! So then indeed I, of myself with the mind and heart, serve the Law of God, but with the flesh the law of sin."*

Paul made some very profound statements in this passage. He made it clear that **all sin, the desire to sin and the temptation to sin originate in the flesh.** As a born again child of God, Paul was given a new nature. There were two different laws operating within him: the law of sin and the law of Christ. At this point, Paul's flesh was overpowering him so that he couldn't overcome it. The very thing he wanted to do, he wasn't able to do. He ended up doing the very thing he didn't want to do. His "willpower" wasn't strong enough to overcome his flesh. Then he said, "Oh, wretched man that I am. Who will deliver me from this?" He got the right answer! "Thank God. Jesus will deliver me."

Paul had to learn to separate himself from his carnality and his fleshly nature and start appropriating the power of God. He had to use the power he had been given at salvation to overcome his flesh and become a son of God. In Romans 8:1 and 2, he says, *"Therefore, [there is] now no condemnation (no adjudging guilty of wrong) for those who are in Christ Jesus, who live [and] walk not after the dictates of the flesh, but after the dictates of the Spirit. For the law of the Spirit of life [which is] in Christ Jesus [the law of our new being] has freed me from the law of sin and of death."*

Romans 8:3a, *"For God has done what the Law could not do, [its power] being weakened by the flesh [the entire nature of man without the Holy Spirit]..."* The Law was good and righteous, but man couldn't keep it. The carnal man has only the nature of flesh and it cannot fulfill the dictates of the Law. Continuing in the same verse, *"...Sending His own Son in the guise of sinful flesh and as an offering for sin,* **[God] condemned sin in the flesh** *[subdued, overcame, deprived it of its power over all who accept that sacrifice]."*

The reason you feel condemnation in the flesh is because **all sin is condemned in the flesh.** You cannot be in the Spirit and sin. You have to get in the flesh to sin. **When you are in the flesh, you cannot be righteous regardless of the good works you may do.** You will never please God or be in right standing with him if you are in the flesh. It doesn't matter how holy or how spiritual you try to act. **The flesh will never be righteous!** Contrarily, when you are in the Spirit, you are in right standing with God. You are holy, just and righteous and you can't sin!

Jesus has given each child of God a new nature. Sin is excluded from the new nature, which is in the Spirit (in the kingdom of God). Sin is condemned in the flesh, which is why you are commanded to kill your old nature and give no place to it. (Colossians 3:5) Instead, you are to yield to your new nature and walk in obedience to God. He will write his laws on the tablets of your heart. (2 Corinthians 3:3) He will give you the power to overcome your flesh if you allow him to lead you by his Spirit. Then you will become a son of God.

Romans 8:4 and 5, *"So that the righteous and just requirement of the Law might be fully met in us who live and move not in the ways of the flesh but in the ways of the Spirit [our lives governed not by the standards and according to the dictates of the flesh, but controlled by the Holy Spirit]. For those who are according to the flesh and are controlled by its unholy desires set their minds on and pursue those things which gratify the flesh, but those who are according to the Spirit and are controlled by the desires of the Spirit set their minds on and seek those things which gratify the [Holy] Spirit."*

It is very important that you see this clearly! You are either being directed by your flesh or by the Spirit. **If you are in the flesh, you will seek to satisfy your carnal desires, because that is where your heart is set.** If your mind is always on natural things and all you want to do is to satisfy the cravings and desires of your carnal nature, you are walking in the flesh. If you are walking in the flesh, you are not seeking God or trying to find out what would really please him. You are doing the things that please you. Those things may not be evil in the eyes of the world, but they are still carnal.

Those who are in the Spirit set their minds on the things that gratify the Holy Spirit. On what is your mind set? Do you seek God daily because you want to do the things that gratify him? That will require you to deny yourself and not do the things that would gratify your flesh.

Romans 8:6-8, *"Now the mind of the flesh [which is _sense_ and _reason_ without the Holy Spirit] is death [death that comprises all the miseries arising from sin, both here and hereafter]. But the mind of the [Holy] Spirit is life and [soul] peace [both now and forever]. [That is] because the mind of the flesh [with its carnal thoughts and purposes] _is hostile to God_, for it does not submit* *itself to God's Law; indeed it cannot. So then those who are living the life of the flesh [catering to the appetites and impulses of their carnal nature] cannot <u>please</u> or <u>satisfy</u> God, or be acceptable to Him."*

<u>Your Choice</u>
    I don't know about you, but it looks to me like we don't have a choice. **The problem today is that false teachers and pastors are giving you other choices.** They are teaching doctrines that give you permission to fulfill the desires of the flesh. They teach that you can seek to satisfy all your cravings and still be in right standing with God. God will understand and you can adjust your morality to the situation. That is a lie from the devil. **The Bible is clear! If you are yielding to your reasoning and the appetites of your flesh, you are not pleasing to God.** You cannot satisfy God and you are not acceptable to him. Romans 8:9a explains what God expects of his children. *"But you are not living the life of the flesh, you are living the life of the Spirit, <u>if</u> the [Holy] Spirit of God [really] dwells within you [directs and controls you]."* As a Christian, you know the Spirit of God dwells in you, but does he direct and control you?

    My first book, *My Sheep Hear My Voice*, reveals the privilege of knowing God and also the responsibility of bowing your knee to the Lordship of Jesus Christ. Through the Spirit, God will direct and control your life. He is to be the functional Lord of your life <u>now</u>.

    That is what God requires, yet I find people all over the world resisting this. They don't want Jesus to literally control and direct their lives. They want to direct their own lives through their reasoning and understanding, but that is flesh! They want to fulfill the desires and appetites of the flesh. If they will yield to Jesus and let him control and direct their lives, he will turn their focus to the things of God that have eternal value.

    We are back to that choice again. **You can live the life of the**

flesh or live in the Holy Spirit because he directs and controls you. Let's continue in Romans 8:9b-12, *"...But if anyone does not possess the [Holy] Spirit of Christ, he is none of His [he does not belong to Christ, is not truly a child of God]. But if Christ lives in you, [then although] your [natural] body is dead by reason of sin and guilt, the spirit is alive because of [the] righteousness [that He imputes to you]. And if the Spirit of Him Who raised up Jesus from the dead dwells in you, [then] He Who raised up Christ Jesus from the dead will also restore to life your mortal (short-lived, perishable) bodies through His Spirit Who dwells in you. So then, brethren, we are debtors, but not to the flesh [we are not obligated to our carnal nature], to live [a life ruled by the standards set up by the dictates] of the flesh."*

Isn't that a wonderful promise of God? We are not debtors! **We don't owe our carnal, Adam nature anything!** God has not given it any authority over us at all. We owe it nothing but to deny it. Verse 13a says, *"For if you live according to [the dictates of] the flesh, you will surely die."* This is not talking about physical death. It is talking about spiritual death. If you live by the Spirit, even though the flesh will die, you live.

Putting the Flesh to Death

Romans 8:13b, *"...But if through the power of the [Holy] Spirit you are [habitually] putting to death (making extinct, deadening) the [evil] deeds prompted by the body, you shall [really and genuinely] live forever."* This is an important point. No one is perfected to the level that he or she never sins or makes a mistake. Your flesh is never going to give up trying to get you to yield to it. **Living in the Spirit means that you habitually, consistently and regularly put to death and resist the evil deeds prompted by the body.** That means you are resisting the temptation of the flesh today. You are also going to resist it tomorrow and the day after that! You are going to consistently and habitually resist whatever the devil tries to tempt you with in the flesh. If you do that, you are going to walk in the Spirit. The flesh is going to get weaker and weaker until it dies and has no power over you.

I keep reminding you of Galatians 5:16. If you walk in the Spirit (consistently and habitually), you cannot fulfill the lusts of the flesh. **The way to mortify the flesh is to consistently walk in the Spirit.** This is one of the benefits of walking in the kingdom of God <u>now</u>. As you walk in the Spirit, you will start getting victory over the flesh.

<u>The Sons of God</u>

Now we are back to Romans 8:14. *"For all who are led by the Spirit of God are sons of God."* Now you understand what it takes to be a son of God. You cannot yield to the dictates of the flesh, fulfill the desires of your carnality and say that you are a son of God just because you are born again. You can choose to be a carnal Christian instead.

We have gone through several scriptures that compare the difference between walking in the flesh and walking in the Spirit. The Bible clearly reveals what it takes to walk in the Spirit. When you walk in the Spirit you are yielded to and controlled by the Lord. You are not controlling and directing him. You yield to the Lordship of Jesus Christ through the Spirit. As many as are led by the Spirit, these are the sons of God.

Let's go on to Romans 8:15-17a, *"For [the Spirit which] you have now received [is] not a spirit of slavery to put you once more in bondage to fear, but you have received the Spirit of adoption [the Spirit producing sonship] in [the bliss of] which we cry, Abba (Father)! Father! The Spirit Himself [thus] testifies together with our own spirit, [assuring us] that we are children of God. And if we are [His] children, then we are [His] heirs also: heirs of God and fellow heirs with Christ [sharing His inheritance with Him]..."*

We are asking in this particular chapter, "What are some of

the particular benefits in the future?" If you are walking in the kingdom of God, which is being in Christ, then the fruit is that you become a son of God. You are a joint-heir with Christ and you are going to share his inheritance with him. As we look at future events, what is the next major manifestation of Christ that will take place? Right now Jesus is sitting at the right hand of his Father. The next major event is Christ coming for his bride. We will become part of his bride if we have met God's conditions. Jesus is going to bring his bride back and set up his kingdom here on earth. Those who qualify will rule and reign with him on this earth for a thousand years.

Are you going to share in this? It is conditional! Those who are going to share in his heritage, which includes his reign for a thousand years, are those who become the sons of God because they are led by the Spirit and conform to God's will. Their minds are set on the things that glorify God, not what satisfies their carnal instincts. If you meet those conditions as a son of God, you are an heir with Christ and you will share in his heritage.

Sharing in Jesus' Suffering

Look at the rest of Romans 8:17. *"...only we must share His suffering if we are to share His glory."* Those who are led by the Spirit of God and become the sons of God must also share in his suffering. It is very clear that if you do not share in his suffering, you will not share in his glory. Verse 18 says, *"[But what of that?] For I consider that the sufferings of this present time (this present life) are not worth being compared with the glory that is about to be revealed to us and in us and for us and conferred on us!"*

2 Timothy 3:12 (KJV), *"Yea, and all that will live godly in Christ Jesus shall suffer persecution."* There are many wonderful benefits from living in God's kingdom now. You are in right standing with God and you have peace and joy, but you are also going to be persecuted. Many people may get offended by that

statement, because they believe you shouldn't go through any trials if you are a Christian. 2 Timothy 2:12 (KJV), *"If we suffer, we shall also reign with him: if we deny him, he will deny us."*

Many believers think you can continually deny Jesus' right to be Lord of your life and when it gets to the end, everything is going to be fine because he wouldn't deny you. That is not what the Word of God says. **If you deny him, he will deny you.** That is a pretty sobering thought. However, if you suffer with him, you will also reign with him.

Many people resist the Lordship of Jesus Christ, because they know persecution is going to come. They make every kind of excuse to remain lord of their own lives so that doesn't happen. No one has gone through more persecution than Paul did. Yet Paul came to the point that he learned to be content when he fell into all kinds of trials, temptations and persecutions. (Philippians 4:11 and 12) **He <u>learned</u> to count it joy!** In 2 Corinthians 12:9, God told Paul that his grace was sufficient.

Grace is God's unmerited favor. When we have to suffer for Christ's sake, God gives us sufficient grace to walk through it in a way that we can actually count it joy! **That is kingdom living now.** It doesn't matter if we are persecuted or we have to suffer something for Christ's sake. We are in right standing with God, we have the peace of God and we have joy! How can anything be that bad if you have peace and joy?

<u>Creation Waits for the Sons of God</u>

Romans 8:19-24a, *"For [even the whole] creation (all nature) waits expectantly and longs earnestly for God's sons to be made known [waits for the revealing, the disclosing of their sonship]. For the creation (nature) was subjected to frailty (to futility, condemned to frustration), not because of some intentional fault on its part, but by the will of Him Who so subjected it-[yet] with the hope That nature (creation) itself will be set free from its bondage to decay and corruption [and gain an entrance] into the*

glorious freedom of God's children. We know that the whole creation [of irrational creatures] has been moaning together in the pains of labor until now. And not only the creation, but we ourselves too, who have and enjoy the firstfruits of the [Holy] Spirit [a foretaste of the blissful things to come] groan inwardly as we wait for the redemption of our bodies [from sensuality and the grave, which will reveal] our adoption (our manifestation as God's sons). For in [this] hope we were saved."

When Jesus comes back for us and we get our glorified bodies, the rest of creation will be set free from the bondage of sin and we will enter into a glorious time in God's kingdom. That is when our hope will be fulfilled and manifested. In the meantime, we have the earnest of that inheritance. We have the earnest of the kingdom of God <u>now</u>! We have the earnest of the Spirit <u>now</u>! Our inheritance will be fully manifested when we rule and reign with Christ.

<u>Being Manifested as a Son of God</u>

In this chapter, we have gone through the steps of being a carnal person to being born again and on to becoming a son of God. With the new nature of Christ in us, we begin to fight the battle of subduing our flesh. As we mature, bring our bodies under subjection and yield to the control of the Holy Spirit, we will grow in the grace of God. As we consistently walk in the Spirit, we reach the position of being called the sons of God.

If we are still living at the end of the age, God will pour out his Spirit on all flesh. (Acts 2:17) **The level to which you allow God to prepare you in his kingdom now will determine the level of additional power you will receive as the Spirit manifests in the last days.** Many glorious things are going to take place in closing the church age right before we move into the millennial reign. The manifestation of the sons of God will begin.

By living in the kingdom, you start taking on the character and nature of the Lord himself. As you become like him, you will get to know him and understand what he is like. When you consistently stay in his presence, you will begin to enjoy very personal and intimate fellowship with him. You will begin to take on his nature and his character more and more because you are allowing him to manifest through you. **Your righteousness will actually be him manifesting within you.**

It is important that you understand this progression. **You only become a son of God if you learn how to walk in the Spirit.** If you learn how to walk in the Spirit, you can live in the kingdom of God now. When you live in the kingdom, all of God's promises will be added to you. You will qualify to be a joint-heir with Christ. You will qualify to rule and reign with him, but you'll also qualify to be persecuted. You will also learn how to appropriate the sufficient grace that is necessary in the time of persecution. You'll start enjoying a lot of the other benefits that are available to you as a child of God.

Eternal Rewards

Another future benefit of walking in the kingdom of God is the kind of rewards you will receive when you stand before the Father in judgment. 1 Corinthians 13:1-3 talks about doing many great works. However, if you do those works and they are not motivated out of love and obedience to God, it profits you nothing and you are nothing. Every work you do will be tested by fire. (1 Corinthians 3:13) If it passes God's test, you will receive a reward. If it doesn't pass God's test, it will burn up and you will suffer the loss of the reward.

The test is your motive! Did you do the work out of your love for God and your obedience to him or was it done from selfish ambition? If you walk in the kingdom of God consistently now, the works you are doing in obedience to him will have great eternal value. They won't burn up and you will receive your reward. Your position in the eternal kingdom of our Father is going to be determined by how you walk now.

You Have a Choice.

You can either walk in the kingdom now by being led by the Spirit or you can spend the rest of your life walking in the flesh and being lord of your own life. You have the choice. **If you want to be the best you can be, you need to get into the kingdom of God now. Jesus is Lord now.** He is the author and the finisher of your faith. (Hebrews 12:2) He is preparing you to live in the eternal kingdom with him and the Father.

God said in 1 Peter 1:16 (KJV), *"Because it is written, Be ye holy; for I am holy."* **You have to walk in the Spirit to be holy.** If you are not walking consistently in the Spirit, you are not holy. If you are not abiding in Christ, you are not holy. If you are not walking in the kingdom of God now, you are not holy. **If Jesus Christ is not the literal, functional Lord of your life (which means he is controlling and directing your life), you are not holy and you are not in right standing with God.** You are in the flesh and you will reap the consequences of living in the flesh. Don't let anyone deceive you. If you choose to stay out of the Spirit, you will reap the consequences because you have denied Christ and what he requires of you.

You need to understand the danger of Christ denying you. There are people who will stand before the Lord and say. "Lord, Lord, have not we done all these things in your name?" (Matthew 7:22) This verse doesn't say that Jesus controlled and directed the works that were done. These people did good works in his name, which is what many of you do. **You do many good works in his name, but you direct it.** This group cast out demons, healed the sick and did all kinds of great miraculous works, but the Lord said, "I never knew you! Depart from me, you workers of iniquity." (Matthew 7:23) Don't let the devil put you in that spot.

Now is the time for repentance. One of the greatest lies that many Christians believe is that you don't have to totally yield to Jesus' Lordship until he catches you up in the rapture. If you don't bow your knee <u>now</u> to his Lordship, you won't be enjoying his Lordship in the millennial reign either. It is as simple as that. Now is the testing time. You have a choice. He is not forcing anyone to rule and reign with him.

Those who deny themselves and yield to Christ will become the sons of God, because they are led by his Spirit. They will mature and become Jesus' bride. They will keep their garments spotless. If anything spots their garments, they will immediately confess their sins and seek his forgiveness. They will be wise virgins who are ready for the Bridegroom to come. When he comes, they will go with him and enjoy the blessings of the marriage supper of the Lamb. They will enjoy the future blessing of ruling and reigning with him in his kingdom.

Those who choose to be foolish and reject his kingdom now (which includes his Lordship now) also reject the right to rule and reign with him. As I said earlier, you have a choice. **Will you accept God's kingdom in your heart <u>now</u> so that you can enjoy the future benefits of his kingdom? Or will you continue to reject what he is offering you?**

Chapter 10

Why Has the Kingdom of God Now Been So Hard for Some to Understand?

<u>Natural Versus Spiritual</u>

As I have ministered around the world, it has become evident to me that there is very little understanding in the body of Christ about how to walk in the kingdom of God now. I asked the Lord why his children lack knowledge in this area and he answered, *"They have substituted the natural for the spiritual."*

God had me write this book for his children, because so few have any real revelation on the kingdom of God, communion and fellowship with God, or how to hear the voice of the Lord. It goes back to the same root problem. The natural has been substituted for the spiritual. It isn't because believers aren't trying to serve God and walk by faith. They are trying to walk in the Spirit. They want to be part of the kingdom of God, so it has nothing to do with their desire to know or understand the things of God.

Many of you reading this book are searching for the answer, but you can't seem to come up with clear, simple truth. If you have substituted the natural for the spiritual, it is because you have believed that this method would work.

Satan disguises lies as truth and tries to convince you that you can produce spiritual results when you operate in the natural. Satan loves to deceive believers with ways that <u>seem</u> right which never lead to life. They never lead to truth but instead lead to confusion, which confirms that satan is the author of them.

We are going to look at different passages in the Bible to get some insight into how and why people have substituted the natural for the spiritual. Real Christians know when they are in blatant rebellion and operating in the flesh (the natural). They know that in such a condition, they are not going to have fellowship with God and they are not going to enjoy the blessings of God.

This is not the "natural" I am talking about. I'm talking about the natural realm where satan deceives those who are really sincere with ways that seem right. He leads them into what I call "spiritualized flesh". **They are doing "spiritual" things that are "good" but they are doing them <u>out of the wrong nature</u>.** They are doing them out of their carnality (the natural, fleshly nature) rather than out of the Spirit, and it just doesn't work.

Luke 12:31 and 32, *"Only aim at and strive for and seek His kingdom, and all these things shall be supplied to you also. Do not be seized with alarm and struck with fear, little flock, for it is your Father's good pleasure to give you the kingdom!"* As I travel around the world, I see very few of his flock who are enjoying the benefits of the kingdom of God now. Most believers I meet are not even aware that the kingdom of God is available nor do they enjoy the benefits of that kingdom. Even when they plainly see what the Word says, they don't believe they can actually appropriate the kingdom or it is confusing to them.

2 Corinthians 4:18 says, *"Since we consider and look not to the things that are seen but to the things that are unseen; for the things that are visible are temporal (brief and fleeting), but the things that are invisible are deathless and everlasting."* Our senses discern things that are temporal. The Word of God says that **the things you can't see are eternal**.

The problem is that satan continues to tempt you to function in the natural. It doesn't matter if you are trying to <u>act</u> spiritual. In the natural, you cannot have eyes to see and ears to hear in the eternal realm. God and his kingdom are in the eternal realm. The blessings God has for you are in Christ, and Christ is in the kingdom of God. God's kingdom is the most permanent thing that exists, but it can't be perceived in the natural realm. We can't see his kingdom now, nor can we comprehend his love, joy, peace or anything that is received by faith unless we are living in his kingdom. None of these things are visible to the natural man.

The external, visible part of us is temporal. The eternal house God is building within each of us can't be seen. We have a tendency to judge what we see on the outside, but that temporal building will pass away. God does not look at the outward appearance. He looks at the eternal spirit within. God doesn't put his focus on temporal things. He puts his focus on eternal things, and we are supposed to be like our Father.

Matthew 6:33a (KJV) says, *"But seek ye first the kingdom of God and his righteousness."* We have need of temporal things, but we are not to put our <u>focus</u> on them. Put your focus on the eternal realm (God's kingdom) and all the natural things will be added to you. If there is a choice between a temporal thing and an eternal thing, you should always choose the eternal thing because it is far more valuable.

As people try to understand eternal things, they get very frustrated. This is especially true if they are highly educated and very successful in the natural realm. In the temporal realm, you can use your reasoning, understanding and education in order to be successful, but when you try to understand the things of God and his kingdom, you are playing by a different set of rules.

Every child of God has been given the privilege to live in the kingdom of God. Jesus was speaking to his disciples in Luke 8:10 after he shared the parable about the sower and the seed. *"He said to them, To you it has been given to [come progressively to] know (to recognize and understand more strongly and clearly) the mysteries and secrets of the kingdom of God, but for others they are in parables, so that, [though] looking, they may not see; and hearing, they may not comprehend."*

Jesus spoke to the multitudes in parables, and they heard what he was saying <u>in the natural</u>. They did not comprehend what he was talking about in the spiritual realm. It wasn't given to them to be able to see or to hear. However, when he took his disciples aside, he told them that it had been given to them to know and understand the mysteries and secrets of the kingdom of God. (Mark 4:11)

Let's look at Luke 24:45. *"Then He [thoroughly] opened up their minds to understand the Scriptures." Jesus gave spiritual understanding* to the same group of disciples who had been given the opportunity to understand the secrets and the mysteries of the kingdom of God. Before Jesus returned to heaven, he opened their minds to understand the Scriptures.

Has God opened your mind so that you understand his Word? The only way you can understand God's Word is if the Author of the Word illuminates your mind. This work is done by the Holy Spirit. The Holy Spirit was sent to lead us into all truth. (John 16:13) Are you progressively being led into deeper truth or are you going from one error to another? Are you believing false doctrines and following ways that seem right? Or are you progressively learning the secrets of God's kingdom and becoming more like your Lord? Has God <u>thoroughly</u> opened your mind to understand his Word?

<u>Faith or Disobedience</u>?

Look at John 3:36. *"And he who believes in (has faith in, clings to, relies on) the Son has (now possesses) eternal life. But whoever disobeys (is unbelieving toward, refuses to trust in, disregards, is not subject to) the Son will never see (experience) life, but [instead] the wrath of God abides on him. [God's displeasure remains on him; His indignation hangs over him continually.]"* This verse makes it very clear. The one who believes in, trusts in and relies on the Lord possesses eternal life. Many of

God's children say they believe in Jesus. To believe in Jesus means that you have faith in him, you cling to him and you rely on him. If you do that, you have eternal life. John 17:3 describes the gift of life eternal which is the privilege to know the Father and Jesus in a personal, intimate way. If that is happening in your life, it is simply because you believe in and rely on God.

Whoever disobeys is unbelieving and refuses to trust the Son. The one who is not subject to Jesus will never see or experience eternal life. These two methods of living are the opposite of one another. The one who believes will enjoy eternal life and fellowship with God, but the one who disregards the Lord will not have eternal life. It is important that you understand the distinction between these two different groups of people.

True Worship

John 4:23 and 24, *"A time will come, however, indeed it is already here, when the true (genuine) worshipers will worship the Father in spirit and in truth (reality); for the Father is seeking just such people as these as His worshipers. God is a Spirit (a spiritual Being) and those who worship Him must worship Him in spirit and in truth (reality)."* Genuine worshipers will worship the Father in spirit and in truth. You can't see God with your natural eyes, because he's here by the Spirit. Jesus is also here by the Spirit. They're both invisible on this earth, but does that make God any less real? There is nothing more eternal than God yet we can't see him. **This invisible God is seeking true worshipers.**

Worship and praise services have become pretty commonplace around the world. Everyone gathers together to tell God how wonderful he is, but you can leave such a meeting and go right back to distrusting God and disobeying him in everything you do. The word *worshiper* means "an adorer". (Strong's # 4353) Most church people don't really adore God. They don't want too many church meetings and they don't want them to last too long. They get offended if the singing style is different from what they are used to hearing.

In praise and worship, we have substituted the natural for the spiritual. We use professional musicians and singers and sing the latest songs. Multitudes may come and say it's the greatest singing they've ever heard. The question remains, **did it move the heart of God?** God is looking for true worshipers. He doesn't care who sings with the best voice. **He wants those who adore him to sing from that heart of adoration.** He looks for those who worship him in spirit, which means they are trusting in him and adhering to what he says. They adore him so much they yield to his Lordship in their lives day by day. They are walking in truth in their daily lives.

You need to spend some time thinking about this. God is seeking people who will worship him in spirit and in truth. To really worship God and adore him, you must be in the Spirit and in truth. When you sing a worship song, are you lying or telling the truth? Do you adore Jesus enough to lay down your life in order to obey him? Most believers have never laid their lives down to take up the cross of Jesus, yet we sing songs every Sunday as if that is how we live. Many believers are hypocritical instead of really living what they profess.

The Pharisees and Sadducees of Jesus' time were the epitome of hypocrisy. They appeared to be upright, but inwardly they were full of lawlessness. (Matthew 23:28) They didn't know the Father even though they were the religious leaders of that time. They looked better than anyone else outwardly, but they were not walking in truth and truly worshiping God. They didn't even belong to God! Their father was the devil. (John 8:44)

God Will Not Excuse Your Flesh.

Some of you reading this book may realize that you don't even belong to God. **He loves you, but he is not going to excuse your flesh.** You must answer for everything you do from your fleshly, carnal nature. Jesus died to give you a chance to be cleansed. You have the opportunity to go to Jesus in humility and adoration for what he has done for you. You have to be honest and repent of your sins. If you will do that, he is faithful and just to forgive you, cleanse you and give you the gift of eternal life. You can stop right now and accept what he did for you on the cross.

If you are born again, you may realize you have been a hypocrite. You have pretended to adore God, but you don't obey him. **If you're not obeying his directions in your life, you are not in the Spirit.**

In 1 Corinthians 2, Paul was addressing the Corinthians who did not understand the mysteries and the secrets of the kingdom of God. He made sure they understood that he didn't come to them with lofty words of man's wisdom. He didn't preach anything except Jesus Christ and his crucifixion. He preached the basics. These Corinthians had been born into God's family, but they tried to be spiritual people from the natural realm. When they should have been mature, they were still babies who had to be given milk. (1 Corinthians 3:2) If you haven't dealt with the basics, you can't handle the deeper things.

Spiritual Wisdom

1 Corinthians 2:6, *"Yet when we are among the full-grown (spiritually mature Christians who are ripe in understanding), we do impart a [higher] wisdom (the knowledge of the divine plan previously hidden); but it is indeed not a wisdom of this present age or of this world nor of the leaders and rulers of this age, who are being brought to nothing and are doomed to pass away."*

I meet pastors and teachers all over the world who would be called the most mature ones in their organization, yet they have very little (if any) understanding about the kingdom of God. Something is wrong because Paul said that full-grown, mature Christians are ripe in understanding.

There is knowledge and wisdom in the natural realm. There is also knowledge and wisdom in the spiritual realm. The quality of knowledge and wisdom available to us in the kingdom of God is at a much higher level than that which is available in the natural, worldly system. The education we received in the world's system is not capable of understanding the knowledge in the kingdom of God. That is why it is so hard for some of you to understand the things of God. **What you have learned in the natural does not qualify you to receive the wisdom that is available in God's kingdom.** If you need more information on the contrast between natural and spiritual knowledge, I suggest that you read my book, *Sound Doctrine*.

Continuing in 1 Corinthians 2:7, *"But rather what we are setting forth is a wisdom of God once hidden [from the human understanding] and now revealed to us by God-[that wisdom] which God devised and decreed before the ages for our glorification [to lift us into the glory of His presence]."* Isn't that an awesome statement? There is divine wisdom that has been hidden from human understanding, but now it's being sent forth for our glorification in this present time.

Verse 8, *"None of the rulers of this age or world perceived and recognized and understood this, for if they had, they would never have crucified the Lord of glory."* The religious leaders set out to kill Jesus. The authorization for his death came from the Roman ruler of that area, and satan was behind the whole thing. If they had known that Jesus' death was going to open the way for divine wisdom to be made available to us, they would never have crucified the Lord of glory.

How did Jesus' death make that wisdom available for us now? Because that wisdom is in the eternal realm. There is no way to come into the presence of God and the eternal realm with sin in our lives. Only by Jesus' blood washing away our sins can we boldly come into the throne of grace. (Hebrews 4:16) Through him, we receive the gift of eternal life so that we can come into the presence of God and get to know him. That is the access for divine revelation and wisdom. It is only by the Spirit of God that this wisdom is available, and God has provided the way for us to receive this divine wisdom in our daily lives!

1 Corinthians 2:9 and 10a, *"But, on the contrary, as the Scripture says, What eye has not seen and ear has not heard and has not entered into the heart of man, [all that] God has prepared (made and keeps ready) for those who love Him [who hold Him in affectionate reverence, promptly obeying Him and gratefully recognizing the benefits He has bestowed]. Yet to us God has unveiled and revealed them by and through His Spirit..."* In the natural realm, it has never entered into the heart of man all that God has prepared, made and keeps ready for those who love him. In John 14:15 (KJV) Jesus said, *"If ye love me, keep my commandments."* There are believers all over the world who don't keep God's commandments. They claim to be born again and they want to go to heaven, but they don't prove their love for God through their obedience. Unfortunately, God's promises cannot be received by believers who do not meet the conditions to obtain them.

1 Corinthians 2:10b, *"...For the [Holy] Spirit searches diligently, exploring and examining everything, even sounding the profound and bottomless things of God [the divine counsel and things hidden and beyond man's scrutiny]."* Only the Spirit can reveal the divine counsels and hidden things of God. What really sets you apart as a child of God is the fact that the Spirit of God Almighty actually lives in you. The Spirit within you gives you the ability to perceive and comprehend the divine gifts and blessings God so lavishly bestows upon his children.

1 Corinthians 2:13, *"And we are setting these truths forth in words not taught by human wisdom but taught by the [Holy] Spirit, combining and interpreting spiritual truths with spiritual language [to those who possess the Holy Spirit]."* You have the Spirit of God in you and you can be taught by him. The Holy

Spirit, not a seminary or even the Bible, leads you into all truth. Please do not misinterpret what I'm saying. There is nothing wrong with going to a Bible college, but you will never arrive at truth by reading the Bible unless the Spirit in you interprets what you read. You can read the Word with your own natural wisdom and process the information out of your carnality. If you do that, you will never understand God and his kingdom. You will be ever learning but you will never come to the knowledge of the truth. (2 Timothy 3:7) No matter how smart you might think you are, you will never be able to interpret what the Bible means from your natural reasoning. Yet believers consistently do that and wonder why they never arrive at truth.

However, when God's children cry out to him and start listening to the Spirit, God will start teaching them. They will begin to understand the Word, even though they don't have the natural "credentials" to do so. Even though they have no formal training from a Bible school or seminary, they will develop a deep understanding of God and his kingdom.

1 Corinthians 2:14, *"But the natural, nonspiritual man does not accept or welcome or admit into his heart the gifts and teachings and revelations of the Spirit of God, for they are folly (meaningless nonsense) to him; and he is incapable of knowing them (of progressively recognizing, understanding, and becoming better acquainted with them) because they are spiritually discerned and estimated and appreciated."*

You should stop and read this over several times. The natural, nonspiritual man leans to his own reasoning. **In the natural, you do not accept, welcome or admit into your heart the gifts and revelations of the Spirit of God.** You cannot accept them, because they are meaningless nonsense to you. You are <u>incapable</u> of knowing them because they are spiritually discerned. You can't appreciate what comes from the Spirit of God if you lean to your natural reasoning, understanding and education.

1 Corinthians 2:15, *"But the spiritual man tries all things [he*

examines, investigates, inquires into, questions, and discerns all things], yet is himself to be put on trial and judged by no one [he can read the meaning of everything, but no one can properly discern or appraise or get an insight into him]." No natural person can properly discern a spiritual person, yet the spiritual person can discern all things. This reconfirms the inability of the natural man to discern spiritual things.

Continuing in verse 16, *"For who has known or understood the mind (the counsels and purposes) of the Lord so as to guide and instruct Him and give Him knowledge? But we have the mind of Christ (the Messiah) and do hold the thoughts (feelings and purposes) of His heart."*

Are You Controlled by the Spirit?

Romans 7 and 8 compare the differences between walking after the flesh or after the Spirit. Let's look at Romans 8:4. *"So that the righteous and just requirement of the Law might be fully met in us who live and move not in the ways of the flesh but in the ways of the Spirit [our lives governed not by the standards and according to the dictates of the flesh, but controlled by the Holy Spirit]."* The just requirement of the Law is met in those who walk in the Spirit rather than in the flesh. The Amplified Bible makes it very clear. **Those who are in the Spirit are controlled by the Spirit.**

Romans 8:5, *"For those who are according to the flesh and are controlled by its unholy desires set their minds on and pursue those things which gratify the flesh, but those who are according to the Spirit and are controlled by the desires of the Spirit set their minds on and seek those things that gratify the [Holy] Spirit."* This is a key verse for examining yourself.

What is your mind set on? If your mind is set on gratifying the things of the flesh, you are living in the flesh. If you are seeking the things that please the Spirit, you are being led and controlled by the Spirit.

It's not very complicated. You are either controlled by your flesh or controlled by the Spirit. If you want to know which one you are in, ask yourself what your mind is set on. What is your heart's desire? The Lord said in Matthew 6:21 that **where your treasure is, there your heart is also**. Where are your thoughts focused? <u>Why</u> are you doing what you do?

A spiritual person seeks to please God in everything they do. It doesn't matter whether they are at work, home or play. They are controlled by the Spirit. In everything they do, they are seeking to please God. They don't want to do anything that would grieve him.

Operating in the natural (in the flesh) doesn't mean you are doing "bad" things. It means your heart is after natural things that satisfy the flesh. The bottom line is, flesh doesn't seek to please the Lord but rather to please self. Many things are not evil in and of themselves, but if you are pursuing the desires of your flesh, you are a carnal, natural person.

Romans 8:6, *"Now the mind of the flesh [which is sense and reason without the Holy Spirit] is death [death that comprises all the miseries arising from sin, both here and hereafter]. But the mind of the [Holy] Spirit is life and [soul] peace [both now and forever]."* The life and soul peace of those who are living in the Spirit are the same <u>now</u> and <u>forever</u>. Some have the idea that we are going to live in sin and be miserable now, but when Jesus comes back, we are going to heaven and will have peace and joy from then on. **The kingdom of God is for now.**

Romans 8:7-9, *"[That is] because the mind of the flesh [with its carnal thoughts and purposes] is hostile to God, for it does not submit itself to God's Law; indeed it cannot. So then those who are living the life of the flesh [catering to the appetites and impulses of their carnal nature] cannot please or satisfy God, or be acceptable to Him. But you are not living the life of the flesh, you are living the life of the Spirit, if the [Holy] Spirit of God [really] dwells within you [directs and controls you]. But if anyone does not possess the [Holy] Spirit of Christ, he is none of His [he does not belong to Christ, is not truly a child of God]."*

The Holy Spirit dwelling within you, directing and controlling you is the assurance that you are a child of God. It's easy to say you have the Spirit in you, but does he control you? **If he does not direct and control you, you are in the flesh.** You are being controlled by your carnality and your thoughts and purposes are hostile toward God. Flesh does not submit itself to God. **If you are operating in the flesh, you <u>cannot</u> please or satisfy God.**

You can see the hypocrisy of singing songs to tell God how much we love and adore him yet we won't allow him to control us by his Spirit. We are doing things that don't please God and are actually hostile to God, and we wonder why God doesn't allow us to hear and understand the mysteries of his kingdom. God gives ears to hear and eyes to see to those who trust in, rely on and adhere to him.

<u>Blessings or Curses</u>

God sets before you this day blessings and curses. (Deuteronomy 11:26) It's a blessing to have ears to hear what God is saying. It's a blessing to understand God's kingdom. It is a curse to not hear and not see and to be ignorant of the things of God. You can choose blessings. **In fact, you are choosing blessings or curses on a daily basis.** What you receive is based on whether or not you yield to the control and direction of the Holy Spirit. Jesus is your Saviour <u>and</u> your Lord. Only through his Lordship can you abide in God's kingdom. **You must take your eyes off temporal things and set your heart on eternal things.**

This may be hard for some of you to understand, because you have been substituting the natural for the spiritual. There's nothing complicated about it. If the Spirit of God that lives in you has convicted you about being in the natural man instead of the spiritual man, it's time to repent. Quit being natural and start being spiritual. Start doing Galatians 5:16. Walk in the Spirit and quit fulfilling the desires of the flesh.

If you want more information on how to be guided and controlled by the Spirit or how to hear God's voice, go back to the book, *My Sheep Hear My Voice*. If you learn how to walk in the Spirit, you can start understanding the things of God's kingdom. You can begin to enjoy your heritage and quit letting the devil steal what is rightfully yours.

Chapter 11

How Does Our Enemy, Satan, See the Kingdom of God Now?

Satan is our enemy, and he seeks to destroy the kingdom of God. Satan controls the kingdom of darkness. In 2 Corinthians 4:4, he is referred to as the god of this world. His goal is to control the earth and eliminate anything that represents God or his kingdom. In the last days, satan will gain control of this earth during the time referred to as the tribulation. However, at the appointed time, the Lord will defeat satan's armies, dismantle the kingdom of darkness and set up the kingdom of God. That will usher in the millennial reign of Christ.

The kingdom of God is the number one threat to satan's kingdom. The kingdom of light (the kingdom of God) and the kingdom of darkness are the only kingdoms that exist in the spiritual realm. All of the natural kingdoms of the world are influenced and controlled by these two kingdoms, because the spiritual realm is of greater power. At this time in history, God has given grace so that the kingdom of darkness can't release its full power. However, we know there is a time coming when that restraint will be pulled back. That is when satan will enforce his control over all the nations of this world for a season.

<u>Satan's Plan</u>

Satan's existence originated in the kingdom of God. In the beginning, there was only God's kingdom and satan was one of the higher angels. He was a beautiful, perfect being created by God. He decided to exalt himself above God, establish his own kingdom and overthrow the kingdom of God. (Isaiah 14:12 and 15) One third of the angels followed him as he tried to overtake the established government of God's kingdom. Satan was defeated, but the Word doesn't explain how or when these events took place. We don't fully understand all of this, but for a season of time, even though satan lost the battle, he was still allowed in heaven and had access to God. From that access, he constantly accused the saints of God. When Job was alive, we know that satan complained to God about him. (Job 1:6-12) We don't understand why God didn't completely remove him from heaven the moment he rebelled, but several scriptures indicate that he had limited access to God in heaven at certain times.

About two thousand years ago, God sent his only Son to earth. Because we were lost, Jesus came to redeem us. Part of his mission was to bring the good news to those who were held captive by satan because of sin. The Son came to bring deliverance. Do you think satan was ignorant that God decided to send his Son? Satan was controlling the earth and when Christ was born to the virgin Mary, satan had access to that information. He knew the purpose for Jesus' coming. Satan did not want him to come, because he knew Jesus was coming to set up the kingdom of light and make the way for the people of the earth to leave the kingdom of darkness. Satan wanted to destroy Jesus from the moment he was born. He realized his kingdom of darkness was in jeopardy.

Revelation 12 describes these events. Because this passage uses a lot of symbolism, it is a little difficult to understand. Let's review this move of satan when he came to earth to destroy the Christ Child. Revelation 12:1-6, *"And a great sign (wonder)-[warning of future events of ominous significance] appeared in heaven: a woman clothed with the sun, with the moon under her feet, and with a crownlike garland (tiara) of twelve stars on her head. She was pregnant and she cried out in her birth pangs, in the anguish of her delivery. Then another ominous sign (wonder) was seen in heaven: Behold, a huge, fiery-red dragon, with seven heads and ten horns, and seven kingly crowns (diadems) upon his heads. His tail swept [across the sky] and dragged down a third of the stars and flung them to the earth. And the dragon stationed himself in front of the woman who was about to be delivered, so that he might devour her child as soon as she brought it forth. And she brought forth a male Child, One Who is destined to shepherd (rule) all the nations with an iron staff (scepter), and her Child was caught up to God and to His throne. And the woman [herself] fled into the desert (wilderness), where she has a retreat prepared [for her] by God, in which she is to be fed and kept safe for 1,260 days (42 months; three and one-half years)."*

As I said, the symbolism in this passage is difficult to understand, but it is pretty obvious that this passage is talking about the one who delivered the Christ, which was Mary. A woman (a virgin girl) delivered the Child. You must be careful not to get caught up in the references to the sun, moon and stars and lose the fact that a woman delivered the Christ child.

This passage clearly states that a child was brought forth who was destined to rule all the nations with a rod of iron. This child was caught up to his Father and to his throne. (Revelation 12:5) We can look at the events that took place from the time of Jesus' birth until he was caught up to heaven, and there is at least a thirty-three and a half year gap in only one verse. It goes on to say that the woman fled into a wilderness for three and a half years, because the enemy was trying to destroy her and the baby.

Satan's Attempts to Destroy Jesus

We know that Jesus was born in Bethlehem. Satan moved through King Herod who ordered that all children be killed that were under two years old. (Matthew 2:16) That was satan's first plan to destroy the baby, but he was not able to kill Jesus. At that time, an angel of the Lord came to Joseph and gave the warning that there was a danger to the child so they had to leave the country immediately. (Matthew 2:13) The wise men had just brought them gold, frankincense and myrrh so they had provision to go to Egypt for a season to be protected. The Bible doesn't say anything about what went on in Egypt, but obviously the devil didn't go there and kill Jesus. God provided a place of safety.

From the very beginning, satan wanted to stop Jesus from coming forth, because Jesus was coming to set up his kingdom on the earth and overthrow satan's kingdom. God Almighty had given the authority of this earth and everything in it to his Son. Satan was aware of this and sought every way possible to destroy Jesus while he was on the earth.

It is a mystery as to why satan didn't try to destroy Jesus between the ages of two and thirty. As Jesus was growing up, he obviously had a security force protecting him. Satan did not have direct access to destroy him.

Once Jesus began his ministry, he was baptized. The Father proclaimed, *"This is my beloved Son, in whom I am well pleased."* (Matthew 3:17 KJV) Then Jesus was led into the wilderness to be tempted of the devil. (Matthew 4:1) The Son of God fasted forty days and nights, and God allowed satan to <u>tempt</u> him but not <u>destroy</u> him.

I'm glad to know that God has complete control over an enemy like the devil, aren't you? He can't do whatever he wants to do. **This is an important point to understand.** We need to see how satan operates, but we must also be aware of his limitations. It is clear that he is limited by God. The Bible is clear about this. Satan wanted to kill the Son of God, but he couldn't do it. He would like to destroy everyone who is part of God's kingdom, but he can't do that either.

Going back to Revelation 12, when satan tried to kill God's Son and failed, verse 7 says war broke out in heaven. *"Michael and his angels went forth to battle with the dragon, and the dragon and his angels fought."* This doesn't say satan and his angels went to fight against God or his angels. It was the other way around. When the war broke out, Michael and his angels battled the devil and his angels. Verse 8 says, *"But they were defeated, and there was no room found for them in heaven any longer."*

Looking at this chronologically, up until this point there was a place in heaven for satan and his angels. They had access to God. The Bible doesn't explain why or how this operated, but once satan tried to destroy the Christ Child and was unsuccessful, Michael and the other angels went to war against him. They defeated him and removed him from God's presence.

If you don't see it as being in chronological order and conclude that it happened some other time, it really doesn't matter. What is important is that Michael and his angels fought against the other angels who had followed satan. They defeated them to the point that satan and his band of angels could no longer find any place in heaven.

Let's look at Revelation 12:9 and 10, *"And the huge dragon was cast down and out-that age-old serpent, who is called the Devil and Satan, he who is the seducer (deceiver) of all humanity the world over; he was forced out and down to the earth, and his angels were flung out along with him. Then I heard a strong (loud) voice in heaven, saying, Now it has come-the salvation and the power and the kingdom (the dominion, the reign) of our God, and the power (the sovereignty, the authority) of His Christ (the Messiah); for the accuser of our brethren, he who keeps bringing before our God charges against them day and night, has been cast out!"*

The time when satan was cast out was the same time that the kingdom of God's Son was manifested. A lot of people have a problem with this, because in their thinking, Jesus' kingdom is not coming until the millennial reign. If the devil is not cast out of heaven until then, how did he get control over all the earth and set up his kingdom here? It is clear in the Bible that satan is already on this earth and he is trying to destroy the church. He has fought against it since its inception. He has been coming against God's people for thousands of years and this fight will culminate in him setting up his throne on this earth before Jesus comes back to defeat him.

Deliverance From Satan

Jesus told his followers not to look for his kingdom to come with signs. It was set up on the earth by God and functions in the spiritual realm. It has not yet been set up physically nor has it overthrown the governments of this world as it will in the millennial reign. It is here for God's children, because Christ's death and resurrection made a way for us to be translated out of the kingdom of darkness and into the kingdom of light. We have become children of God, even though we are still living on an earth which is contaminated by satan and his kingdom. Satan doesn't have full control of every kingdom on this earth, but he has influence in all of them. He is a tremendous threat to God's children because he wants to destroy them. God has given us a safe haven in his kingdom so we can be protected from satan's attacks. We can dwell where the power of darkness has no access. This removes us from the control and imprisonment of the kingdom of darkness.

Continuing in Revelation 12:11, *"And they have overcome (conquered) him by means of the blood of the Lamb and by the utterance of their testimony, for they did not love and cling to life even when faced with death [holding their lives cheap till they had to die for their witnessing]."* Those who are in Christ will overcome satan by the blood of the Lamb and the word of their testimony. They could not have completely overcome satan before the cross, because the blood of the Lamb had not yet been shed. Until he died on the cross and shed his blood, we didn't have the provision to be the overcomers that verse 11 talks about.

We realize there is a time gap between when satan made a strong move to destroy the Christ Child at about two years old and the time when Christ became a man. When Jesus was around thirty years old and beginning his ministry, satan tempted him and tried to disqualify him. Satan knew the only way anyone could break the curse that separated people from God was for someone to live a sinless life in order to be a sacrifice for sinners. The devil was not ignorant of the conditions of the law. He knows them better than we do! Satan didn't have to destroy Jesus. If he could get Jesus to sin, that would also stop him. That would destroy his authority to set up the kingdom of God on earth and to rescue us out of darkness. Therefore, before Jesus began his ministry, satan set out to tempt him with everything on this earth. (Matthew 4:1-10) The Father allowed Jesus to be put through that test. Jesus had to endure the temptations without sin. Praise God! The devil failed again!

<u>Jesus Overcomes the Enemy</u>

As time went on, Jesus began to minister. Everywhere he went, satan tried to hinder him. Satan manifested through his demons and worked through those who were in positions of authority. Jesus overcame everything satan did. Everywhere Jesus went, he proclaimed the good news of the kingdom of God. As the time to establish Jesus' kingdom grew closer, satan became more desperate. He moved in every way he could to destroy the Saviour.

At one point, Jesus was reading in the Temple and he proclaimed that the Spirit of the Lord was upon him because God had anointed him. (Luke 4:18) The people took Jesus out to the edge of a cliff to throw him off because they were so upset. Jesus simply passed through the midst of them. (Luke 4:29 and 30) It wasn't his time to die so the devil couldn't kill him.

Satan moved through the carnal religious leaders of Jesus' time. He also used the Roman rulers and Pontius Pilate to set a trap for Jesus. Satan was able to get Jesus accused by false religious leaders before Pilate and he was crucified.

Satan did not have full knowledge of God's plan. God's plan of redemption was not available to him. Satan really believed he had destroyed Jesus. The Son of God was crucified on the cross, and satan mistakenly believed that he had defeated the kingdom of God.

Satan didn't realize that when Jesus died on the cross, he was the Lamb without blemish who would take away the sins of the world. Through his death, the curse was removed. He qualified to be King of Kings and Lord of Lords. God Almighty gave him the power to lay down his life, but he also gave him the power to take it back again. (John 10:18) He rose from the dead!

Before Christ died, everyone who died with faith in God went to Abraham's bosom. Luke 16:22 and 23 describe this as Paradise, which was separated from Hades by a great gulf. Those in Hades were waiting for final judgment, while those in Paradise were waiting for the Messiah.

When satan thought he had destroyed Jesus, it was time to celebrate. You can imagine what kind of rejoicing was going on in hell. I don't know if those in Paradise could hear their celebration. Ephesians 4:8-10 says that before Jesus ascended to heaven, he first descended into the earth to bring the good news to those who were in captivity. Colossians 2:15 says Jesus made a show of the devil openly! Jesus didn't defeat satan in a hidden corner. He did it right in front of everybody. Jesus put the devil under his feet and took the keys to death, hell and the grave away from him. He went into Paradise and brought the good news that his blood was available to remove their sins. They were separated from God, but once Jesus applied his blood, their sins were removed. Ephesians 4:8 says he led captivity back to his Father.

Jesus took those who had been waiting for him back to his Father. He went in to the Holy of Holies and sprinkled his blood on the mercy seat. He came back to earth and rose from the dead on the third day. When the devil wanted to celebrate, he instead lost everything. When he thought he had finally gotten the victory over God's kingdom, he was completely defeated.

Keep in mind that satan's purpose was to destroy Jesus before he could set up his kingdom. The very thing satan thought would stop the kingdom of God (Jesus' death on the cross) was the thing that brought it in. In 1 Corinthians 2:7 and 8, Paul is talking about the wisdom that he shares with mature people when he says, *"But rather what we are setting forth is a wisdom of God once hidden [from the human understanding] and now revealed to us by God [that wisdom] which God devised and decreed before the ages for our glorification [to lift us into the glory of His presence]. None of the rulers of this age or world perceived and recognized and understood this, for if they had, they would never have crucified the Lord of glory."*

If satan had known or understood what was going to take place, he would not have wanted the Lord crucified. In fact, he would have fought harder than anyone else to keep Jesus off the cross. Jesus came to this earth to die for us, but no man took his life from him. Jesus <u>voluntarily</u> laid down his life. God used the devil in this situation and made a fool out of him.

Let's turn to Revelation 12:17 and take a look at satan's attitude toward all of this. *"So then the dragon was furious (enraged) at the woman, and he went away to wage war on the remainder of her descendants-[on those] who obey God's commandments and who have the testimony of Jesus Christ [and adhere to it and bear witness to Him]."* What is satan doing now? He is furious and he wages war on those of us who obey God's commandments, have the testimony of Jesus Christ and bear witness to him.

2 Timothy 3:12 (KJV) says, *"Yea, and all that will live godly in Christ Jesus shall suffer persecution."* What is this persecution we are going to suffer? It is satan trying to destroy us.

You may not have realized it before, but God had a calling on your life before you ever knew it. The devil knew it and he wanted to destroy you, but he could not get it done because there are limitations as to what he can do. Each one of us has guardian angels, and even though satan would like to destroy us, he is unable to do so.

The War Continues

The war is continuing and satan has not given up. From the time Jesus died on the cross, satan's plan has been to take full control of the earth and destroy every person who believes on the Saviour. There is a time coming when he will have control, but he won't destroy us. He will get close enough that, if it wasn't for the grace of God, even the elect would be destroyed. (Matthew 24:22) Before he can get the job done, Jesus is going to come and take his bride out of this earth for a season. Before the millennial reign begins, our Lord will come back again and defeat the devil.

We are now living in the time after Christ's death but before his return for the church. In the meantime, the war is raging. We are dealing with a furious enemy whose kingdom is established here on earth and getting stronger. Why is the kingdom of God such a threat to satan's kingdom? The answer is simple. God's kingdom is more powerful and it will destroy satan's kingdom. Another reason why satan is threatened is because the devil cannot penetrate the defenses of the kingdom of light. He cannot access a believer who is abiding within the kingdom of God.

Divine Protection

Today, the kingdom of God is only available for God's children. It doesn't protect those who are lost. Satan has continual access to them. However, if you are abiding in the kingdom of God, satan cannot penetrate God's defenses and you can enjoy the safe haven of living in the Spirit. In addition, you who live in God's kingdom can penetrate satan's domain. You can destroy his works. You can rescue someone who is in satan's kingdom and bring them out of darkness. If you will use the authority God has given you and let God equip you, your weapons will defeat the weapons satan has in his kingdom.

The only way satan can get access to you is to tempt you to leave God's kingdom. You do that by yielding to the lusts of the flesh and sinning. Once you have sinned, you are outside the protective shield of the kingdom of God. Then satan has access to steal, kill and destroy in your life, even though he has limited power because you are a child of God. (Ephesians 4:27 and James 4:7) This limited access is not something God gives him. You give it to him!

You have been given the right to live in the kingdom of God now, but you also have the freedom of choice. You can choose to leave God's kingdom and let the devil steal from you. God does not want you to be ignorant of satan's devices. He wants you to be aware of the devil's tricks, and he doesn't want you to yield to them. Keep Revelation 12:17 in mind. Satan is furious and his goal is the total destruction of God's children.

Satan is a Thief.

Satan's kingdom survives by what it steals, and he cannot steal from those who are living in the kingdom of God. Matthew 28:18 says that all authority in heaven and in earth has been given to the Lord. That leaves none for the devil. The Lord didn't give him any authority here on this earth. God has only shared his authority with his children. The devil had to steal it from the Lord or from us, so where do you think he got it? **Whatever power or authority satan has in your life is what you have given him.**

There are mature Christians who are not ignorant of satan's devices. They are not afraid of the devil, and they know who they are in Christ. It is no different than who you are in Christ. Yet satan can attack both of you and you get overcome while the other person doesn't. You may wish you had the faith they have, but **you have the same Spirit!** The difference is, they hold on to their God-given authority. You give it away, because you believe the lie of the devil that he can overcome you. When you believe that lie, you give him the authority to defeat you.

Satan may try to use authority he got from someone else to attack you, but it doesn't make any difference. The God who lives in you is greater than the god of this world. Satan doesn't like to lose battles. You will find that a person who really walks in the Spirit consistently is rarely attacked directly. Satan uses guerrilla warfare on that person. He has to use human agents close to that person to mount an indirect attack. He can't use a frontal attack against someone who is living in the kingdom of God now, because he can't get into God's kingdom to attack them directly.

You may be wondering what satan steals from us as Christians. The first thing he steals is our authority. All authority (power) in heaven and earth was given to Jesus and he shares it with his joint heirs. (Matthew 28:18 and Romans 8:17) If satan has any authority to function, which he obviously does, it is because he stole it from God's children. He also wants to steal our heritage. If the children of God understood their inheritance as much as the devil understands it, they would be walking in a much greater spiritual depth.

Satan is a Liar.

Satan operates in the realm of lies. He is the father of lies, and everything he speaks to you is intended to deceive, steal from or destroy you in some way. (John 10:10) He knows who you are in Christ, but he also knows you must meet God's conditions to receive God's promises. **He will deceive you into trying to do everything else but the one thing that will qualify you for God's promises.** In doing this, he has robbed you of your inheritance. He wants to steal your inheritance because the more you walk in your inheritance, the more of a threat you are to him. Satan doesn't want you to become a vessel equipped by your

Father to do the same works that Jesus did, which is to destroy the devil's works.

Satan knows we can have fellowship with God. When we have that fellowship, satan doesn't have any access to us. He wasn't able to keep you from becoming a child of God, so he will do anything he can to keep you from having fellowship with God. **Satan will tempt you to do anything other than to make God happy.** Why do you think you have to deal with thoughts that accuse God of doing something that is unfair? Satan wants you to be angry at God. Satan is the accuser of the brethren and he loves to accuse God, too. If you have thoughts that accuse God of wrongdoing, to whom are you listening? Satan wants you offended at God (which is sin because you are judging God), because he knows that sin will separate you from God. Then satan has access to you. **When you listen to satan's lies, he has stolen your fellowship with God from you and you allowed it!**

God has ordained positions of authority for you. Each one of you has the potential to rule and reign with Christ in his kingdom. The devil wants to make sure you don't qualify for that position. He wants to keep you from being a part of the kingdom that will overthrow his rule.

In Philippians 4:19, God promises to supply all our needs according to his riches in glory. Instead of receiving that provision, the devil wants you to struggle all the time. He wants you to be at war with him but unequipped to defeat him. **If the devil can get you to believe that God hasn't given you what is necessary to overcome him, then you will be defeated.**

Every child of God has access to the provisions that are available to those living in the kingdom of God. You can have peace, joy and contentment, but the devil will try to steal them from you at every opportunity. He wants as many people as possible to be judged with him.

<u>Staying in the Kingdom of Light</u>

Colossians 1:11-14 says, *"[We pray] that you may be invigorated and strengthened with all power according to the might of His glory, [to exercise] every kind of endurance and patience (perseverance and forbearance) with joy, Giving thanks to the Father, Who has qualified and made us fit to share the portion which is the inheritance of the saints (God's holy people) in the Light. [The Father] has delivered and drawn us to Himself out of the control and the dominion of darkness and has transferred us into the kingdom of the Son of His love, In Whom we have our redemption through His blood, [which means] the forgiveness of our sins."*

When you got saved, the Father translated you out of darkness and into the kingdom of light. When Jesus' blood was applied to your sins, you were forgiven. You were immediately moved into right standing with God, which means you were in the kingdom of God. You felt the Spirit and it was wonderful.

The question is, why did you leave? Somebody lied to you! They told you the honeymoon period would wear off and you would no longer feel God's presence consistently. I am not judging the people who told you this lie because someone lied to them, too. They sincerely believe this "doctrine" to be the truth, but they are sincerely wrong. **God never intended for you to leave his presence or his kingdom.** This lie is a trick of satan to move you out of God's kingdom, because if he doesn't get you out, he can't steal authority from you and he can't make you miserable. If the devil gets access to bring harm to you, you are in a place where you are not supposed to be. If you are doing what God says, even if his purposes may involve suffering, God will give you grace that is sufficient to joyfully endure anything that takes place. When you suffer for his glory, there is an immense reward in heaven for you.

The enemy wants to keep you out of God's kingdom at all costs. He will tell you that God's kingdom doesn't exist now. If he can convince you that God's kingdom won't exist until Jesus comes back, then you'll believe the doctrine that you can live any way you want and still rule with Christ. 2 Timothy 2:12 plainly says that if you aren't willing to suffer for Christ's sake, you are not worthy to reign with him. It is time to look at what the Word really says.

We don't fully understand God's timing, but we do know that if we stay in Christ, we will know him and we will be like him when he returns. (1 John 3:2) If you are living in the kingdom of God, you are becoming like him already.

If you could see God's kingdom as clearly as the devil sees it, you would be rushing to get into it. You wouldn't be remotely tempted to get out of the kingdom if you could see what access the devil has to you when you get out. The devil is a whole lot more afraid of you than you realize. God has not given us a spirit of fear, so we shouldn't be afraid of the devil at all. The devil trembles because he knows you have the potential to destroy his works. He also knows that this destruction can only be accomplished from within the kingdom of God. You must abide there in order to destroy the works of the enemy.

You have a chance to move into the kingdom of God now. You can grow up in Christ and become a soldier the Father can use to destroy the works of the devil. You can also rescue others from the kingdom of darkness. Many Christians feel threatened by the devil, but you need to understand that he is far more threatened by you than you are by him. If you yield yourself to God, you can destroy satan's works and he can't do anything about it.

Chapter 12

What Should I Do to See the Kingdom of God Now?

What is your attitude toward satan, considering what was revealed in the previous chapter? What is your attitude toward your Adam nature? Satan fights against God's kingdom because it is such a threat to him. If you realize at this point that satan has robbed you of your heritage through the years, it is time to adjust your attitude toward him <u>and</u> your flesh, as well as toward God.

When I realized how much satan had been robbing from me, I got angry at the devil. My attitude toward him changed. I wasn't complacent and I didn't ignore him. I realized that satan wants to destroy my life. He wants to prevent me from enjoying my heritage as a child of God, and he will use any method necessary to defeat me. I soon realized that I had been cooperating with him by yielding to the flesh. That really made me angry so I began to resist him instead.

<u>Your Attitude Toward the Devil</u>

If you don't get an attitude of resistance toward the devil, you won't do anything about him. Many people get a little frustrated with the devil. However, when they try to resist, they get "beaten up" by him. They often decide it's easier to stop trying to resist him. They decide his attack or influence in their lives isn't that bad, so they put up with it.

It's important to understand that the most evil person who has or will ever live is not nearly as evil as satan. Can you imagine having a close relationship with an evil, perverted person?

Would you let them talk to you and yield to their counsel? Most believers know from the Word that satan is the author of all sin. We have been clearly commanded to cast off the works of darkness. (Romans 13:12) Even with all these warnings from God, his children still listen to the devil.

Satan is the accuser of the brethren, and there are many divisions in the body of Christ because believers are listening to him. When you judge others, which God has told you not to do, you are under the direction of and in obedience to satan. Many believers are listening to and obeying him without even knowing they are doing it. He is a liar and the father of lies. (John 8:44) He wouldn't tell the truth if his life depended upon it. So what is your attitude toward this wicked one and his access into your life?

Change Your Attitude

The truths in this book should be doing one of two things in your life. They should be confirming what you are already obeying and encouraging you as they shed additional light on how to walk with God more closely. Otherwise, they should be convicting you if you are not walking in the kingdom of God now. You may not have known it was possible to live in God's kingdom now because you were deceived. If you were deceived, it is because satan (the deceiver) has blinded your eyes. He has been able to do that because you have yielded to him through the years whether you were aware of it or not. If you have desired God's best but have been blinded, satan has tricked you.

It's time to change your attitude! You ought to get angry at satan for what he has stolen from you. This book is not intended to bring condemnation on anyone but it is intended to bring conviction. **Conviction is a blessing for the children of God.** Convictions is intended to convince you that something is out of order. All the evidence presented in this book is intended to convince you of the reality of the kingdom of God now and your place in it, as well as expose some tricks the devil uses to keep you from enjoying your inheritance. If you don't get angry at the devil, you aren't going to do anything to resist him.

I'm going to share with you where I was when I realized how much satan had stolen from me. I was disgusted with myself for allowing my Adam nature to control me. My carnal, Adam nature gave access to the devil and he destroyed many things in my life. As angry as I was with the devil, I realized that he could not have had access to me if my own Adam nature had not cooperated with him. **My Adam nature gave satan place because I had released my Adam nature to run my life.** God gave me a free will, and I can decide to yield to Christ or yield to the flesh. Satan was robbing from me because I had yielded my will and my flesh to him. When you trace it back to the root, it started with me. **I had the choice.** If I had chosen to yield to Christ, God would have never allowed satan to overpower that choice. Instead, I made the wrong choice for many years.

Many of you reading this book have made wrong choices throughout your life. The question is, are you going to continue making the wrong choices and allowing satan to steal from you until he finally destroys you? If not, you can take a stand like I did and say, "This is as far as it goes! I am giving no more place to the devil. I'm fed up with him and I am fed up with my own Adam nature. I'm going to start doing what God says, whether the flesh and the devil like it or not. I'm going to serve God."

The Right Attitude

You must develop a right attitude toward God. If you have yielded to satan and your Adam nature, you ought to be repenting and than thanking God for his forgiveness. You can then move on to stirring up the gifts that are within you. At the same time, seek for new insights into who you are as a child of God and what God has made available for you. You should also praise God that he loves you in spite of all the failures in your past. You should constantly praise him because he still has a purpose for you in his kingdom. **God still wants to bless you.**

Many of you have gifts and callings on your lives. You have abilities that God has given you that have either lain dormant or have been used for something other than God and his kingdom. You need to stir up the faith you have in God. Get before God and start taking back the faith you have released into lies and the things of the flesh. Start releasing faith into God alone.

Choose This Day

You have come to the valley of decision. The choice is yours. You need to choose this day whom you will serve. If the Lord is God, serve him. (1 Kings 18:21) If you really think the devil and the flesh are gods, serve them. It is time to make up your mind. Which one are you going to serve?

Revelation 3:14-22, *"And to the angel (messenger) of the assembly (church) in Laodicea write: These are the words of the Amen, the trusty and faithful and true Witness, the Origin and Beginning and Author of God's creation: I know your [record of] works and what you are doing; you are neither cold nor hot. Would that you were cold or hot! So, because you are lukewarm and neither cold nor hot, I will spew you out of My mouth! For you say, I am rich; I have prospered and grown wealthy, and I am in need of nothing; and you do not realize and understand that you are wretched, pitiable, poor, blind, and naked. Therefore I counsel you to purchase from Me gold refined and tested by fire, that you may be [truly] wealthy, and white clothes to clothe you and to keep the shame of your nudity from being seen, and salve to put on your eyes, that you may see. Those whom I [dearly and tenderly] love, I tell their faults and convict and convince and reprove and chasten [I discipline and instruct them].*

So be enthusiastic and in earnest and burning with zeal and repent [changing your mind and attitude]. Behold, I stand at the door and knock; if anyone hears and listens to and heeds My voice and opens the door, I will come in to him and will eat with him, and he [will eat] with Me. He who overcomes (is victorious), I will grant him to sit beside Me on My throne, as I Myself overcame (was victorious) and sat down beside My Father on His throne. He who is able to hear, let him listen to and heed what the [Holy] Spirit says to the assemblies (churches)."

This church claimed it didn't have need of anything. It was a very prosperous church, but God gave them a warning. He said, "You are <u>lukewarm</u>. If you don't repent, I will spew you out of my mouth." God would rather you be hot or cold than lukewarm.

<u>Are You Lukewarm</u>?

What are you today? Are you cold, hot or lukewarm? **In order to be hot, you must humble yourself and submit to the Lordship of Jesus Christ.** You have to walk in the Spirit consistently. You must obey God with a right attitude and a pure motive of love for him. If you draw close to God, he will draw close to you. (James 4:8) **If you are in continual fellowship with God, you are hot.**

However, if you "get your act together" for Sunday morning and get in the Spirit for a little while but immediately get back in the flesh, then sometimes you are hot and sometimes you are cold. When you mix hot and cold together, the result is being lukewarm. A lukewarm person isn't cold (or hot) all the time. Lost people are cold all the time. Those who are sold out for God are hot all the time. **Those who alternate between the kingdoms of light and darkness by submitting to God one moment and then submitting to their flesh end up being lukewarm.**

If you are in that category, you have a decision to make. Satan is setting you up for destruction. Now is the time to repent. Today is the day to make up your mind. You need to have the same attitude Joshua had in Joshua 24:15b (KJV) as he said, *"...but as for me and my house, we will serve the Lord."*

My service to God is not dependent upon anyone else serving

him with me. I made a decision to serve the Lord, and I haven't changed my mind since the day I made that decision. I'm still serving God. I renew that decision daily. When I make a mistake, I repent quickly and get right back in the presence of the Lord. I don't let enough "cold" in to make me lukewarm.

We all sin and come short of the glory of God. (Romans 3:23) We all make mistakes. If you start becoming cold, how long does it take before you repent and get hot again? That will determine whether you become lukewarm or you stay hot. It is crucial that you take some time to meditate on this truth and repent from your heart for being lukewarm in any area of your life.

Do You Lack Knowledge?

In Hosea 4:6a, God said, "*My people are destroyed for lack of knowledge;...*" That's why many of you have gotten into trouble. You've lacked knowledge on how to walk with God. You have lacked knowledge about the kingdom of God, as well as how to get in the kingdom and stay there. Some of you have gotten frustrated because those who are in authority in your lives haven't taught you about living in God's kingdom. The reason most of them didn't teach you is because they were never taught themselves. Lack of teaching doesn't excuse you. You have a Bible. Everything you are reading in this book came out of the Bible. You are commanded by God to study to show yourself approved so you will be a worker that needs not be ashamed, rightly dividing the word of truth. Even if you think you had an excuse up to this point, you don't have one anymore. Having read this book, you are certainly not ignorant any longer.

In 2 Corinthians 2:11b, Paul told the Corinthians that they were not ignorant of satan's devices. Satan uses our ignorance of him and God against us, but God does not want you to be ignorant. That's why this teaching is being put into book form. When truth comes, it convicts you of sin. When it is embraced, it sets you free. All of this information is given so you can rescue yourself from the snares of satan.

In 2 Timothy 2:24, Paul instructed Timothy not to be angry or debate but in gentleness to tell the truth. These truths are being given so you can rescue yourself from the snare that satan has set for you. If you don't know truth and apply it, he can take you captive at his will.

Make the Adjustment

It is imperative that you adjust your attitude toward the devil (your arch enemy), your flesh and God your Father. If you will yield to God and make the decision to serve him and love him, you will begin learning how to live in God's kingdom now and throughout eternity. **If you determine that you are not going to yield to your flesh or give place to the devil, you can make rapid progress spiritually.** Regardless of how much you may be convicted at this point, God loves you. He is faithful to forgive you of your sins and cleanse you from all unrighteousness if you will simply repent and confess your sins. (1 John 1:9)

Chapter 13

If I Embrace The Kingdom Of God Now, How Will That Affect My Life?

Living in the kingdom of God now will dramatically change your life for the better. I think it is important that we focus on the word "change". **This walk will change your life.** If you embrace the truth and make the decision to yield to Jesus' Lordship and walk in his kingdom, your life and everything in it will be dramatically affected in a positive way.

<u>Becoming a New Creation</u>
2 Corinthians 5:17, *"Therefore if any person is [ingrafted] in Christ (the Messiah) he is a new creation (a new creature altogether); the old [previous moral and spiritual condition] has passed away. Behold, the fresh and new has come!"* Many people are familiar with this scripture and quote it as if it is an automatic thing that happens the day you get saved. Some of you may be new believers and some of you may have been saved for fifty years. Nobody knows you like you know yourself, and **you know whether your old nature has been passing away or not**. You know whether everything is continually being made new or whether you are alternating between being hot and cold. You know when you are in your new nature, but at other times you may realize you are in the old nature.

<u>Bow Your Knee to Jesus' Lordship</u>.
If you embrace what I am talking about, **you must bow your knee to Jesus' Lordship**. I continue to repeat this truth because

it is absolutely crucial! **Lordship is the very foundation of kingdom living.** As this becomes a way of life, old things will pass away and all things will become new. With the right attitude and trust in the Lord, the process of change is very exciting. **When you have a clear vision of where you are going, letting go of the old things becomes much easier.**

Most people do not like to change. That is why some of you have struggled throughout the years. **You have tried to find some way to please God and walk with him <u>without actually changing</u>.** You have allowed the flesh to influence your character for a long time. **Not only has your flesh formed your character, you have become comfortable with that character.** You may not like the way you act sometimes, and you may not like the way you react to certain things. You may smile on the outside while you are angry in your heart, and you probably don't like that either. Yet at the same time, such behavior has been "normal" for you. The effort to change seems too difficult.

Most people make excuses for their behavior or they make a token effort to change. Some excuse themselves by saying, "That is just the way I am and I can't help it. I guess God made me this way." <u>That is a lie!</u> If you do not reflect the nature of God's Son, then God didn't make you act that way. The new creation God desires to develop in you will resemble God. Your nature and character can either be like God or like the Adam nature, which is sensuous (controlled by the senses) and carnal. It can even be like satan. **If your character is carnal and selfish, that is the fruit of your lordship.** You may even have traits you allowed satan to form in you. The negative aspects of your character result from submitting to ungodly influences, regardless of whether they are from the Adam nature or satan.

<u>Acquiring a Taste for Change</u>

The good news is that you can repent and renounce your old nature. You can do as Paul did and put no confidence in or dependence on your flesh. (Philippians 3:3) You can yield yourself totally to Christ for him to create a new nature in you. **That will start the change!** God will start exposing old things that need to pass away. When God exposes something, it passes away through repentance. When you make the decision to turn around and go the other way (repentance), it will start the process of old things passing away and all things becoming new.

The most immediate fruit of embracing the kingdom of God now is that you will move into right standing with God. You will begin to have peace and joy. That is a pretty good place to start, but that's just the beginning. More changes are on the way! **You need to acquire a taste for change.** Change is only negative if you are changing to something worse. There will be a dramatic, <u>positive</u> difference when you move out of the flesh and into the Spirit. 2 Corinthians 3:18 says you can move from glory to glory! **The longer you remain in right standing with God, the more your character will change.** As the negative things begin to pass away, you will begin to enjoy a deeper walk with God.

Some of you are being destroyed for lack of knowledge. You don't really know where God wants to take you. Some of you are afraid to let go of where you are. Even if you can't see where you are going, you can trust the One who is leading you. **God loves you and wants only the best for your life.** If you walk in humility before him, he will test you for a season and purify your faith, then he will exalt you. (1 Peter 5:6) You have to decide to trust God. **Faith in God is simply believing that he is trustworthy to do what he said he would do.** God also tells us if we turn from the flesh and walk after the Spirit, he will make us vessels of honor in his house. (2 Timothy 2:20)

As the old things pass away and all things become new, you will begin to see the wonder of God's plan for your life. You need to eagerly expect change and the good things it brings. As you seek the kingdom of God first, he will add everything you need according to his riches in glory. (Philippians 4:19) It's not complicated. Matthew 6:33 tells us to seek first the kingdom of God and his righteousness. Then all the other things you need will be added to you.

Expect Wonderful Changes in Every Area of Your Life.

Most importantly, you will begin to have fellowship with your Father and Jesus. You'll learn to hear the Lord's voice and get to know him. You will grow rapidly in the Spirit. Every area of your life will be affected by walking in the kingdom of God. That doesn't mean God is going to change everything you are doing in your life, but he will change the way you are doing things. You may be working the same job you've worked before. However, instead of doing your job out of your reasoning and your secular education, you will begin to acknowledge him and allow him to direct you in that profession. You will find out that he knows much more about that job than you do. He will start blessing you with his wisdom and insight. With his direction and favor, you can become far more effective in the very same job.

God will also bring change in your home life. Everything is going to work better as you learn to live in the kingdom of God, because you have access to better equipment than you would have had if you had continued to live in this world's system.

For example, as you begin to obey God, you are sowing agape love into him. (John 14:15) God promises that whatever you sow, you will also reap. (Galatians 6:7) You will always reap more than you sow. As you continue this process, the level of your capacity to love will increase. The immediate benefit will be your ability to love your family more than ever before. Your love will continue to grow until you have enough for it to be shed abroad from your heart.

Again, if you embrace this message, everything in your life will begin to change. How you do things, why you do things, and for whom you are doing them will change. Your motive is going to change dramatically. Your attitude toward God and what he does in your life will change. Many of your "methods" are going to change. Some new things will need to be learned and some things will need to be "unlearned", because you didn't learn the right thing. God will make those adjustments. There is nothing negative about God's dealings in your life when you are walking in obedience to him.

If God tears something down, it's because it is in the way of something better he wants to build. God does not want to be Lord of our lives in order to take us backward. He wants to be Lord to move us forward. Just like building a great building, you have to go down before you can go up, because you need a solid foundation. Simply trust and obey! Develop a positive attitude that embraces the wonderful changes God will bring into your life. Attitude makes all the difference!

Chapter 14

If I Reject the Kingdom of God Now, How Will That Affect My Life?

Learning to live in the kingdom of God now is the key to much of your inheritance as a believer. Rejecting what God has made available <u>now</u> will dramatically affect your <u>future</u>. Do not allow satan to steal the many blessings God has planned for you.

<u>The Story of Esau</u>

Let's consider the story of Esau, which is referred to in Hebrews 12:16. *"That no one may become guilty of sexual vice, or become a profane (godless and sacrilegious) person as Esau did, who sold his own birthright for a single meal."*

This refers to the story in Genesis 25:29-34 when Esau was coming home from the fields. He was very hungry and his brother, Jacob, was making stew. Esau asked him for food but Jacob refused. Verse 31-34, *"Jacob answered, Then sell me today your birthright (the rights of a firstborn). Esau said, See here, I am at the point of death; what good can this birthright do me? Jacob said, Swear to me today [that you are selling it to me]; and he swore to Jacob and sold him his birthright. Then Jacob gave Esau bread and stew of lentils, and he ate and drank and rose up and went his way. Thus Esau scorned his birthright as beneath his notice."* (Esau was the firstborn, so he was the heir.) Esau counted his birthright as "beneath his notice", because **he was thinking more about his natural desires than the life-long consequences of his decision**. He made an oath that gave up his birthright as the firstborn just to get something to eat.

Later on, Esau wanted to change his mind. He probably planned to get out of this oath. Hebrews 12:17 says, *"For you understand that later on, when he wanted [to regain title to] his inheritance of the blessing, he was rejected (disqualified and set aside), for he could find no opportunity to repair by repentance [what he had done, no chance to recall the choice he had made], although he sought for it carefully with [bitter] tears."*

Just to give you a little background, the name Jacob means *supplanter*. (Strong's #3290) This means "trip up the heels; to remove or displace by stratagem; to overthrow; to undermine." Jacob and Esau were twins, but Esau was born first. Jacob was holding Esau's heel as he was being born, thus giving Jacob his name.

Esau had hairy skin but Jacob was smooth skinned. When the twins' father (Isaac) was losing his sight, Jacob took the skin of a young goat and put it over his arms and neck. He went to his father while pretending to be Esau. He also brought food that had been prepared just like his brother Esau would have done. His father, being convinced that he was Esau, gave the blessing and inheritance to Jacob. When Esau found out about Jacob's trickery, he was very angry and plotted to kill Jacob. Esau later explained everything to his father, but it was too late. The blessing had already been given. (Genesis 27:36) There was no way to reverse it.

Esau made a foolish mistake because his flesh was weak. He wanted food badly enough that he was willing to give anything to get it. He probably thought he could reverse his decision later on. By the time he realized he had made a serious mistake and was genuinely willing to repent, he could find no place of repentance. It was too late.

<u>The Ten Virgins</u>

Matthew 25:1-13 relays the story of the ten virgins. Five virgins were wise and five were foolish. **All were virgins**

looking for the bridegroom. The five wise virgins went with the bridegroom when he came because they were prepared. The five foolish virgins didn't go in and were rejected. We are warned to watch for the bridegroom's coming in verse 13. *"Watch therefore [give strict attention and be cautious and active], for you know neither the day nor the hour when the Son of Man will come."*

This passage in Matthew is talking about ten virgins. It doesn't say there were five virgins and five harlots. This passage isn't about five people looking for the Lord and five people serving the devil. All ten were looking for the Lord. All ten wanted to be part of the bride. All ten wanted to go in and spend eternity with the Lord. They were all waiting for him, but five were prepared and five were not ready.

At the time the bridegroom called, all of the virgins rose up to trim their lamps. The five wise virgins had <u>brought extra oil</u> for their lamps but the foolish had not. While they slept their lamps had gone out. The foolish virgins wanted oil from the wise virgins, but the wise ones didn't have time or supply enough to share with the virgins who were unprepared. It was time to go. The foolish virgins were willing to go get the oil like the wise ones had done, but it was the wrong time. Once they realized they had made a mistake, they went to get the oil. Matthew 25:10 and 11 imply that they actually got it. The only problem was, the door had already been shut. It never reopened and they were not allowed to enter in. They had procrastinated until it was too late.

Procrastination is Dangerous.
Procrastination is the most foolish and dangerous thing you can do. You don't know the hour when the Lord is coming. **Having good intentions will not save your inheritance but faithfulness will.** Hell is being filled daily with people who had good intentions. Thoughts of procrastination come from satan.

Now is the time to repent! You should now realize that the

Word of God speaks clearly about the kingdom of God now. It is clear to you that you should be living and walking in God's kingdom daily. The Bible clearly teaches that you should be in fellowship and communion with God. (1 Corinthians 1:9 and 1 John 1:3) You should be hearing his voice and obeying him.

Many people desire fellowship and communion with God but they never do the necessary things to achieve it. They make a token effort, but when it gets a little uncomfortable because things have to start changing, they put it off a little longer.

I don't know anything about the people who will read this book, but **the Holy Spirit knows everything about you**. The Holy Spirit who has been moving on me while preparing this book is the same Spirit who is ministering to you now as you read it. He will speak to your heart based upon where you are.

I have seen a dangerous habit that is common among many Christians. It is the habit of procrastination. They have a tendency to put things off just a little longer. They want to deal with what God is saying tomorrow. Yet every morning you can read your newspaper or turn on your television and find out that someone else has died. What if they were going to repent and get right with God tomorrow? Many people are waiting until tomorrow or a more favorable time to repent.

There will never be a more convenient time to obey God. Today is the day of salvation. If you are hearing God speak to your heart today, do not harden your heart. (Hebrews 3:15) The <u>moment</u> God convicts you that you are doing something wrong, you need to make the change. Now is the best moment in time to deal with it. There is never a better day than today. The maximum amount of grace to deal with any issue is the moment God first convicts you. It may be something you need to quit doing or something you haven't been doing and should do.

Because this is very critical, I am going to say it again. **The temptation to procrastinate comes from a demonic spirit speaking to you.** Satan knows that if he can get you to put off this decision a little longer, he has successfully stolen a little more from you. Even if you deal with it later, he has stolen the benefits you could have had from walking in it now. From the moment God first began to deal with you to the moment you actually do it, satan has stolen everything that could have been accomplished and what you could have received of your inheritance during that time.

There is not a person on the face of this earth who has not procrastinated the things of God to some measure. If the Spirit of God is convicting you, you are not alone. All have sinned and come short of the glory of God, but <u>all do not keep on sinning</u>. You are called to repent, turn from your sins and go the other way. Like Paul says in Galatians 5:16, you can walk in the Spirit. When you do that, you cannot fulfill the lusts of your flesh.

<u>Repent of Rejecting the Kingdom</u>.

You have to change your mind. You need to repent of the sin of procrastination. Quit listening to the devil. Listen to God and do what he says. This book makes God's standards for his children very clear. If you <u>knowingly reject</u> these truths, it will be much harder for you to find a place of repentance should you decide to procrastinate once again. Such rejection will open a major door to satan. It is one thing to make mistakes and miss God because you are ignorant, but it is quite another thing to know the truth and knowingly reject it by choosing your flesh instead of God. This is very, very serious. It falls into the same category as having put your hand to the plow and then turning back. (Luke 9:62)

Since you have gotten to this point in the book, it should have dawned on you by now that you really don't have an option. You need to make the necessary adjustments and recognize your heritage as a child of God. You belong in the kingdom of God and you belong there <u>now</u>! It is where you are supposed to live and move and have your being. (Acts 17:28) Any time you choose to reject living in the kingdom of God now, you are giving satan direct access to steal your inheritance from you. Your pride will also put you in a place where God will resist you! (1 Peter 5:5b) Obviously, that is not a good place to be. This choice will dramatically affect your life. Now is the time to repent of rejecting God and his kingdom. They are available to you <u>now</u>!

Chapter 15

God Has a Plan

In Genesis 1, when the Lord created everything, God had a plan. Before the creation of the heavens, the earth and mankind, he had a plan. Revelation 21 describes how God will destroy the heavens and the earth and create new ones. At that point, he will still have a plan.

God's Purposes
Ecclesiastes 3:1, *"To everything there is a season, and a time for every matter or purpose under heaven."* Ecclesiastes 3:11, *"He has made everything beautiful in its time. He also has planted eternity in men's hearts and minds [a divinely implanted sense of a purpose working through the ages which nothing under the sun but God alone can satisfy], yet so that men cannot find out what God has done from the beginning to the end."* Continuing in verse 14, *"I know that whatever God does, it endures forever; nothing can be added to it nor anything taken from it. And God does it so that men will [reverently] fear Him [revere and worship Him, knowing that He is]."*

These verses in Ecclesiastes contain great truths. Solomon was seeking to understand God and his wisdom. He tried everything under the sun to see if there was value in any of it. He also learned that there is a season for everything under the sun. He came to the conclusion that, except for the worship of and obedience to God, everything was futile and vain.

Ecclesiastes 12:8 and 13, *"Vapor of vapors and futility of futilities, says the Preacher. All is futility (emptiness, falsity, vainglory, and transitoriness)! All has been heard; the end of the matter is: Fear God [revere and worship Him, knowing that He is] and keep His commandments, for this is the whole of man [the full, original purpose of his creation, the object of God's providence, the root of character, the foundation of all happiness, the adjustment to all inharmonious circumstances and conditions under the sun] and the whole [duty] for every man."*

God's Timing

One of the favorite tactics of satan against the children of God is to get us doing the right thing at the wrong time. God has a plan. As his children, we are part of that plan. Our problem is that we try to get God to do something he said he would do at a time he doesn't plan to do it. The Lord God is not slack concerning his promises, but he is long suffering. (2 Peter 3:8 and 9) If it takes ten thousand years to get it done, he will still do what he says. However, he will do it when he planned to do it, not when we think he ought to do it. This is where we get into trouble. God's plan began long before we came along. His plan will still be in effect after we all die. This little space we call "time" is just a moment in eternity. It is a part of God's plan, but it certainly isn't the whole of his plan. God's plan covers everything that has ever been or ever will be.

A very common problem among Christians is the inability to get into God's timing for his plan. Occasionally, we stumble across God's timing. When we do this, we see God move. That is what is commonly called a "divine appointment". What that really means is that the kingdom of God and God's plan happen to coincide with where we are and what we are doing. If you happen to be the instrument that he uses at that time, you will see God work through you. All he asks you to do is give him the credit for what he did. Give him all the praise and glory and he will honor you for being the vessel that was used.

Some of you may not have experienced being used by God.

In fact, most believers do not experience a sovereign move of God on a regular basis. Living in the kingdom of God now is all about bringing your daily life into alignment with what he has planned for you! This is part of his overall plan and you can be in his plan at the right time and the right place. The sovereignty of God flowing in your life will confirm it. **God intends for this to be a way of life for his children.**

Eternity in Your Heart
Ecclesiastes 3:11a, *"...He also has planted eternity in men's hearts and minds."* **If you don't sense eternity within you, it is because you have seared your conscience and hardened your heart.** Now is the time to humble yourself under the mighty hand of God so that in due season he may exalt you. (I Peter 5:6) This is the time to let God take out your stony heart and give you a tender heart of flesh so you can sense the eternal things God is doing. (Ezekiel 36:26 and 11:19) **Your heart and mind should have a sense of longing that God alone can satisfy.**

God has placed within every person the need to connect with him. Nothing but God can satisfy this need. Yet people (even believers) try to satisfy this need with everything but God. All these other things sear their hearts a little more, because they are counterfeits that are being substituted for what will really satisfy. When all has been accomplished, the same emptiness that only God can fill remains. **Many people try to dull their hearing so they cannot hear their heart cry out for God.**

God's plan is for that heart longing to be in you and that it would draw you to him. He does not wish that any should perish but that all should come to repentance. (2 Peter 3:9) **If you dull your hearing so that you can't hear God speaking to you, what will you do when it is time to stand before him and give an account for your life?** What will you do on judgment day when it is decided whether you will spend eternity with God or in hell? You will be like Esau who was willing to repent but was unable to find a place of repentance. Don't wait until it is too late.

Ecclesiastes 3:14 says, *"...whatever God does, it endures forever..."* His works are not temporal. We spend the majority of our time trying to accumulate temporal things, even though the Word warns us that these things will not last. The things we cannot see will last for eternity. People struggle with the kingdom of God now, because they can't see it. **2 Corinthians 4:18 says the things you can't see are everlasting, but the things you see are temporal.** We don't understand that so we don't believe it.

God gave us the gift of faith which is the substance of things we hope for and the evidence of things we have not yet seen. (Hebrews 11:1) We have hope for the future as God's children, and we can have an earnest of our inheritance now. We can start becoming part of God's plan now. He hasn't changed his mind about his plan and our part in it.

"I know that whatever God does, it endures forever; nothing can be added to it nor anything taken from it. And God does it so that men will [reverently] fear Him [revere and worship Him, knowing that He is]." (Ecclesiastes 3:14) All that God does endures forever. He allows us to see his sovereignty so we can know that he is God. This is done so that we may worship him and have a reverential fear of him. Proverbs 9:10 says that the fear of the Lord is the beginning of wisdom.

God Will Abide with Us.

Revelation 21:1-7 describes the events which happen immediately after the new heaven and the new earth are created. *"Then I saw a new sky (heaven) and a new earth, for the former sky and the former earth had passed away (vanished), and there no longer existed any sea. And I saw the holy city, the new Jerusalem, descending out of heaven from God, all arrayed like a bride beautified and adorned for her husband; Then I heard a mighty voice from the throne and I perceived its distinct words, saying, See! The abode of God is with men, and He will live (encamp, tent) among them; and they shall be His people, and God shall personally be with them and be their God. God will wipe away every tear from their eyes; and death shall be no more, neither shall there be anguish (sorrow and mourning) nor grief nor pain any more, for the old conditions and the former order of things have passed away.*

And He Who is seated on the throne said, See! I make all things new. Also He said, Record this, for these sayings are faithful (accurate, incorruptible, and trustworthy) and true (genuine). And He [further] said to me, It is done! I am the Alpha and the Omega, the Beginning and the End. To the thirsty I [Myself] will give water without price from the fountain (springs) of the water of Life. He who is victorious shall inherit all these things, and I will be God to him and he shall be My son."

God not only has a plan, he has included us in his plan! His plan is to be our God and for us to be his people. His plan is to wipe away all our tears and our sorrows and remove all pain and death.

The Victorious Shall Inherit All Things.

God gives a condition to his plan. *"He who is victorious shall inherit all these things."* In this book, I keep asking you to examine yourself. Do you meet God's conditions? Have you decided to receive your inheritance now or are you going to let the devil continue to steal it from you? **Receiving the earnest of your inheritance now is God's plan!** God has a plan for where you are right now. He also has a plan for you and all his children through the millennial reign, the white throne judgment and in the new Jerusalem. He intends for you to be a part of his eternal plan, but there are conditions that must be met if you want to be part of his plan.

He who is victorious shall inherit these things. All the exciting things that are listed in Revelation 21:1-7 have a condition attached to them. Many Christians believe that it doesn't matter what they do. They expect to inherit God's promises. They believe that because they accepted the Lord as Saviour, they will get it all. God has the plan and in this passage, particular benefits of this plan are described. God gives very clear instructions regarding the condition required to be part of that plan. If we aren't required to be victorious, why does he mention it in this passage?

Let's look at the other side of the picture in verse 8. It begins by saying, "*But as for the cowards...*" For you to be victorious in Christ, you must humble yourself and let Jesus Christ be the literal, functional Lord of your life. You're also called to be a soldier. You must yield yourself to God and resist the devil. You must be able to destroy the devil's works and set captives free. That makes you a victorious soldier in Christ.

Why aren't you victorious? Why do you resist when God tells you to do something that looks impossible to you? Because you are afraid. A spirit of fear attacks you and you yield to it. You obey that spirit and become a coward who is unwilling to do what God says. Believers make every kind of excuse as to why they are not victorious and why they can't keep the devil out of their lives.

Does the whole church have to be focused on you as you drag in your problems every Sunday? Are you the first in the prayer line at every meeting because the devil continues to defeat you? **It is because you are a coward!** Are you going to stand in judgment before God and be rejected because you haven't met his conditions? When are you going to look in the mirror and realize you are the problem? I know this sounds like a hard saying, and I would like to be able to say it in an easier way, but you must see that it won't do you any good for someone to tell you this when it's too late!

Missing God's Plan

Revelation 21:8a, *"But as for the coward and the ignoble and the contemptible and the cravenly lacking in courage and the cowardly submissive..."* Notice the term, "the cowardly submissive". When you act like a coward and refuse to submit to God, to whom do you submit? You submit to your flesh and satan. Like a whipped puppy, you lie down and roll over so the devil can steal from you or do whatever he wants to do in your life.

Concluding verse 8, *"...and as for the unbelieving and faithless, and as for the depraved and defiled with abominations, and as for murderers and the lewd and adulterous and the practicers of magic arts and the idolaters (those who give supreme devotion to anyone or anything other than God) and all liars (those who knowingly convey untruth by word or deed)-[all of these shall have] their part in the lake that blazes with fire and brimstone. This is the second death."* **Note that an idolater is one who gives supreme devotion to anyone or anything other than God.** This includes your career, your spouse, your children or any other thing you worship more than you do God.

Choose God's Plan

God has a plan for you to be his child, to be victorious and to rule and reign with him. He wants you to rejoice in his fellowship. He also has a plan for cowards who refuse to trust him. All who reject him and do not have their names written in the Lamb's Book of Life will be cast into the lake of fire.

In Revelation, we see the description of what happens after the new heavens and earth are created. God's plan continues! Our vision is limited, but his plan is not. Malachi 3:6 (KJV) says, *"For I am the Lord. I change not..."* **Jesus is the Lord and he does not change.** God's plan has very clear conditions, and he doesn't change them. It is important that we understand this truth.

The question remains. Are you going to enjoy the goodness

of God or face the severity of God? Which part of his plan will you experience? God says in Deuteronomy 11:26, *"Behold, I set before you a blessing and a curse."* **Which one are you choosing?** It is inevitable that you are making a choice. You will be in one category or the other. It is a sobering thought. Study the Word of God to get a clearer vision of his plan. Now is the time to move into God's plan for you.

Chapter 16

God Has a Place for You in His Plan

God's ultimate plan is for his kingdom to be filled with saints who will rule and reign with him throughout eternity. **God has a place for each one of his children in his kingdom.** In Matthew 22:14 (KJV), we are given a sober warning. *"For many are called, but few are chosen."*

<u>Many Are Called</u>
This is where many people make a tremendous mistake. They know God has spoken to them and called them to be a certain thing, but they believe a lie from the devil that says because you are called, you are automatically chosen. The Word clearly states that **<u>many are called</u>, but <u>few are chosen</u>**. The word *called* means that you have been invited or appointed. (Strong's #2822) God doesn't want anyone to perish but for all to come to the saving knowledge of Jesus Christ. He has invited every person who has ever lived on the earth to become a part of his family.

You realize, of course, that not every person gets saved. There are conditions that must be met. If you humble yourself, repent of your sins and accept what Jesus did on the cross, then you will be saved by grace through faith, not of works lest any man should boast. (Ephesians 2:8 and 9) Only under these conditions will God accept you so that you become chosen. If you try to get to God any other way (even though you have been invited), you will not be accepted. The word *chosen* means you've been selected. (Strong's #1586) It is one thing to receive an invitation and another to be accepted.

God has extended the invitation for us to become his children, to rule and reign with Christ as part of the eternal kingdom, and to be vessels of honor in his household. As you study each of these invitations God has given us, you will see a corresponding responsibility or condition that goes with receiving each particular invitation. If you meet the conditions, God accepts you and you become chosen to receive what you were invited to have. **If you don't meet the conditions, you won't be chosen!** God is not mocked. Whatever you sow, you are going to reap. (Galatians 6:7) You cannot pervert the truth and disobey God's standards and expect God to excuse your disobedience.

Part of Christ's Body

Paul talks about being called to the body of Christ. If you are born into the family of God, you are also called to be part of Christ's body. 1 Corinthians 12:18 says, *"But as it is, God has placed and arranged the limbs and organs in the body, each [particular one] of them, just as He wished and saw fit and with the best adaptation."*

This is where some of you get into trouble. **You decide where you want to be in the body of Christ and how you want to function.** God has placed and arranged the parts of his body as he sees fit. God has a plan! He has a plan for the body of Christ, and he has a plan for your part in the body of Christ. He has already decided <u>what part you are</u> in the body, <u>where you are</u> supposed to function, and <u>how you are</u> to function.

God will prepare you and supply everything you need. If he has chosen you to be a little toe, you can't be a nose, because little toes wouldn't look good on your face! When you were born into God's family, you were created to be a particular part of the body of Christ. All parts are important and must function properly.

In Ephesians 4:11 and 12 (KJV), Paul describes five different offices of authority God has given in order to equip you for your part. *"And he gave some, apostles; and some, prophets; and some, evangelists; and some pastors and teachers; For the perfecting of the saints, for the work of the ministry, for the edifying of the body of Christ."* These gifts were given for your equipping so that you can come to maturity in the body of Christ and function properly. Verse 16 says you are to be fitly joined together where you belong, receiving and giving what has been effectually worked in you by God. He has given you five offices to help you. He has also given you his Spirit to live within you and lead you into all truth. He has given you gifts and abilities as well as every good thing you need to be successful.

A Good Soldier

In 2 Timothy 2:3-5, Paul was instructing Timothy about being a good soldier. In order to master something, it has to be done lawfully. If you want to grow up and become an effectual part of the body of Christ, there is a lawful way to do it. **You must present yourself to God as a living sacrifice, holy and acceptable, which is your reasonable service.** (Romans 12:1) When you do this, God will prepare you, equip you and place you in the body where he intends for you to be. God will supply everything you need, whether it is one of the offices listed above, giftings, abilities, grace or the working of the Holy Spirit, so that you can function properly in your place in the body of Christ. 1 Corinthians 12:23 says the uncomely parts that don't seem as important are more necessary. God gives even more grace to these parts to balance things out.

God is not a respecter of persons. (Romans 2:11) If you find yourself thinking that someone else in the body of Christ is more important than you are, you are entertaining a lie. If someone else can do a job better than you can, it is only because God has given them the grace necessary to do the job.

Spiritual Rewards
We tend to think that our rewards are based on the

volume of work we do or what the world considers important, as opposed to faithfulness, trustworthiness and obedience to God with a right motive. The person who sets up chairs in the church may be far greater in the eyes of God than the one who does the preaching. He may also receive a greater reward because he has a right attitude and motive and he is functioning where God wants him to function. If God has called this person to set up chairs, but the one preaching is actually called to do something else, then the preacher is in rebellion every time he preaches. He is out of order and he won't receive any eternal reward from God. Even though it may appear that the preacher would have more importance due to his position, only God knows the heart and callings of each person.

A Place Prepared for You

In 1 Corinthians 2:9, God talks about the place he has for you in his plan. Many of you may have dreamed about what it is going to be like when you get to heaven. You may have read the description of the new Jerusalem in Revelation. The Lord told the disciples that he was going to prepare a place for them so that where he was they would be also. (John 14:3) God's plan includes his children living with him in the new Jerusalem. As we read earlier in Revelation 21:4, there will be no sorrow or crying in that place.

This is a wonderful part of God's plan, but it is only the beginning. We will live in the new Jerusalem in our glorified bodies after the Lord creates new heavens and a new earth. If you are an overcomer, you will rule and reign with him, but have you ever imagined what you might rule over?

Even though the Word doesn't say it, it's not a big stretch to realize that while God is creating new heavens and a new earth, he could also create living beings to inhabit these places. What has entered your mind regarding the possibilities of God's plan? The Bible stops short of explaining the rest of the plan. It just takes us to the point when it is about to get really interesting. You can assume from what the Bible does say that it is going to be really good! 1 Corinthians 2:9 says, *"But, on the contrary, as the Scripture says, What eye has not seen and ear has not heard and has not entered into the heart of man, [all that] God has prepared (made and keeps ready) for those who love Him [who hold Him in affectionate reverence, promptly obeying Him and gratefully recognizing the benefits He has bestowed]."*

Meeting God's Conditions

God has a plan, but our eyes haven't seen nor our ears heard all the things God has prepared for us. This plan is for those who love God and hold him in affectionate reverence, promptly obeying him and recognizing the benefits he has bestowed! **This is another one of those conditional promises.** 1 Corinthians 2:10, *"Yet to us God has unveiled and revealed them by and through His Spirit, for the [Holy] Spirit searches diligently, exploring and examining everything, even sounding the profound and bottomless things of God [the divine counsels and things hidden and beyond man's scrutiny]."*

John 14:15 (KJV), *"If ye love me, keep my commandments."* **Those who love God and promptly obey him with a right attitude will have the privilege of receiving revelation about the deep things God has prepared for us.** God has a plan for you and he has a plan for me! He wants to start revealing our part in his plan.

You will never see or hear what God has prepared if you don't start loving him. If you don't promptly obey him, get a right attitude toward him and become more appreciative of the benefits he has given you, you will not receive the deeper revelations of his plan.

How many times have we taken the benefits God has given us and cast them away for a bowl of stew like Esau did? When we are hungry and uncomfortable, we throw away the great things of God carelessly. We think we can reclaim a pearl of great price we've cast away anytime we want, but people are dying every day who have never retrieved what they lost spiritually.

Now is the Time

The only time we have is now. Take time to humble yourself before God. Get in his presence and accept his plan. **Conduct yourself daily with the recognition that he is God.** Hebrews 11:6 says that those who come to God must first believe that he is God and that he is a rewarder of those who diligently seek him. Realize that God has a good plan for your life. Accept the conditions for receiving God's promises in your life. Don't waste your time trying to get God to adapt himself to your plans. Submit to him and receive the wonderful plan he has for you!

Ask the Lord to prepare you to be in a condition that allows him to unveil more things about his plan for you. Humble your heart before him and recognize that you can do nothing without him. **Set your heart to be part of God's plan.** Repent of any hindrance God shows you. Believe that God will supply every need you have according to his riches in glory. (Philippians 4:19) Ask him for his plan for you at this time and get a vision of what he has planned for your future. **You can live in God's perfect timing and his plan every moment of every day.** To do that, you must quit directing your life and let him take control.

I want to encourage you to meditate on these chapters and **thoroughly repent at the root level, rather than simply dealing with the bad fruit in your life**. The root of all sin is taking over the lordship and control of your life. God has a place for you in his plan. It is your heritage if you are a child of God. You can throw it away as Esau did or you can stir up the Spirit of God who lives in you. **The same power that raised Jesus from the dead is in you.** If you'll make the decision from your heart to serve God, he will rise up within you and drive the enemy back.

The devil will actually have to flee from you. (James 4:7)

Prepare your heart and make sure you are cleansed in every area the Holy Spirit has revealed to you. Repent and let it go. Repentance is wonderful because it gives you a fresh start. If you will confess your sins, God will forgive your sins and cleanse you from all unrighteousness. He not only forgives you and cleanses you, he won't remember your sins anymore. (Hebrews 8:12 and 10:17)

It doesn't matter how many mistakes you have made up to this point or how many lies you have believed. Today you are promised a fresh start. If the Holy Spirit has been revealing things to you, you may be feeling very uncomfortable. You are blessed! The fact that God is chastening you and convicting you is because he loves you. Every son that God loves, he thoroughly purges and chastens. (Hebrews 12:6) Why? Because he wants you to lay aside every sin and weight that besets you so that you may run the race that is set before you. (Hebrews 12:1)

God has a glorious plan set before you. He has a glorious plan for each of his children. You are important to God, but you cannot drag the sins of this world into a perfect kingdom. God has made the provision for your robe to be white. Let the blood of Jesus cleanse you from all your sin.

Chapter 17

Jesus is the Author and Finisher of God's Plan in and for You

Hebrews 11 details the great witnesses of faith who trusted God through many difficult situations. Verse 39 states that all of these believers won divine approval by means of their faith, but they did not receive the fulfillment of what they were promised. Because God had us in mind, these heroes and heroines of faith did not come to perfection apart from us. Hebrews 12 begins by discussing this great cloud of witnesses who have gone on before us.

Hebrews 12:1-4, *"Therefore then, since we are surrounded by so great a cloud of witnesses [who have borne testimony to the Truth], let us strip off and throw aside every encumbrance (unnecessary weight) and that sin which so readily (deftly and cleverly) clings to and entangles us, and let us run with patient endurance and steady and active persistence the appointed course of the race that is set before us, Looking away [from all that will distract] to Jesus, Who is the Leader and the Source of our faith [giving the first incentive for our belief] and is also its Finisher [bringing it to maturity and perfection]. He, for the joy [of obtaining the prize] that was set before Him, endured the cross, despising and ignoring the shame, and is now seated at the right hand of the throne of God. Just think of Him Who endured from sinners such grievous opposition and bitter hostility against Himself [reckon up and consider it all in comparison with your trials], so that you may not grow weary or exhausted, losing heart and relaxing and fainting in your minds. You have not yet struggled and fought agonizingly against sin, nor have you yet resisted and withstood to the point of pouring out your [own] blood."*

In understanding God's plan and our place in that plan, it is critical to recognize that he has entrusted that plan into Jesus his Son. Jesus is the author and finisher of our faith and God's plan for our individual lives. (Hebrews 12:2) All the saints who have gone on before us are monitoring what we are doing. We need to lay aside every sin and weight so we can run the race that is set before us. Verses 3 and 4 describe Jesus' attitude toward his place in God's plan. **He was willing to endure shame and immense suffering in order to accomplish God's plan for him.**

Paul is reminding us in Hebrews 12:4 that we have not resisted sin to the point of pouring out our blood like Jesus did. If you haven't gotten to that point in your obedience to God, what are you complaining about? Jesus never wavered as he pressed toward the mark, and that is the same attitude we need to have.

The Correction of the Lord

Hebrews 12:5, *"And have you [completely] forgotten the divine word of appeal and encouragement in which you are reasoned with and addressed as sons? My son, do not think lightly or scorn to submit to the correction and discipline of the Lord, nor lose courage and give up and faint when you are reproved or corrected by Him."* We don't always understand the way God functions in our lives. We don't really know him, and that is part of our problem.

Many believers never get to know God. They won't trust him enough to meet the conditions to get into his presence and stay there long enough to actually get to know him. Paul is reminding us that God is speaking to us as his children and he has a plan for us. God wants to prepare us so that we can start fulfilling his plan for our lives.

Hebrews 12:6-8, *"For the Lord corrects and disciplines everyone whom He loves, and He punishes, even scourges, every son whom He accepts and welcomes to His heart and cherishes. You must submit to and endure [correction] for discipline; God is dealing with you as with sons. For what son is there whom his father does not [thus] train and correct and discipline? Now if you are exempt from correction and left without discipline in which all [of God's children] share, then you are illegitimate offspring and not true sons [at all]."*

This is important. God makes no exceptions. **Everyone whom the Lord loves, he disciplines, chastens and corrects.** You must endure this correction for discipline, because God is dealing with you as a son. This verse includes an important warning. **If you are exempt from correction, you are not really a true son at all.** You are illegitimate.

Mortifying the Flesh

How many times have you wished (or even prayed) that God's corrections would go away? Why is it so uncomfortable to your flesh? Because that is where the correction is directed. All sin is contained in the flesh. It is condemned and God is going to purge and cleanse you from your carnal nature every chance he gets. **The flesh cries out because it doesn't want to be killed, but God wants it totally mortified!** He wants your new nature in Christ to grow. He wants your old nature to be completely destroyed. Through the Spirit, he can fulfill his plan and purpose for you as your old nature dies.

God has no good plan for your flesh. **Everyone whom God receives must go through this process of killing the flesh and letting the new nature come forth.** You need to quit fighting this as if it is something strange. The more you submit to God and cooperate, the sooner the work will get done. You can get past the uncomfortable stage and on to the joy of walking in God's kingdom. You can enjoy your inheritance without the devil constantly making you miserable through fleshly accesses. God knows you don't really want that. You want what God wants, yet you ignorantly give satan permission to harass you. You may even resist God who is trying to deliver you.

It is important that you meditate on these scriptures and let God reveal his truth to you. It is very critical that you stop resisting God's corrections. In the end, this causes you to give up the right of being treated like a son.

<u>For Our Certain Good</u>

Hebrews 12:9 and 10, *"Moreover, we have had earthly fathers who disciplined us and we yielded [to them] and respected [them for training us]. Shall we not much more cheerfully submit to the Father of spirits and so [truly] live? For [our earthly fathers] disciplined us for only a short period of time and chastised us as seemed proper and good to them; but He disciplines us for our certain good, that we may become sharers in His own holiness."* God's dealings are compared to those of natural parents. If you happened to have godly parents, they corrected you when you needed it. Many of you may not have liked the corrections at the time, but now you realize that it was done for your good. You have an appreciation for parents who loved you enough to resist the things you wanted to do in the flesh.

You must yield to your Father as he corrects you. **When God corrects you, it is for your <u>certain</u> good.** He has the plan and he knows exactly what you need to do. When he corrects you, he is not doing it out of frustration or anger, but for your good so that you may become a sharer in his holiness.

Look at Hebrews 12:11. *"For the time being no discipline brings joy, but seems grievous and painful; but afterwards it yields a peaceable fruit of righteousness to those who have been trained by it [a harvest of fruit which consists in righteousness-in conformity to God's will in purpose, thought, and action, re-*

sulting in right living and right standing with God]." **The correction God brings may not seem pleasant, but it will yield good fruit after you have been trained by it.** It will help you conform to God's will in purpose, thought and action.

You have to ask yourself if you want to be in right standing with God. God is trying to conform you to his will, because that's his plan for you. He wants you to be in right standing with him by living according to his standards and purposes for your life. The corrections are not punishment. They are part of your training! God is teaching you how to stay in right standing with him by letting you understand what is not acceptable and what will cause fellowship with him to be broken. You must learn to yield to God and let him do whatever is necessary to keep you in right standing with him.

Your Reaction to God's Corrections

Hebrews 12:12-14, *"So then, brace up and reinvigorate and set right your slackened and weakened and drooping hands and strengthen your feeble and palsied and tottering knees, And cut through and make firm and plain and smooth, straight paths for your feet [yes, make them safe and upright and happy paths that go in the right direction], so that the lame and halting [limbs] may not be put out of joint, but rather may be cured. Strive to live in peace with everybody and pursue that consecration and holiness without which no one will [ever] see the Lord."*

It is easy to look at a scripture like this and see yourself in it. Many of us grumble when God corrects us. We don't like it! **You can tell by your reaction to God's dealings in your life how well you really understand what he is doing.** As you begin to understand what God is trying to do, your attitude toward God's training will change. You will be able to count it all joy. (James 1:2) **Even though you may go through trials and testings, keep focused on the fact that you are getting to know Christ.**

In Hebrews 12:12, Paul is reminding us to be invigorated and set right our slackened hands. He goes on to say that God will direct your feet and you will have happy paths. The steps of a righteous man are ordered by the Lord. (Psalm 37:23) For many of us, that revelation comes from hindsight. You may remember things God did in your life and realize you would have had a different attitude if you had understood what God was doing.

What is your reaction to the things God is dealing with you about today? Every truth God reveals to you should bring rejoicing to your heart because it is either confirming your walk or exposing areas that need to be adjusted. Either way, it is positive. If you have ears to hear where you are missing God, you are blessed. If you get convicted as you are reading this book, you are blessed because God is dealing with you as a son.

There is a point when you have gone through enough chastening that you begin to see the fruit of righteousness it produces. That helps you develop a more positive attitude toward the whole process. As your attitude improves in accepting God's chastening, you will find that the discomfort of the chastening lessens. You can actually come to the point that Paul reached and begin to count it as joy for God to correct you, because you know that is the only way you are going to grow. **You must receive truth and be convicted of what is wrong in your life in order for you to let it go.** Through the gift of repentance, you can turn from sin and become more like Christ. Each time you go through this process, you grow a little more in the grace and knowledge of the Lord.

Most Christians do not think of chastening as a positive thing. They prefer to avoid it. That is why there are so many dead churches. Most people want a preacher who won't tell them any truth that will convict them, because they don't want to be chastened by the Lord. If you want to grow up and walk with God, you have to get to truth. If it isn't being preached at your church, you should go where it is preached.

It's important that you let God speak to you and quit listening to the lie that chastening is negative. You either believe the Word or you don't. **You won't always understand why God works the way he does, but God is love.** If it weren't necessary for you to go through this process, you wouldn't be going through it. **You must quit fighting against God and resisting his instructions.** You must yield to what God says. As it says in Hebrews 12, you must learn to submit to God and get on with growing up.

God's Timing

Ecclesiastes 3:1 says there is a season and time for every purpose. One common trick of the enemy is to get you out of God's timing and purposes. If there is something God purposes for you to do now, the devil will tell you to do another "good" thing as long as it isn't what God said. If you are determined to obey God, satan will try to get you to obey at the wrong time. There is a right plan and a right time for that plan. **If you struggle with God and procrastinate on doing what God says, you are interfering with the timing of God's plan for you.** If it weren't time to deal with a particular sin, the Lord wouldn't be bringing it up.

We each have many flaws and the Lord knows them all. If God brought them up all at once, it would overwhelm us and no one would obey. That's why you should yield to the Lord, because he knows exactly what you need to deal with now. He is trying to bring you to the fulfillment of his plan for you. **You need to process his corrections quickly so you can move on to the next level of God's plan and stay in God's timing.**

Timely Obedience

When God starts dealing with any area in our lives, it is time for that area to pass away. At that moment, there is abundant grace to deal with it. Typically, we resist the correction and procrastinate. We plan to obey at a more convenient time, but it seems that time never comes. We never really repent, and we resist God's conviction. The more we procrastinate, the less grace there is to obey what God says. **When we miss God's timing, we lose part of God's purpose and plan for your life.** He will still deal with us, but we are suffering loss both now and in the future by procrastinating our obedience.

Romans 8:28 is a beautiful promise. *"We are assured and know that [God being a partner in their labor] all things work together and are [fitting into a plan] for good to and for those who love God and are called according to [His] design and purpose."* God is working as a partner with you.

It takes two things for you to flourish in the kingdom of God and his plan. First of all, accept God's invitation to be part of his plan. Humble yourself before God. Find out what he wants in your life. When you yield to the Lord, who is the author and finisher of your faith, he will fulfill his plan for you. Secondly, start obeying God when he brings correction and instruction. **No matter what happens in your life, all things will work to your good if you are following God's plan and loving him.**

Those who love Jesus keep his commandments. You can't separate loving God from obedience to him. As God is chastening you, simply yield to him and express your love through obedience. He is communicating his love for you by bringing truth to you and revealing the things satan is doing to steal from you.

Chapter 18

How Do I Get Started?

Settle the Lordship Issue

In order to move into God's plan for your life, you must settle the Lordship issue. Jesus is Lord. He is the author and finisher of God's plan for you. In order for Jesus to accomplish God's plan in you, he must be functioning as Lord of your life. It is not enough to call him Lord. You must humble yourself, acknowledge him in all your ways and submit to him to direct your paths. **If you disregard the Lordship issue, you will <u>never</u> be able to abide in his kingdom now.**

God wants you to know what his kingdom is and what is available to you now. He wants you to understand some of the benefits of being in his kingdom as well as the cost of rejecting it. **In order for Jesus to put God's plan for your life into motion, you must set your heart to submit to Jesus Christ as the literal, functional Lord of your life.** That will happen as you humble yourself under the mighty hand of God. God will exalt you at the proper time. As explained in Hebrews 12:5-7, God will chasten and instruct you in order to get rid of the things that will hinder his ability to exalt you in his kingdom. In order for Jesus to be the author and finisher of your faith, you must obey what he directs you to do because you love him.

The Fruit of Repentance

Many believers have made that decision numerous times in their lives, but they have never followed that decision with the appropriate fruit of repentance. Proverbs 3:5 and 6 explain the simple walk of Jesus being the Lord of your life. Trust him with all your heart. Quit leaning to your reasoning, which is trusting yourself instead of God. Start acknowledging him in all your ways (which is trusting him), and he will direct your paths.

When you decide to obey God's directions, you have a choice about your attitude toward that obedience. You can obey out of love or obey out of duty or fear. You can obey instantly or you can procrastinate. Remember, there is a time and place for everything under the sun. The Lord gives his children timely directions. That's why we need to develop the habit of obeying instantly. This will keep us in God's perfect timing for our lives.

When God is correcting you, he gives you a space of time to deal with the issue he has revealed. God will provide the maximum time to deal with whatever he has said. It is important that you become sensitive to God so that you can tell if you are getting behind on his timing. You don't want to get ahead of God either. **For God's sovereignty to flow, you need to be in the right place at the right time.** That only happens if you acknowledge him in all your ways.

Hearing the Lord's Voice

The basic problem some of you may have in asking him to direct you is that you don't "hear" anything. That is a common problem. You may be willing to let Jesus be Lord of your life, but you have never learned to hear his voice nor have you stopped the habit of leaning to your own understanding. It may take a little time, but it can be done. You can't live in the kingdom of God if you haven't learned how to let Jesus direct your life. You can't obey God if you can't hear his voice. That skill has to be developed in you.

If you need to know how to hear the Lord's voice speaking to your spirit, I again suggest that you study *My Sheep Hear My Voice*. Numerous scriptures in that book teach the mechanics of how to get into God's presence, how to stay there, how to hear his voice, and how to test to make sure it really is his voice. If you bypass this crucial step, you aren't really going to be able to live in the kingdom of God now. Study the book at your own pace and begin practicing what it teaches.

<u>The Kingdom Can Be Yours</u>.

You need a clear vision of where Jesus wants to take you. Begin to trust and obey him because you love him. **The kingdom of God can be yours <u>now</u>.** It's as simple as that. It starts with the decision to relinquish the throne of your life and to give Jesus his rightful place. Follow that up with studying to show yourself approved and learning what is necessary to be able to hear his voice. **Bring your body under subjection so it doesn't resist what the Lord commands.** Purify your motive and develop a proper attitude toward God and what he says, then everything else will fall into place and be very simple.

Chapter 19

Getting in His Kingdom Now and Growing Up

Every child of God has the potential to enter into and live in the kingdom of God. It is important that you understand God's kingdom and what is required to get in and stay in so that you can grow up in the presence of God. John 14:6, *"Jesus said to him, I am the Way and the Truth and the Life; no one comes to the Father except by (through) Me."*

Jesus is the Way.
Nothing profane or corrupt is allowed in the kingdom of God. God our Father is holy and his kingdom is holy. Isaiah 59:2 says your iniquities separate you from your God, because sin cannot come into the presence of his holiness. Everyone has sinned and come short of the glory of God. We were all born into sin and separated from God. We could not live with God in his kingdom because of sin. The curse of the law could not be removed until someone qualified to be the sacrificial Lamb by fulfilling every letter of the law without sin. This Lamb without spot or blemish laid down his life to take away the sins of the world. (John 1:29)

Until Jesus met the conditions to be the sacrifice, the curse was still in effect. His shed blood cleanses us from sin. Our sin is completely removed so that we are without sin. We can be holy and unblamable, because our righteousness is Christ's righteousness in us. That is why Jesus said, "I am the Way."

The only way you can get to the Father and live in his kingdom is by entering through the way Jesus has provided. His way is the blood. As a child of God, you can humble yourself, repent and apply the blood of Jesus to your life. You can come into the very presence of God. At the moment of repentance, you can enter into the kingdom of God now, which is righteousness, peace and joy in the Holy Ghost. (Romans 14:17)

You can stay in God's kingdom until you sin. As soon as you sin, the <u>conscious</u> presence of the Lord leaves. You do not "lose" your salvation. The Lord doesn't quit loving you and he doesn't disown you. You are still his child, but your sin has separated you from him. God doesn't want you separated from him. If you confess your sin, he will forgive your sin and cleanse you from all unrighteousness. You can come back into his presence very quickly. It is crucial that you understand this principle.

James 4:6b-10, *"...God sets Himself against the proud and haughty, but gives grace [continually] to the lowly (those who are humble enough to receive it). So be subject to God. Resist the devil [stand firm against him], and he will flee from you. Come close to God and He will come close to you. [Recognize that you are] sinners, get your soiled hands clean; [realize that you have been disloyal] wavering individuals with divided interests, and purify your hearts [of your spiritual adultery]. [As you draw near to God] be deeply penitent and grieve, even weep [over your disloyalty]. Let your laughter be turned to grief and your mirth to dejection and heartfelt shame [for your sins]. Humble yourselves [feeling very insignificant] in the presence of the Lord, and He will exalt you [He will lift you up and make your lives significant]."*

<u>True Repentance</u>

James 4:8 says if you will come close to God, he will come close to you. You must first recognize that you're a sinner. As a sinner, you can't come close to God. That is why you are commanded to get your soiled hands clean. **Only by repentance can you be made clean.** These verses remind you to be deeply penitent. Don't play games and tell God you're sorry when you

don't really repent. **Being sorry you got caught isn't repentance, and it won't move you back into the presence of God.**

Many believers get frustrated over this issue. They think they have repented of their sins and wonder why they can't draw near to God or feel his presence. In reality, they haven't repented because **repentance is turning from sin** (you stop doing it) and going the other direction. Many believers don't have deep sorrow for sinning against God. Because they get convicted and want the discomfort to leave, they ask for forgiveness to get some relief. They never get a total cleansing that allows them to really draw close to God. Real repentance means you humble yourself and submit to God as you turn from your sin.

Hebrews 4:16, *"Let us then fearlessly and confidently and boldly draw near to the throne of grace (the throne of God's unmerited favor to us sinners), that we may receive mercy [for our failures] and find grace to help in good time for every need [appropriate help and well-timed help coming just when we need it]."* When you are truly repentant as you confess your sins, God cleanses you and you can boldly come before the throne of grace once again. It is at that point that you draw near to God and he draws near to you.

As you walk in humility, God is going to exalt you at the appointed season. He will reveal to you why you keep sinning, because he wants you to close the doors that separate you from him. When you are in God's presence, he doesn't want you to leave. God doesn't convict you because he is angry. He does it because he loves you and it is good for you. He wants you to come into his kingdom and stay there. That's where your heritage is and where you will spend eternity. He wants you to become familiar with his kingdom.

Cooperate with God

Most Christians seem to have a hard time consistently cooperating with God as he deals with their carnal natures.

They keep trying to procrastinate or look for some way to excuse their carnality, but there is no excuse. They listen to satan's deceptions and ways that seem right rather than deal with the things of the flesh because it makes them uncomfortable. They don't even realize how much they are giving away, because everyone around them is doing the same thing. James 4:6-10 explains how you should approach your flesh so that you can have a right attitude that moves God's heart.

1 Peter 2:1 and 2, *"So be done with every trace of wickedness (depravity, malignity) and all deceit and insincerity (pretense, hypocrisy) and grudges (envy, jealousy) and slander and evil speaking of every kind. Like newborn babies you should crave (thirst for, earnestly desire) the pure (unadulterated) spiritual milk, that by it you may be nurtured and grow unto [completed] salvation."* You should have a heart to do away with the sins of the flesh. **Develop a hunger and thirst for God so that you won't settle for anything less than the truth.** Don't look for something to deceive you and lead you in a way that seems right. Desire God and his will above all else. Once you receive truth, process it by immediately obeying from a heart of love.

Jesus, the Cornerstone

1 Peter 2:3-5, *"Since you have [already] tasted the goodness and kindness of the Lord. Come to Him [then, to that] Living Stone which men tried and threw away, but which is chosen [and] precious in God's sight. [Come] and, like living stones, be yourselves built [into] a spiritual house, for a holy (dedicated, consecrated) priesthood, to offer up [those] spiritual sacrifices [that are] acceptable and pleasing to God through Jesus Christ."* God has a place for you in his plan. Part of the plan is for all of us to become living stones which are put together for the habitation of God. That is a high calling, but you have to put away the manifestations and habits of the flesh to walk in it.

1 Peter 2:6 and 7, *"For thus it stands in Scripture: Behold, I*

am laying in Zion a chosen (honored), precious chief Cornerstone, and he who believes in Him [who adheres to, trusts in, and relies on Him] shall never be disappointed or put to shame. To you then who believe (who adhere to, trust in, and rely on Him) is the preciousness; but for those who disbelieve [it is true], The [very] Stone which the builders rejected has become the main Cornerstone."

Jesus is to be the cornerstone of your life, and you are called to be a living stone. That is God's plan! When you trust in, adhere to and rely on Jesus, his position as the Lord of your life becomes very precious to you. It takes two things to make Jesus your cornerstone. First, you must accept him as the literal, functional Lord of your life. Secondly, you must obey him because you love him.

Those who reject Jesus as the cornerstone are described in 1 Peter 2:8. *"And A Stone that will cause stumbling and a Rock that will give [men] offense; they stumble because they disobey and disbelieve [God's] Word, as those [who reject Him] were destined (appointed) to do."* In other words, Jesus is either a precious cornerstone to you or he is a stumbling block. For those who disobey, he is a stumbling block because they disbelieve God's Word. Those who reject him are destined and appointed to doom.

God is calling us to be a chosen generation and a royal priesthood who display the virtues of him who called us out of darkness and into light. (1 Peter 2:9) This is all part of his plan.

Ephesians 4:11-16 explains the gifts of apostles, prophets, evangelists, pastors and teachers who are sent to the saints so that we can be equipped and grow up in the Spirit. God's purpose is for us to be fitly joined together and no longer tossed to and fro by winds of doctrine. He desires that we grow up to the fullness of the measure of Christ and supply and receive what has been worked in each one of us. Ephesians 4:15 says, *"Rather, let our lives lovingly express truth [in all things, speaking truly, dealing truly, living truly]. Enfolded in love, let us grow up in every way and in all things into Him Who is the Head, [even] Christ (the Messiah, the Anointed One)."*

<u>Get in the Kingdom and Grow Up</u>.
In this particular chapter, I am dealing with how to get into the kingdom of God and grow up there. When Jesus is the Lord of your life, you become fitly joined into the body of Christ. You begin to supply what has been worked in you. As you listen to the authorities God has placed in your life and do what God says, you are going to grow faster in a few months' time than you have grown in years.

Your life should lovingly express truth in all things. That is part of kingdom living! In God's kingdom you hear truth, not deceptions and half-truths. You will start speaking truly, dealing truly and living truly. This will cause you to mature in the Spirit continually. Acts 17:28a says, *"For in Him we live and move and have our being;..."* You are supposed to have your very being in Christ. You have the Spirit of God <u>in you</u> if you are a child of God, but kingdom living is you <u>getting into</u> Christ. You must get in the Spirit, live there and learn how to function there.

John 15 talks about Jesus being the true Vine and the Father being the Vinedresser. We are the branches and we are supposed to abide in him. John 15:1 and 2, *"I am the True Vine, and My Father is the Vinedresser. Any branch in Me that does not bear fruit [that stops bearing] He cuts away (trims off, takes away); and He cleanses and repeatedly prunes every branch that continues to bear fruit, to make it bear more and richer and more excellent fruit."* If we don't bear any fruit, the Father cuts us off. We are separated from union with Christ and we are no longer in him. If we stay in Christ and bear fruit, the Father cleanses and prunes us so that we bear richer and more excellent fruit.

John 15:5, *"I am the Vine; you are the branches. Whoever lives in Me and I in him bears much (abundant) fruit. However, apart from Me [cut off from vital union with Me] you can do nothing."* That is a pretty sobering statement. As a child of God, you have a choice. **You can either trust in, rely on and adhere to the Lord or you can trust in yourself.** You can be either hot, cold or lukewarm (a hypocrite). **The Lord said you can do nothing unless you abide in him.**

Obviously, unbelievers do all kinds of things without acknowledging God, much less abiding in him. Unfortunately, God's children do the same thing. We can be lord of our lives as well. Yet the Lord said that outside of him, you can do nothing. In John 15:5, Jesus is saying we cannot bear fruit outside of him.

You cannot move into God's kingdom without being under the headship of Jesus Christ. You cannot even cross the border. You can't do anything of eternal value because you are not in the kingdom. The only way to bear fruit in the kingdom of God is by abiding in the Vine. The life that goes through the branch to produce the fruit comes from the vine rather than the branch. The branch is merely the channel through which it comes.

John 15:8, *"When you bear (produce) much fruit, My Father is honored and glorified, and you show and prove yourselves to be true followers of Mine."* Each of us will give an account of himself or herself before God. (Romans 14:12) Do you want to hear, "Well done, thou good and faithful servant?" Or will you be in the group that the Lord says he never knew?

The only way to bear fruit is by abiding in the Vine. This is made very clear in John 15. When you bear fruit, you honor the Father and prove you follow Jesus. Bearing much fruit is the result of the Father's work within you. He cleanses and repeatedly prunes every branch that abides in him so that it bears more excellent fruit. Saying you are a follower of Jesus doesn't prove anything. Abiding in him (trusting him rather than yourself) is the real proof.

Many doctrines today allow for rotten fruit that is obvious to everyone. This is one of the signs of the last days. What is bad is called good, even within the church. The Lord said not to be deceived. You will reap whatever you sow. A good tree cannot produce bad fruit, and a bad tree cannot produce good fruit. A tree is known by its fruit. **What is in your heart always manifests and it proves whether or not you are abiding in the Vine.**

Isaiah 46:9-11, *"[Earnestly] remember the former things, [which I did] of old; for I am God, and there is no one else; I am God, and there is no one like Me, Declaring the end and the result from the beginning, and from ancient times the things that are not yet done, saying, My counsel shall stand, and I will do all My pleasure and purpose, Calling a ravenous bird from the east–the man [Crus] who executes My counsel from a far country. Yes, I have spoken, and I will bring it to pass; I have purposed it and I will do it."*

God has declared the end from the beginning. When he purposes something, he brings it to pass. God doesn't deviate from his plan. He is not slack concerning his promises. (2 Peter 3:9) Everything he has said, he will fulfill to the letter, no matter how long it takes. **There is no power in heaven or hell that can stop God from doing what he has said.**

Are you going to get into God's plan or not? God's plan is for you to abide in the Vine and bear fruit. God's plan is for you to be a true follower of Jesus and one who honors the Father. God has authorized everything it takes for that to be done, but you have to cooperate. If you refuse to endure his corrections, he will not deal with you as a son.

The "Parable" of the Acorn

An acorn contains the genetics within it to create an oak tree. When God looks at an acorn, he sees the full grown oak tree. He not only sees an oak tree, he sees a <u>particular</u> oak tree because no two oak trees are identical. If an acorn is set on a counter for the next fifty years, it won't produce an oak tree. If that same acorn is planted in the earth, fifty years later everyone will be able to enjoy a beautiful, large tree. The acorn has the potential to be an oak tree, but it may or may not become that tree. The tree's potential is determined by what is done with the seed (acorn).

When you were born into the family of God and his Spirit came into you, a seed was placed in you with all the "genetics" to fulfill God's complete purpose for you. When God looks at that seed, he sees the fullness of what he has purposed you to be. He sees your full potential. The seed has to abide in God's kingdom in order to grow and reach its potential. It can't grow in the world. As a matter of fact, if you leave it in the world a long time, it will become dormant even though it is still alive. If you put it back into God's kingdom, it will start growing again. God is the only one who can bring the seed to maturity, because he is the master gardener. You have to be planted in his kingdom and submitted to the Father continually. He will cleanse and fertilize your seed and provide everything it needs to become what he has purposed it to be. **God has it all under control.**

All satan has to do to rob you of your potential in God's kingdom is to get you to stay in charge of your own life. As long as you are lord, you are disqualified from living in the kingdom of God and the spiritual "seed" in you will never mature. You will continue to be a baby spiritually because you choose to live in the flesh rather than in the Spirit.

Never Underestimate God's Grace.

As you study this book, you may realize you've wasted many years by not living in the kingdom of God. It would seem that there isn't enough time to make up what you have lost. In the natural, that is true. However, by grace, God can make up any time that has been lost. **You can never underestimate God's potential to change you into what you are ordained to be.**

In Matthew 20:1-15, a parable describes a master who hired

laborers who agreed to work all day for a certain wage. Later on, other groups agreed to work for the remainder of the day. Finally, one group agreed to work the last little bit of the day. At the end of the day, the master paid the first group what he had promised, but he also paid the other groups the same amount. God, by his grace, has the option to do what he wants. You may be behind, but we serve a gracious God who loves to bless us.

If you don't move into humility where grace can be found, there is no hope for you to reach your potential. However, God will stop resisting you and he will begin to assist you if you quit being lord. God can take you to the fullness of what he has purposed for you. One of the most wonderful things about God is that he forgives us of our sins and he also forgets them. He gives us a clean start when we humble ourselves and repent, and we can move right back into his kingdom.

You can enjoy a relationship with God far beyond what you qualify for in the natural. God sees the end from the beginning. This is true when he speaks a word to us. That word is a seed and it is intended to produce good fruit in our lives. If you receive the seed and don't process it properly, nothing happens. When you embrace what God says and yield to his Lordship, the seed goes into good ground and starts growing. When you set your heart to obey God's word for you, he can bring it to fullness in his timing. He will start treating you as if you've already fully obeyed, because he can see the fullness of that seed when your obedience is completed. That is a glorious blessing! Some people don't understand this provision and have a hard time believing it.

The fact that God sees the end from the beginning also works in the opposite way. If I get angry at someone in my heart and decide to punch them in the nose the next time I see them, does God wait until I actually commit the act to convict me? No! He begins to speak conviction in my heart as soon as I entertain the thought to commit a sin. When I purpose to run my own life, God will begin to treat me as if I have sinned when it is still in the thought stage. Why? He wants me to repent because even the sinful thought separates me from him. He also wants to keep me from walking out the fullness of that sin, which is blatant rebellion against his control in my life.

When God speaks to me to do something I can't yet do, he knows I am unable to do it. Because I recognize that he is the author and finish of my faith, I accept the commandment and set my heart to obey anyway. As I acknowledge him in all my ways, God looks at my heart of obedience and he sees the fullness of the obedience as if I have hit the mark. He encourages me to continue pressing toward the mark of total obedience. As I obey, I become able to do what I was unable to do before. If I don't obey, I remain unable to do what God has said and I am considered an unfaithful servant.

It's important that you don't run from the things God speaks to you. **Don't get under condemnation by thinking you have to walk fifty levels above where you are.** Many people resist God because he speaks something they are incapable of doing at that moment. They think they have to walk in the fullness of obedience immediately. All you have to do is accept God's standard, yield to his Lordship, and press toward obedience. God will treat you as if you are obeying completely because of his grace.

Getting into the kingdom begins with yielding to Jesus' Lordship. I have said this many times, but it bears repeating. **Even though this seems to be a simple issue, it is the cornerstone of developing a close relationship with God and abiding in his kingdom.** Without making any excuses, embrace every word God speaks to you and believe that he will complete the work he has ordained to be done in you.

Chapter 20

Qualifying to Reign with Christ

An important part of growing up in the kingdom of God now is becoming qualified to reign with Christ in the millennial kingdom. Our time on this earth now is the time of preparation. The kingdom of God is here now for our security and safety. It also gives us an earnest of what is coming. We can learn how to flow with Jesus Christ as the ruler of his kingdom. We can learn how to be under his authority now so that we qualify to rule with him for eternity.

<u>A Vision</u>
Proverbs 29:18a (KJV) says, *"Where there is no vision, the people perish..."* Many people in the body of Christ have no idea that God's kingdom is available now. They don't know it exists, so they are not seeking it. They are looking forward to God's future kingdom, but they do not realize it is available to them now. They have no vision of their potential now and wonder why they are perishing! Hosea 4:6 (KJV) says, *"My people are destroyed for lack of knowledge..."* There are many wounded and imprisoned believers who lack the knowledge of how to live in the kingdom of God now. They are perishing and being destroyed because they are ignorant of how to use their inheritance to become overcomers.

Many Christians never surrender to Jesus' Lordship because they are afraid of what will happen if they lose control. Isn't it amazing that the Lord we trust for our salvation is the same Lord we won't trust to run our lives? We trust him to deliver us into eternity, but we won't trust him now. We are scared that he is going to lead us into something rather that lead us out of it.

In this chapter, we are going to get a little insight into what it takes to reign with Christ. Every Christian hopes they will reign with Christ, but will they? Most Christians assume that because they have accepted Jesus as their personal Saviour, they will reign with Christ in his millennial kingdom. Unfortunately, that way of thinking is in direct contradiction to many scriptures.

Many believers seem to think that we are not responsible for our own actions. They think that it really doesn't matter what you do, because the Lord is going to act as if it didn't happen. Many believe that it doesn't matter if you are faithful, because we end up with the same rewards in the end. Unfortunately, it is possible to perish because of your ignorance. It is too late to find out the truth after you die. You may only have this day to repent and make the necessary adjustments so that satan doesn't steal your inheritance.

Qualifying to reign with Christ is something every child of God should desire. It is very clear in the Word that this is a privilege rather than a right. It is a privilege with conditions. Jesus paid the price for everything you need to qualify to rule with Christ, but you must embrace your inheritance and meet the conditions in order to receive the provision.

Satanic Fear Versus Godly Fear

One of the major hindrances Christians face today is fear. Many dread what God might do. In addition to that fear, they also fear satan and what he will do if they start serving God. They believe the devil is going to attack them, and because they are ignorant of who they are in Christ, they get defeated. This defeat increases their fear of the enemy.

Proverbs 1:7a (KJV) says, *"The fear of the Lord is the beginning of knowledge..."* Most people do not think of fear as bringing knowledge. Their fear of God is not reverence but rather dread. They have the very kind of fear that God has not given us. (2 Timothy 1:7) It is futile for you to seek divine wisdom without getting the fear of the Lord first. **The foundation of your ability to gather divine knowledge is based on your reverential fear of the Lord.** Let's look at all of Proverbs 1:7 to get a clearer understanding of the fear of the Lord. *"The reverent and worshipful fear of the Lord is the beginning and the principal and choice part of knowledge [its starting point and its essence]; but fools despise skillful and godly Wisdom, instruction, and discipline."*

That is pretty simple, isn't it? **The kind of fear that brings wisdom is the worshipful fear of the Lord.** This is the foundation of knowledge. Contrarily, fools despise godly wisdom, instruction and discipline. Christians can be intimidated when worldly people scoff at the wisdom of God. When you walk in truth and godly wisdom, some people may laugh at you. This may sometimes cause you to become embarrassed, but why would the opinion of a fool concern you? God said that those who despise his wisdom are fools, so you ought to pity them instead of feeling intimidated by them. You should be convicting them with the truth that is in you.

If you want to qualify to rule with Christ, you need to agree with what God says about his kingdom now as well as later. Decide if you are going to believe God or not. If you aren't going to believe what the Word says, you can't walk in God's kingdom now or in the future.

It sometimes amazes me that Christians can read plain, simple scriptures on a subject then discard them when they hear a fool teaching something totally contrary to God's Word. If you do this, you must be a fool as well. Romans 3:4 (KJV) says, *"...let God be true, but every man a liar;..."* I'm talking about the rightly divided Word of God, not the devil's interpretation of it. The Spirit was sent to bear witness to the truth. If he won't bear witness to a doctrine, it is not the rightly divided Word of God.

Agree with God Without Understanding.
You do not have to understand God's Word to agree with it. The fact that he is God and you have a reverential fear of him means that you trust him. He knows what he's doing. Don't forget that he is much smarter than you are! If God explained everything, you still wouldn't understand because his ways are so high above your ways. (Isaiah 55:9) **You don't have to understand everything about how God operates to enjoy the benefits of his work in your life.** Agree with what God says about his kingdom and seek that kingdom as your top priority. Matthew 6:33 says to seek the kingdom first, and all the other things you need will be added to you.

Revelation 1:6 says God has made us kings and priests unto himself. That is your potential, but you can allow satan to steal it from you. Many of you reading this are not enjoying your inheritance because the devil has stolen it from you. You don't believe the Word of God and you won't meet the conditions for walking in his kingdom. God is no respecter of persons. (Acts 10:34) You are his child and you have access to your inheritance as long as you meet his conditions. It is God's desire that you reach your potential in his kingdom now and that you also rule and reign with Christ in the future.

If you want to know the conditions for reigning with Christ, ask the Lord what you must do. You can talk to him and find out how you stand. If you don't qualify, he will show you why and you can make the adjustments. If you can't hear his voice, read *My Sheep Hear My Voice* again. Learn how to hear the Lord and come into his presence so that you can communicate with God. When the Lord speaks to you, start obeying what he says and trust him with all your heart.

Preparing to Rule with Christ
The most important thing to remember about qualifying to reign with Christ is that you learn to rule by first being

ruled. No one is fit to be in authority who hasn't first learned how to be under authority. Reigning with Christ will put you in a position of high authority. God doesn't give that kind of responsibility to someone who doesn't qualify. **Your ability to rule comes from your ability to serve.** If you refuse to be under authority, you are not qualified to be in authority.

One of the hardest teachings I preach is submission to authority. People don't want to hear about it because it makes them uncomfortable. Why? Because it challenges their lordship. **When you have a problem with an authority you can see, you already have a problem with the Lord, because he is the one who established that authority.** If you have a problem with this, go before the Lord and ask him if this statement is true or not. If you are in the Spirit, he will bear witness to it. There are also <u>many</u> scriptures that confirm it. **In the flesh, you can come up with reasons why you shouldn't submit, and the devil will give you a few more if you listen to him.** However, if you will humble yourself, make sure you are in the Spirit and ask God, he will confirm that this is truth.

Let's look at Mark 10:42 and 43. In this passage, some of the disciples were asking to sit on the right and left side of Jesus on his throne. These verses explain that things in God's kingdom are much different than they are in the world. *"But Jesus called them to [Him] and said to them, You know that those who are recognized as governing and are supposed to rule the Gentiles (the nations) lord it over them [ruling with absolute power, holding them in subjection], and their great men exercise authority and dominion over them. But this is not to be so among you; instead, whoever desires to be great among you must be your servant."*

If you have the ambition to "be up front" (a lot of believers do), is your desire to lord over others or do you have a heart to serve? The desire to control someone else should not be in the heart of a Christian. **You qualify to lead by serving everyone.** That is how God wants his children to lead, but that isn't what many leaders want. They go to Bible school or seminary and learn how to be in charge of a congregation so everyone will serve them. This attitude is shared by many authorities in the world. Many of those who want to be in charge do not have the desire to serve their people. Mark 10:44 and 45, *"And whoever wishes to be the most important and first in rank among you must be slave of all. For even the Son of Man came not to have service rendered to Him, but to serve, and to give His life as a ransom for (instead of) many."*

Jesus is the King of Kings and Lord of Lords. He is coming back to set up his kingdom and rule this world with a rod of iron, but how did he qualify for the Father to give him that kind of authority? He qualified by giving up his position with the Father to take on the form of man. He humbled himself as a servant, even unto death. Because of his servant's heart, he has qualified to rule with the Father.

Jesus is the example. In the millennial kingdom, those who rule and reign with Christ will also rule with a rod of iron. (Revelation 2:26 and 27a) Why would God entrust us with that kind of awesome power if we haven't met the qualifications for it? Jesus, being the first born, is heir to everything. **He said himself that he did not come to be served but to serve.** This same standard is required of us as God's people. The higher the position of authority, the more of a servant you must be to qualify for it. **You cannot bypass this training.**

Many of you may take offense at this and proclaim that you are sons rather than servants. I hope you will closely examine your heart if that is your reaction, because **you will never become a manifested son of God if you don't first learn how to serve.** Those who rule and reign with Christ will be serving Jesus. **It is not our kingdom. It is God's kingdom.** Yes, we are sons and we will serve him as his children, but we will <u>serve</u> him.

Qualifying to Rule

In 2 Timothy 2, Paul was speaking to Timothy about being a good soldier and the need to endure hardness. I encourage you to read this entire chapter. Paul made it clear that you can only master God's principles by doing so lawfully. This is what God is emphasizing in this chapter. If you want to reign with Christ, there is a lawful way to qualify for such a position. If you don't meet the lawful conditions, you will not rule and reign with him. The devil will do anything he can to disqualify you, including lie to you about the things that will qualify you.

It is convenient to believe that it doesn't matter what you do, as long as you are born again because you are going to reign with Christ regardless of how you live in this life. If that is true, Paul lied and he wasn't inspired by the Holy Ghost to write 2 Timothy 2:10-12. Let's go over these verses and see what they really say.

"Therefore I [am ready to] persevere and stand my ground with patience and endure everything for the sake of the elect [God's chosen], so that they too may obtain [the] salvation which is in Christ Jesus, with [the reward of] eternal glory. The saying is sure and worthy of confidence: If we have died with Him, we shall also live with Him. If we endure (KJV says, *"if we suffer"*), *we shall also reign with Him.* **If we deny and disown and reject Him, He will also deny and disown and reject us."**

That's pretty plain, isn't it? If we endure (suffer) for his name's sake, we will reign with him. Do you realize that it isn't easy to suffer for Christ's sake? **Many Christians suffer because of sin instead of suffering for Christ.** They endure much pain and suffering because they are reaping what they have sown. This is another law of God. Don't be deceived. God is not mocked. Whatever you sow, you are going to reap. Many sow to the flesh and then proclaim they are suffering for the glory of God. No, they are suffering because of their flesh. There is no reward for that! **However, if you have done right and suffer, great is your reward.** (Luke 6:22 and 23)

Paul said he was ready to persevere, stand his ground and patiently endure everything for the sake of the elect. When we serve God, he requires us to endure many things for the sake of those he wants to be part of the family or those satan has imprisoned. Sometimes he requires one of his soldiers to rescue those who are captured and set them free. To do that, the soldier has to endure some hardness.

Every time God gives me a command that requires me to serve with discomfort, I have to <u>endure</u>. Some of you reading this book may have also heard me preach. I travel all over the world to many nations each year. That is not easy, especially when you consider I'm not getting any younger! I endure a heavy travel schedule because I love God and he sends me. When I open my heart and share my testimony, many people in the audience judge me when they don't know anything about me. I also have to endure this. I do all of this so people have an opportunity to hear truth and be rescued from the snares of the devil. That is the work of a soldier. I'm not offended by it and I don't regret it. I do it because I love the Lord and I love his people. I get my orders as a soldier and follow those orders because I love the commander who is giving the orders. For the elect's sake, I will endure whatever is needed.

Once you've been set free, God is going to prepare you as a soldier and you will have to endure some things to get freedom to somebody else. 2 Timothy 3:10-12, *"Now you have closely observed and diligently followed my teaching, conduct, purpose in life, faith, patience, love, steadfastness, Persecutions, sufferings-such as occurred to me at Antioch, at Iconium, and at Lystra, persecutions I endured, but out of them all the Lord delivered me. Indeed all who delight in piety and are determined to live a devoted and godly life in Christ Jesus will meet with persecution [will be made to suffer because of their religious stand]."*

The King James Bible simply says, *"Yea, and all that will live godly in Christ Jesus shall suffer persecution."* I have seen many Christians who will quote a promise of God that they want but don't have. They say, "God, you said this. I believe you are going to do what you said you would do. I want what you have promised. I claim it now! I speak it as if it is done!" They demand that God does what he says in his Word.

These same people claim to be living godly but how many have claimed 2 Timothy 3:12? Do they "claim" the promise that if you live godly, you shall suffer persecution? They might make a little more progress if they did! **Are you willing to let God do what he wants in your life regardless of whether it is a blessing or persecution?** That's the attitude we should have if we are faithful soldiers.

Many people will not submit to the Lord, become equipped as soldiers or endure hardness and suffering because <u>they are afraid</u>. They fear that God is going to put them into something they cannot handle. They are also afraid that if they do what God says, the devil will counter-attack and destroy them. Fear grips their hearts and their flesh is so strong, they fit Paul's description in Romans 7. They want to obey God and may make a token effort to do so, but they can't carry it out. Their flesh overpowers them because fear has crippled them. 2 Timothy 1:7 and 8, *"For God did not give us a spirit of timidity (of cowardice, of craven and cringing and fawning fear), but [He has given us a spirit] of power and of love and of calm and well-balanced mind and discipline and self-control. Do not blush or be ashamed then, to testify to and for our Lord, nor of me, a prisoner for His sake, but [with me] take your share of the suffering [to which the preaching] of the Gospel [may expose you, and do it] in the power of God."*

Paul is saying to take your share of the suffering that comes from the persecution for preaching the Word of God. As I minister all over the world, I go through some suffering. Some judge me as if I should not go through it. Very rarely has anyone ever said, "What can I do to help? I want to share in your suffering. I should be standing with you and sharing in your hardships." Most people don't want to stand too close to me. They are afraid that if they do, whatever comes against me might get to them, too.

There are some carnal, self-righteous believers who actually proclaim that if the apostle Paul had been as spiritual as they are and had known what they know, he would have never suffered the things he suffered! This conclusion is an abomination. I hope that, before they face God's judgment, they have to look Paul in the eye and repeat that statement. If they don't go through any persecution, when the Bible says all who live godly in Christ Jesus will suffer persecution, what does that tell you? As I said, it is not easy to suffer for Christ's sake.

Most people don't suffer for Christ's sake because they don't qualify to do so. If the devil attacks you or you go through a little persecution, you ought to praise God. You just qualified to suffer a little bit for Christ's sake.

Grace for Persecution

You need to ask God how to deal with persecution. In 2 Corinthians 12:7, we read about Paul's thorn in the flesh, which was a messenger of satan that was given to him by God to buffet him. Because of the abundance of revelation that had been given to Paul, this messenger was sent lest Paul be exalted above measure. Paul wasn't happy with his thorn at the time. Verses 8-10 tell us, *"Three times I called upon the Lord and besought [Him] about this and begged that it might depart from me; But He said to me, My grace (My favor and loving-kindness and mercy) is enough for you [sufficient against any danger and enables you to bear the trouble manfully]; for My strength and power are made perfect (fulfilled and completed) and show themselves most effective in [your] weakness. Therefore, I will all the more gladly glory in my weaknesses and infirmities, that the strength and power of Christ (the Messiah) may rest (yes, may pitch a tent over and dwell) upon me! So for the sake of Christ, I am well pleased and take pleasure in infirmities, insults, hardships, persecutions, perplexities and distresses; for when I am weak [in human strength], then am I [truly] strong (able, powerful in divine strength)."*

Paul's ministry lasted for many years, during which time he learned a great deal. He spent fourteen years in the wilderness with the Lord before he ever started preaching! He was given an abundance of revelation because he was called to lay the foundation of the Gospel to the Gentiles. There wasn't time to deepen his foundation enough to handle that kind of revelation without getting puffed up, so God gave him something to keep him on the ground. It wasn't comfortable but it worked!

Meditate on these scriptures. In the beginning, Paul didn't understand what was going on. He begged God to take the thorn away, but once God told him that his grace was sufficient, Paul's attitude quickly changed. He understood that God's strength was manifested in his weakness. This is a marvelous revelation. Paul didn't take forty years to change his attitude. As soon as he understood God's purpose, he agreed with what God said!

Is this what is being preached today? If a man of God is going through infirmities, insults, financial burdens or hardship of any kind, many believers judge him. Yet Paul said he took pleasure in these things! **Discomfort is not popular in Christian circles today, but it is spiritually profitable.** For a season, if you choose to be godly, you will suffer persecution. For a season, if you are going to have an abundance of revelation from God, he may allow things in your life to keep you from being exalted above measure because he wants to give you more. He may allow you to be perplexed, distressed or go through hardship. **When you have no answers and no way out, your reverence and worshipful attitude toward God will bring you sufficient grace when everything looks hopeless.** You can still count it all joy and have the peace of God that passes all understanding. God will sovereignly move and manifest his strength in your weakness, and you will glorify God because you know his grace is sufficient to keep you.

Everyone wants a testimony of God delivering them, but you have to get delivered <u>into a situation</u> before you can get delivered <u>out of it</u>. There are times when you may stumble into something and God has to snatch you out by his grace to keep you from being destroyed. There are other times, if you live godly and learn to endure hardness as a good soldier, that God will deliver you into situations because you are able to suffer for God's people. For the sake of helping someone else get free from the devil, God can put you in a "prison" then bring you out again to show others that they can trust him to bring them out as well.

That is why Paul said he would be all things for all men. (1 Corinthians 9:22) He didn't keep himself aloof from everyone else. He endured many things yet he was victorious and had a right attitude. Paul got to the point where he could count it all joy. Even when he fell into diverse trials, it didn't matter. Paul counted everything he had received or achieved as dung when it was compared to the privilege of knowing the Lord. (Philippians 3:8)

Such hardness may not feel comfortable, but it is preparing you to rule and reign with Christ throughout eternity. God's grace is available to each one of us. **There is nothing God will lead you into that his grace isn't sufficient to handle.** Don't run from the hardness God may allow in your life.

The devil will try to shield you from suffering for the glory of God by keeping you ungodly. He'll even supply you with doctrines that say you can be ungodly and everything will be all right. You can be comfortable because you don't go through any persecution for Christ's sake and the devil leaves you alone, too. Everything looks great until this little speck of time we are in passes away, then it will not be so great.

There is a time appointed for every one of us to stand before God in judgment, and we must all give an account of how we lived our lives. It will be too late to make a change at that point. We must change now. Some of you are afraid to trust Jesus as Lord. You are afraid to walk in his kingdom because you cannot handle the attacks of the enemy. However, someone who truly walks with God has no fear of the devil whatsoever.

I don't have a spirit of fear. I'm not afraid to open my heart to someone I know will try to wound me. I can open my heart and love others even if I get wounded. I have the power to go to God and get immediate healing of that wound and do the same thing again. I'm not anxious or worried about anything. God gives me peace that keeps my heart and my mind. I have to endure hardness, but I don't dread it. For Christ's sake, it is a pleasure and an honor to be counted worthy to suffer.

If God finds you worthy to suffer, he will also give you sufficient grace to endure it with joy. With God's grace you can do anything. The weaker you are, the more glory you bring to God. **God's strength is made perfect and manifested in your weaknesses.** If you really want to reign with Christ, you must humble yourself, yield to his Lordship and let him prepare you as a soldier. Learn to serve God in humility. If you do this, God will exalt you to a high position as a king and priest. You will rule and reign with Christ in his kingdom.

Chapter 21

Enjoying God Manifesting You as His Child

If you are beginning to qualify to rule and reign with Christ, it is because you have already bowed your knee to the Lord. You are already learning to walk in his kingdom now. As described earlier, God's kingdom is righteousness, peace and joy in the Holy Ghost. Consistently walking in the Spirit and being directed by the Lord Jesus qualifies you to rule with Christ.

<u>The Manifested Sons of God</u>
Romans 8 describes the manifested sons of God who will rule and reign with Christ. Let's take a look at these verses and see some of the conditions that are required before God will manifest his sons to the world.

Romans 8:11-19, *"And if the Spirit of Him Who raised up Jesus from the dead dwells in you, [then] He Who raised up Christ Jesus from the dead will also restore to life your mortal (short-lived, perishable) bodies through His Spirit Who dwells in you. So then, brethren, we are debtors, but not to the flesh [we are not obligated to our carnal nature], to live [a life ruled by the standards set up by the dictates] of the flesh. For if you live according to [the dictates of] the flesh, you will surely die. But if through the power of the [Holy] Spirit you are [habitually] putting to death (making extinct, deadening) the [evil] deeds prompted by the body, you shall [really and genuinely] live forever. For all who are led by the Spirit of God are sons of God.*

For [the Spirit which] you have now received [is] not a spirit of slavery to put you once more in bondage to fear, but you have received the Spirit of adoption [the Spirit producing sonship] in [the bliss of] which we cry, Abba (Father)! Father! The Spirit Himself [thus] testifies together with our own spirit, [assuring us] that we are children of God. And if we are [His] children, then we are [His] heirs also: heirs of God and fellow heirs with Christ [sharing His inheritance with Him]; only we must share His suffering if we are to share His glory. [But what of that?] For I consider that the sufferings of this present time (this present life) are not worth being compared with the glory that is about to be revealed to us and in us and for us and conferred on us! For [even the whole] creation (all nature) waits expectantly and longs earnestly for God's sons to be made known [waits for the revealing, the disclosing of their sonship]."

It is not a question of whether or not there will be manifested sons of God. The question is, will you be one of them? I deal with this issue in detail in my book, *The Manifested Sons of God*. (If you have not read this book, I suggest that you get a copy for your own study.)

The manifested sons will have glorified bodies. They will be caught up in the first resurrection with Christ to the marriage supper of the Lamb. They will return with him on white horses as witnesses to the destruction of satan and the literal establishment of Jesus' throne on the earth. They will be honored because they honored Jesus. It is very clear in the Bible that no one will reign with Christ if they have not first bowed their knees and served Christ in the kingdom of God <u>now</u>. **If you aren't willing to be a servant under his Lordship, you certainly aren't qualified to reign with him.** If you have not been willing to obey Christ and live a godly life that may bring persecution to you, you are not worthy to suffer for his sake nor are you worthy to reign with him.

When God manifests his sons, the whole world will know who has bowed their knees to Jesus. Everyone will know who was willing to suffer for Christ's sake and who actually walked in the Spirit during their lifetime. It won't be hard to figure out who the manifested sons of God are. They will rule this earth with Christ.

How to Qualify

In the mean time, how do you qualify to be one of the manifested sons of God? Bow your knee <u>now</u> and yield to his Lordship <u>now</u>. **Allow him to prepare you so that you can trust God with all your heart.** Quit leaning to your own understanding. Break that habit! When you obey God because you love him, he will start manifesting himself through you in ways that confirm you are his child. The Spirit will bear witness that you are a child of God. Romans 8:14 says that those who are led by the Spirit of God are the sons of God. You can have joy in knowing that you are God's son and you meet the conditions to be a manifested son.

If you continue to live according to the dictates of the flesh, you will surely die, but if you subdue your flesh through the power of the Spirit, you shall live. (Romans 8:13) This is an important point! Acts 1:8 says, *"But you shall receive power (ability, efficiency, and might) when the Holy Spirit has come upon you, and you shall be My witnesses in Jerusalem and all Judea and Samaria and to the ends (the very bounds) of the earth."* We all want the empowering of the Holy Spirit. It was given primarily so that you could <u>be a witness</u> for Christ.

It takes a whole lot more power to <u>be</u> something than it does to <u>say</u> something. Talk is cheap. When you start walking in the Spirit, your fruit will bear witness to that fact. You have been given the power of the Spirit so that you can habitually and consistently put to death and make extinct the evil deeds prompted by the body. You must live in the Spirit and no longer yield to the dictates of the flesh. You can resist the flesh until it has no more power over you. God will make you a vessel of honor in his house if you will bring your flesh under control. (2 Timothy 2:21)

The Spirit is Power!

Most believers think the only reason they were filled with the Spirit was so they could speak in tongues. The Spirit is power! The Greek word *dynamos* describes the Spirit's power, which is supposed to act like "dynamite" in you to blow Adam up! If you have dealt with your flesh by appropriating this power, it is soon obvious to you and others that you are becoming a son of God.

Paul learned to walk in the Spirit and no longer fulfill the lusts of the flesh, but he had to struggle just like everyone else does. We can all relate to Romans 7! Sometimes Paul did the wrong thing because his flesh was strong, but he didn't stay in that condition as many believers do.

Many of you keep making excuses for your flesh. If you continue to excuse yourself, your flesh will still be strong thirty or forty years from now when it should have been made extinct. It should have been killed so it couldn't stop you from doing what God says.

Godly Fruit

You cannot consistently walk in the Spirit if you will not submit to the Lordship of Jesus Christ. **If you don't trust God with all your heart and obey his directions because you love him, you will never walk consistently in the Spirit.** It is not enough to "act spiritual" and proclaim that you are in the Spirit. You are either in the Spirit or you are in the flesh. If you are in the Spirit, the fruit you produce will prove it. Galatians 5:22 and 23 list some of this godly fruit. *"But the fruit of the [Holy] Spirit [the work which His presence within accomplishes] is love, joy (gladness), peace, patience (an even temper, forbearance), kindness, goodness (benevolence), faithfulness, Gentleness (meekness, humility), self-control (self-restraint, continence). Against such things there is no law [that can bring a charge]."*

Many believers pursue miraculous manifestations of the Spirit, but such supernatural events are not proof that you are in the Spirit. Godly fruit is the real proof. Meditate on these verses in Galatians 5 and open your heart for the Lord to reveal to you the areas that he desires to develop more fully in you. These fruits should be present in you and ever increasing in quality and quantity. This work is done as you continually abide in the Vine.

Walking consistently in the Spirit is synonymous with being a son of God. The Father is going to manifest those who abide in the Spirit as his sons. These are the ones who will be the bride of Christ. They will be without spot, wrinkle, blemish or any such thing because they have kept their robes clean in the blood of the Lamb. (Ephesians 5:27 and Revelation 7:14) When they sin, they quickly repent and the Lord immediately cleanses them from all unrighteousness. They stay in right standing with God. All who abide in the Spirit will be filled with the peace that passes all understanding and joy that is not affected by external circumstance. They are the sons of God now, but the fullness of their manifestation will come when Jesus sets up his throne during the millennial reign.

Erroneous Doctrine

If you have been believing an erroneous doctrine that says you can accept Jesus but live like the devil the rest of your life and still reign with Christ, you better get rid of your doctrine! **You are not going to reign with Christ if you continually live in the flesh in this life.** If you will not serve him now, you will not rule with him later. You may not like what I'm saying, but you must face the lie you've been believing. Please make the adjustments while there is still time. Otherwise, satan will steal everything that God desires to give you.

There are vessels of honor and vessels of dishonor in God's house. You choose which one you will be. In fact, you are making the choice every day. **If you continually make excuses for your flesh, you will not be a vessel of honor.** The choice you make every day will determine your future.

Manifested Sons Act Like Jesus.

God's manifested sons are those who act like his first Son. The manifested sons of God do not seek their own will. They only seek to do the Father's will. In fact, they love to please the Father. It is not a chore for them. True sons of God want God's direction in their lives. They continually sow love into God through obedience and they are reaping love from him at the same time.

When you walk in the Spirit, you are in a position that God can manifest himself through you in a variety of ways. 1 Corinthians 12 explains the gifts of the Holy Spirit. The Spirit gives gifts as God wishes and as it pleases him. It pleases God to manifest himself through those who are his sons. He delights in moving through you to meet the needs of others. It is a joy to watch the Father work! When he manifests through you, he is doing eternal works.

The End of the Church Age

As we come to the close of the church age (before the sons of God are fully manifested), there is going to be an increase in darkness such as the world has never seen. There will be strong persecution against the body of Christ. Satan and his followers will make war with the saints during this time. (Revelation 13:7) There will be a group who overcomes the enemy by the blood of the Lamb and the word of their testimony. (Revelation 12:11) These are the sons of God. These are the ones who are walking in the Spirit now. They are living in the kingdom now. These are those who are enjoying shelter from the kingdom of darkness now. Shelter from the devil cannot be found in a particular church or denomination. It is only in God's kingdom. The sons of God who continue to walk in the Spirit will become more evident as the end grows nearer.

You have the privilege of enjoying God manifesting in your life now, as well as when he catches up his bride for the marriage supper of the Lamb. Don't put off the decision to submit to his Lordship any longer. If you are abiding in the Spirit, you should become more and more excited as you see darkness increasing. You can rejoice because your redemption draws nigh. (Luke 21:28) There will be an abundance of grace given to you as you continue to humble yourself before God. This will enable you to overcome whatever the enemy may bring your way.

On the Side of Victory

Don't put yourself in a place where the devil has access to you and God also resists you. That ensures that you will be overcome. If you want to be on the side of victory, get in the Spirit now and stay there. Move into the kingdom of God and abide there. **Quoting the salvation scriptures in a church does not guarantee your place in the kingdom of God.** You are only guaranteed a future place in God's kingdom if you learn to abide there now. It is only in the kingdom that you have freedom from satan.

Don't let satan lie to you any longer. You cannot abide in the kingdom of God and the kingdom of the world at the same time. **Examine the choices you have been making.** Who is the Lord of your life? To whom do you submit your will on a daily basis? Take time right now to submit to the Lord Jesus and move into his kingdom. Determine that you will do whatever is necessary to abide in the Spirit and become a manifested son of God.

Chapter 22

Being Part of the Solution and Not Part of the Problem

Three Basic Requirements

There are three basic things that are required for you to be used of God in such a way that you become part of the solution rather than part of the problem. In the English language, I use the acronym, "P.A.W.", to identify these three areas. The "P" in P.A.W. stands for "prepared". God can't use you to be part of the solution if you are not prepared. In addition, if you are not prepared for God to use you, you are actually part of the problem.

Many people are prepared, but they are not "available". That's what the "A" stands for in P.A.W. During the Revolutionary War in America, soldiers were called "minutemen" because they had to be ready to fight at a moment's notice. They worked on their farms, but when the alarm sounded, they would immediately leave their plows. They carried their rifles with them at all times so that they could be available to fight whenever they were needed.

2 Timothy 2 says a good soldier cannot be entangled with the affairs of this life in order to please him who has called him to be a soldier. Sometimes we get so bound up in the things of this world that we are not available for God to use us. Our lives are filled with many obligations. If God wanted to use us, we would make excuses because we aren't really available.

The "W" in P.A.W. stands for "willing". You can be prepared and even available, but you might not be willing. If you are going to be used as a soldier of Jesus Christ, you must be willing to suffer some persecution. A lot of people aren't really willing because they realize they might have to put up with some hardship. They don't really want to endure hardness as a good soldier. They are willing to pray for other "soldiers" and prefer to send someone else to fight the enemy as long as they don't have to go themselves.

We tend to want to hire someone to go to the front line in our place. If that is your attitude, you are part of the problem instead of part of the solution. However, if you have bowed your knee and you are learning to walk in the kingdom of God now, then <u>the Lord will prepare you</u>.

No soldier goes to war at his own expense. You don't have to figure out how to get prepared because God will do the necessary work in you. God will supply everything it takes to make you an effectual soldier. If you are not available because you are entangled with the things of the world, yield to his Lordship. Ask him to dismantle all the entanglements that would hinder you, and God will start cutting loose everything that is holding you back. If you are not willing, the Lord will help you to become willing. He will bring you to the point that you can see the cost of not being a good soldier. You can change what you are willing to do.

When you are prepared, available and willing, you can start becoming part of the solution rather than being part of the problem. It is wonderful to go through life and know that in any situation or problem, you can let the Lord use you. **Even if you were part of the problem originally, you can repent and start becoming part of the solution.** You can go into hopeless situations and help people who are filled with despair. You can bless others as God manifests his answers through you. It is a good feeling to know that the Spirit of God can move through you in any way he wants. It doesn't matter whether you think you have the ability to solve the problem or not. **God has the answer. Since you are not leaning on your own abilities, you can lean on his abilities.** It is fun to watch God work!

Everything the devil has ever done or will ever do is built upon a lie. He creates problems that overwhelm people to the point of hopelessness. When there seems to be no way out, you can bring the truth. As you begin to truly love people, their hearts will open up and the Spirit of the Lord can move through you to them. God will start exposing the lies that put them in their situation. As you dismantle the works of the devil, you will see people become free from their problems. You have become part of the solution. That's a good feeling!

Problem or Solution?

We've programmed ourselves to think we must wait until the Lord returns before we will see miraculous things happen. If you maintain that mentality, you will not get prepared. **If you can't overcome your flesh and the deceptions that are in your life now, you won't qualify to help others, and you certainly won't qualify to reign with Christ in his kingdom.** Luke 19:17 says if you are faithful and trustworthy in little things now, you will be given authority over greater things. **If you can't rule your own vessel now, you won't rule with Christ later.** Jesus has given you the power to subdue your flesh and everything that would hinder you, so what excuse do you really have?

You are either an overcomer or you are being overcome. You have to decide. You are either part of the solution or part of the problem. The wonderful thing about conviction and repentance is that you can begin to see yourself as God sees you. Praise God! No matter how wrong you have been, he still loves you and wants to forgive you. He wants you to be part of the solution, but you have to make the right choice.

God sets before you blessings and curses. He is encouraging you to receive blessings, but if you are foolish enough to choose the curses, you can't complain when the door shuts and you are left outside. Wake up while there is still time! Make the necessary adjustments and become part of the solution. **It always goes**

back to bowing your knee and presenting yourself to the Lord. He will prepare you. He will change you so that you are available and willing to be part of the solution. Then you will qualify as a son of God to rule and reign with him.

Chapter 23

Being an Eye-Witness to the Destruction of Satan's Kingdom on This Earth

The kingdom of darkness and the kingdom of light have been at war since satan's rebellion. We know that the kingdom of light eventually wins the war. It is an awesome thing to realize that some of us may actually witness the final destruction of satan's kingdom. The sons of God who walk in the Spirit and qualify to be the bride of Christ will be witnesses to that event.

Some of you reading this book have had the truth preached to you time after time. You may have read *My Sheep Hear My Voice*, which teaches you the importance of dealing with the Lordship of Jesus Christ in your life. However, you may have played around with this truth for years and made excuses to get around bowing your knee to the Lord. Something in you doesn't want to do that. That "something" is your Adam nature that gives access to satan.

<u>Are You Ready</u>?

What are you going to do if the trumpet sounds and you are not ready? You will face the remainder of the tribulation if you refuse to be prepared as the bride of Christ. You will have to serve the Lord and be obedient unto death. You will have the pressure to receive the mark of the beast and thereby face the wrath of God. (Revelation 14:9 and 10) **If you think it is hard trying to bow your knee now, it is going to be much harder after the trumpet sounds.** The cost is going to be much greater.

God is preparing Jesus' bride and he is not going to change his standard. His bride will be without spot, wrinkle, blemish or any such thing. **You have deceived yourself if you think being part of the bride is an automatic thing.** It doesn't happen just because you accepted Jesus as your Saviour sometime in the past. That doesn't mean your robe stays clean all the time. You have the responsibility to deny your flesh. **You have the choice every day to either submit your heart to the Lord and do what he says or be your own lord and do what your flesh wants to do.** As long as you are being lord, your robe is getting dirty time and time again because being your own lord is sin. **It is your choice and you are making the choice every moment of every day.**

Satan's Just Punishment

I want to share with you the excitement of those who are going to be witnesses to the destruction of the kingdom of darkness. This makes it all worth while. With everything we've had to go through in fighting the devil, it's going to feel good to see him finally get his just punishment. Revelation 19:7-20:15 relays the progression from the time when the bride is completed to what is going to happen to satan.

"Let us rejoice and shout for joy [exulting and triumphant]! Let us celebrate and ascribe to Him glory and honor, for the marriage of the Lamb [at last] has come, and His bride has prepared herself. She has been permitted to dress in fine (radiant) linen, dazzling and white-for the fine linen is (signifies, represents) the righteousness (the upright, just, and godly living, deeds, and conduct, and right standing with God) of the saints (God's holy people). Then [the angel] said to me, Write this down: Blessed (happy, to be envied) are those who are summoned (invited, called) to the marriage supper of the Lamb. And he said to me [further], These are the true words (the genuine and exact declarations) of God.

Then I fell prostrate at his feet to worship (to pay divine honors) to him, but he [restrained me] and said, Refrain! [You must not do that!] I am [only] another servant with you and your brethren who have [accepted and hold] the testimony borne by Jesus. Worship God! For the substance (essence) of the truth revealed by Jesus is the spirit of all prophecy [the vital breath, the inspiration of all inspired preaching and interpretation of the divine will and purpose, including both mine and yours]. After that I saw heaven opened, and behold, a white horse [appeared]! The One Who was riding it is called Faithful (Trustworthy, Loyal, Incorruptible, Steady) and True, and He passes judgment and wages war in righteousness (holiness, justice, and uprightness). His eyes [blaze] like a flame of fire, and on His head are many kingly crowns (diadems); and He has a title (name) inscribed which He alone knows or can understand. He is dressed in a robe dyed by dipping in blood, and the title by which He is called is The Word of God.

And the troops of heaven, clothed in fine linen, dazzling and clean, followed Him on white horses. From His mouth goes forth a sharp sword with which He can smite (afflict, strike) the nations; and He will shepherd and control them with a staff (scepter, rod) of iron. He will tread the winepress of the fierceness of the wrath and indignation of God the All-Ruler (the Almighty, the Omnipotent). And on His garment (robe) and on his thigh He has a name (title) inscribed, KING OF KINGS AND LORD OF LORDS.

Then I saw a single angel stationed in the sun's light, and with a mighty voice he shouted to all the birds that fly across the sky, Come, gather yourselves together for the great supper of God, That you may feast on the flesh of rulers, the flesh of the generals and captains, the flesh of powerful and mighty men, the flesh of horses and their riders, and the flesh of all humanity, both free and slave, both small and great! Then I saw the beast and the rulers and leaders of the earth with their troops mustered to go into battle and make war against Him Who is mounted on the horse and against His troops. And the beast was seized and overpowered, and with him the false prophet who in his presence had worked wonders and performed miracles by which he had led astray those who had accepted or permitted to be placed upon them the stamp (mark) of the beast and those who paid homage and gave divine honors to his statue. Both of them were hurled alive into the fiery lake that burns and blazes with brimstone. And the rest were killed with the sword that issues from the mouth of Him Who is mounted on the horse, and all the birds fed ravenously and glutted themselves with their flesh.

Then I saw an angel descending from heaven; he was holding the key of the Abyss (the bottomless pit) and a great chain was in his hand. And he gripped and overpowered the dragon, that old serpent [of primeval times], who is the devil and Satan, and [securely] bound him for a thousand years. Then he hurled him into the Abyss (the bottomless pit) and closed it and sealed it above him, so that he should no longer lead astray and deceive and seduce the nations until the thousand years were at an end. After that he must be liberated for a short time.

Then I saw thrones, and sitting on them were those to whom authority to act as judges and to pass sentence was entrusted. Also I saw the souls of those who had been slain with axes [beheaded] for their witnessing to Jesus and [for preaching and testifying] for the Word of God, and who had refused to pay homage to the beast or his statue and had not accepted his mark or permitted it to be stamped on their foreheads or on their hands. And they lived again and ruled with Christ (the Messiah) a thousand years.

The remainder of the dead were not restored to life again until the thousand years were completed. This is the first resurrection. Blessed (happy, to be envied) and holy (spiritually whole, of unimpaired innocence and proved virtue) is the person who takes part (shares) in the first resurrection! Over them the second death exerts no power or authority, but they shall be ministers of God and of Christ (the Messiah), and they shall rule along with Him a thousand years. And when the thousand years are completed, Satan will be released from his place of confinement, And he will go forth to deceive and seduce and lead astray the nations which are in the four quarters of the earth–Gog and Magog–to muster them for war; their number is like the sand of the sea. And they swarmed up over the broad plain of the earth and encircled the fortress (camp) of God's people (the saints) and the beloved city; but fire descended from heaven and consumed them. Then the devil who had led them astray [deceiving and seducing them] was hurled into the fiery lake of burning brimstone, where the beast and the false prophet were; and they will be tormented day and night forever and ever (through the ages of the ages).

Then I saw a great white throne and the One Who was seated upon it, from Whose presence and from the sight of Whose face earth and sky fled away, and no place was found for them. I [also] saw the dead, great and small; they stood before the throne, and books were opened. Then another book was opened, which is [the Book] of Life. And the dead were judged (sentenced) by what they had done [their whole way of feeling and acting, their aims and endeavors] in accordance with what was recorded in the books. And the sea delivered up the dead who were in it, death and Hades (the state of death or disembodied existence) surrendered the dead in them, and all were tried and their cases determined by what they had done [according to their motives, aims, and works]. Then death and Hades (the state of death or disembodied existence) were thrown into the lake of fire. This is the second death, the lake of fire. And if anyone's [name] was not found recorded in the Book of Life, he was hurled into the lake of fire."

Those who have bowed the knee and served Christ will see the beast and the false prophet taken captive and thrown into the lake of fire before the millennial reign. The bride will also be a witness as the angel chains satan and seals him in the pit.

The End of Satan's Kingdom

At the end of the millennial reign, satan will be loosed for a season to stir up the nations in rebellion against Jesus. They will form a great army with as many soldiers as the sands of the sea. They will surround Jerusalem where the kingdom of God is headquartered, right about the time the Father returns with the new Jerusalem. The saints will witness the absolute destruction of satan's army in a moment's time. Satan will be thrown into the lake of fire and then the judgment will take place. Hell and death will be cast into the lake of fire. Everyone whose name is not found in the Lamb's Book of Life will also be cast into the lake of fire where there will be torment for eternity. **That is the end of satan's kingdom.**

You Will Reap What You Have Sown.

God is no respecter of persons. Whatever you have sown, you are going to reap. You are going to get exactly what you deserve and so is the devil. If you have been sowing to the flesh, you are going to reap corruption, but if you have been sowing to the Spirit, you will reap life everlasting and be part of the bride who will witness these events.

Decide now what you want to reap later. If you want to be part of the bride who will witness satan's destruction, you better quit playing games with God. You can either walk in the Spirit or in the flesh. The Bible clearly explains what it takes to walk in the Spirit. Someone telling you that you are in the Spirit isn't good enough. You must meet God's standard.

If you are truly walking in the Spirit, you should see the fruits listed in Galatians 5:22 and 23 manifesting in your life with increasing quality and quantity. If that is not happening, you are not consistently walking in the Spirit. You are not keeping your robe clean. You are not keeping the spots and blemishes out of your garment, and you are not meeting God's qualifications to be Jesus' bride.

Chapter 24

Being an Eye-Witness to the Establishment of God's Kingdom on This Earth
(The Millennial Reign of Christ)

For a short season during the tribulation, satan will set up his kingdom on the earth. His headquarters will be in Jerusalem. When the Lord returns, he will destroy satan's kingdom and chain him for a thousand years. Then the Lord will set up his throne in Jerusalem. (Isaiah 24:23) Those who qualify to rule and reign with him will sit with him on his throne, just as Jesus sits at the right hand of his Father on his throne. As I reiterated time after time in previous chapters, only the saints who qualify will reign with him. (Revelation 3:21 and 20:4)

Those Who Will Reign

Those of us who are going to rule with Christ will be raptured as part of the first resurrection. We will have glorified bodies. We will know even as we are known. (1 Corinthians 13:12) The glorified bodies we receive last throughout eternity. They will never die or feel any pain, and we will have the mind of Christ. This will be a dramatic change for those of us who qualify. The normal inhabitants of the earth will still be functioning as we are now, with natural human bodies.

This is a glorious reward for those who are willing to suffer for Christ's sake. It will be a time to enjoy the fruits of that labor. It will be a time to reap the rewards for serving Christ and being persecuted for righteousness' sake. What was sown in obedience will be reaped in honor and glory.

The Establishment of Christ's Reign

There are many things that will take place in the initial establishment of Jesus' kingdom. There will be a transition of power from satan who was ruling this earth. In one battle, he will be totally defeated and his army destroyed. Christ will step on this earth as the conqueror and proclaim that he is Lord. He will establish his right to the earth which belongs to him. He will put down all resistance. He will bring with him those saints who qualify to rule with him as well as his warring angels. (Matthew 25:31) The angels will be visibly present to establish the Lord's kingdom throughout the earth and subdue all rebellion. (2 Thessalonians 1:7 and 8) Justice will be exact and immediate.

The people on the earth will still be making choices. Some will have submitted to satan and received the mark of the beast on their foreheads or their hands. When Jesus returns, they will have to bow before him. He will not allow any rebellion on the earth. All will serve Christ.

The actual set up of Christ's kingdom will be amazing. The Bible does not explain how he will set up his throne and place of government. Will he simply speak it into being? Or will he call for the greatest craftsman and architects of the world to build what he wants? We don't really know how it is going to come about, but we are going to witness that event.

All the saints who qualify will reign with Christ, but I don't know how we will fit on his throne. Will we actually climb up beside him? These are details that we do not understand, and the throne could possibly be symbolic of a position of authority.

Obviously, if you are going to rule and reign over all the nations of the earth, you have to leave Jerusalem at some point. Someone will either have to leave the city or we will speak from Jerusalem and the angels will enforce what we say. I don't know how it will operate. There are a lot of things that are not answered in the Bible, and it will be exciting to see how it unfolds.

Keep in mind as you read the Bible that God speaks things

that don't make sense to our natural minds. Don't start doubting the Word just because it isn't clear to you. Remember that God's ways are not man's ways. They are higher than the heavens are above the earth. There have been many occasions when God spoke and people misunderstood what he said. We shouldn't be surprised if the establishment of his kingdom does not happen the way we think it will happen. However, when it is completed, it will clearly fulfill what God said would be done.

Amazing Changes on the Earth

During this time, angels will be visibly present to enforce the rule of Christ. I don't know about you, but I think it will be exciting to watch angels function. This is especially awesome because we will be in positions of authority and the angels will be carrying out judgments God may speak through us. 1 Corinthians 6:3 says the saints will judge the angels. Can you imagine such a thing? Obviously, we will be passing on judgments from the Lord, but such a thing is almost beyond our imagination.

As you study this book, you should begin to realize the awesomeness of Christ's reign and the strictness of the qualifications that must be met in order to rule and reign with him. To believe that he would allow you to rule when you never honored him or bowed your knee to him as Lord in this life is foolish. All through the Bible, it is made very clear as to which people will rule with him. He will honor those who have honored him. It is imperative that you think very seriously about this.

During Christ's reign, all ungodly laws will be removed and replaced with godly ones. I don't know if Jesus will do this in one day or if he will send ambassadors to do the job over a period of time. Talk about a dramatic change in the world! Keep in mind that Jesus will be on his throne in Jerusalem, but other people will be thousands of miles away in different countries. Even though people will live all around the world, their laws will change suddenly.

Isaiah 26:9 says that when God's judgments are in the earth, its inhabitants will learn righteousness. There will still be natural people on the earth, so what will keep people from evil? It will be Jesus ruling with a rod of iron and the angels of the Lord. Keep in mind that God knows the thoughts and the intents of men. **God sees in fullness, and he judges us as guilty and convicts us immediately, before we have ever carried out the actual sin.** Those who purpose in their hearts to rebel or create problems will not be given the chance to manifest. I believe God will move swiftly through his angels and bring judgment on them before they get the chance to actually commit a sinful act.

All poverty, grief and affliction will end for those who obey the rules of the kingdom of God. That ought to bring a lot of rejoicing, shouldn't it? Those who bow the knee and accept the rule of God will have no more poverty because God's blessings will be flowing. Obviously, if you choose to be in rebellion against the rules of the kingdom of God, you will be as poor as you are ever going to get, because you are going to lose everything.

All pollution of the earth will end. God clearly says in Revelation 21:27 that nothing which defiles will be allowed in his kingdom. Everything we have done to pollute this earth will be stopped. There will be no more factories dumping filth into our streams and rivers. There will be no more facilities belching out pollution and contaminating the air. Anything that harms this earth will no longer be authorized.

The curse on the land will be removed. (Revelation 22:3) When Adam fell into sin in the garden and yielded to satan's temptation, God cursed the land. That is one reason why all of creation is travailing and waiting for the manifestation of the sons of God. We can only imagine how that curse has affected every part of creation. There will be a dramatic turn about throughout all of nature. Even the waters of this earth will change dramatically.

The nature of the wild beasts will change. Isaiah 11:6 talks about the wolf dwelling with the lamb. Children will even be able to play on the adder's nest and be safe. (Isaiah 11:8) The lion will no longer be carnivorous. (Isaiah 65:25) Such changes will be amazing. Things will go back to the way they were before the fall of man.

The life expectancy of natural humans will increase dramatically. Isaiah 65:20 refers to a child dying at a hundred years old. Perhaps this is because all pollution will be gone and disease and plagues that shorten the human life span will be banished. There will no longer be such corrupting influences on the earth.

All nations that will not obey will perish. (Isaiah 60:12 and Zechariah 12:9) Keep in mind, there are still nations in this earth that have to make a choice. When the Lord establishes his kingdom, there will be clear rules that every nation has to follow. Every nation will have to send representatives to Jerusalem to pay homage to the Lord. They will have to recognize who he is, honor him and bow before him. If a nation refuses to do that, the judgment of God will come on that nation and it will cease to exist.

This is just a partial listing, but it is exciting to realize that you as a child of God have the potential to be an eye-witness to these events. The choices you are making in your life today **determine whether or not you will meet the qualifications to be part of Christ's kingdom during the millennium.**

Chapter 25

God's Kingdom: A More Excellent Way

As the Lord establishes his authority and sets up his government on this earth, we will have the privilege of seeing the curses and corruption removed from the earth. It is going to be a beautiful life that is far beyond description. The following is a partial list of what will occur after Jesus has established his kingdom and the earth has been restored to its original state.

The Earth Will Again Become a Paradise.
 (Isaiah 4:2; 35:1, 2, 6 and 7; 41:18-20; Ezekiel 36:34-36)
Any part of the world that has not been polluted too badly is called a paradise. You may travel to a remote island, hoping to find some natural beauty that hasn't been spoiled by mankind, but the entire earth will become a paradise when all corruption and pollution have been removed.

It will be interesting to see how long this change will take. You may believe that the Lord is going to restore everything immediately. He is certainly capable of doing it that way, but he may just change the rules and allow the change to come about through natural progression. If we stop polluting everything and begin to do what God says, the earth will naturally restore itself just like the human body does if you quit poisoning it. I have a suspicion that this may be the method he will use, because that would show us the difference between his rule and man's rule.

Righteousness, Peace and Joy in the Kingdom
(Isaiah 9:7, 35:10; Zechariah 9:10)

Anywhere you go in the kingdom of God during Jesus' reign, you will experience righteousness. Everybody will be in right standing with God and there will be peace. There will no longer be wars nor fear of terrorism. When Jesus is in charge, righteousness will be evident throughout the earth.

Our Father's Will Shall be Done

Everything on earth that doesn't line up with God's heavenly standard will be changed. Again, is he going to do all this in one day or will it be a progression? I believe there are some basic things that will be done immediately as he establishes his order. That will not be a problem for the saints who have glorified bodies, but the human beings may be overwhelmed by all the diverse changes. There may be a season when the changes seem difficult until they see how wonderful it will be. Our Lord's will is going to be established, whether it is done in one day, a week, a year or the first hundred years. The Father's will shall be done on this earth, just like it is in heaven. Anything out of harmony with his will is going to get adjusted.

The Transformation of the Earth Under God's Rule
(Habakkuk 2:14)

It is hard to imagine this in the natural. We are not only going to see this change, but we are going to have the mental capability to comprehend it because we will have the mind of Christ. We will understand what God is doing, see how it works and be part of the counsel of God as he proclaims what he is going to do. The righteousness of God will manifest. We will understand and enjoy watching the entire earth transformed under his godly rule.

No Corrupting Influences From the Kingdom of Darkness
(Revelation 20:2 and 3)

Isn't that a wonderful thought? No one from the kingdom of darkness will be functioning on the earth during the one thousand year reign. Even the natural people will not be tormented with demonic spirits. There will be no spirits of fear attacking them. There will be no depression, frustration, spirits of condemnation or lying spirits. The jealousy, greed and corrupting influences of demonic spirits over the minds of men will be gone. No one will have to deal with any corrupting influence from satan whatsoever.

No More False Religions or Hypocrites
(Matthew 7:21)

All the false religions on the earth which promote ways that seem right will no longer exist. It will be clearly understood that the only true God is ruling and reigning. Even within the realm of "Christianity", all pretenders and hypocrites will be exposed and done away with. There will no longer be churches with hireling pastors. There will not be anyone on television manipulating the people and using the name of God for personal gain. There will be no more corruption of religion in any form.

The Heavenly Choir in Divine Worship Around the Throne
(Revelation 15:4; 19:5 and 6)

Worship and praise will be just like it is in heaven. We will be able to enjoy the heavenly choirs in holy worship. We will sit at the right hand of Christ around the throne in Jerusalem and praise the King of Kings in pure worship and fullness of joy.

No Abuse of Authority at any Level
(Psalm 103:19; Zechariah 9:10 and 14:9; Revelation 15:4)

Because the actual ruling will be done by Jesus and the saints, there will be no abuse of authority at any level. Only the Father's perfect will shall be done. All decisions will be motivated by pure love. Any variance will not be tolerated. Obviously, there will be varying levels of authority, but no one at any level will abuse their position of authority.

Pure Truth in Education
No theories, half-truths or lies will be taught. The natural people of the earth will need to be re-educated with godly principles because everything will operate under the Lord's rule. These changes will affect businesses and society as a whole. The entire educational system will change for the better.

Removal of All Diseases and Plagues from the Righteous
(Isaiah 35:5 and 6; Revelation 22:2)
It is obvious that the saints will be free from natural illness, but the humans who keep their knees bowed before God will enjoy life without disease.

A More Excellent Way
God's kingdom is certainly a more excellent way. I believe there is a reason why Christ sets up his kingdom on the earth for one thousand years. I believe this will happen so that everyone can see the benefits of godly rule and the restoration of the earth to the glory of God's original creation. This is important because Jesus' control of the earth will stand in judgment against all those who have corrupted the earth. They will have no excuse because they will see the fruit of righteous rule under Christ.

It will be exciting to be an eye-witness to these events! This is only a partial listing of your heritage. You can enjoy this or allow satan to steal it from you. **The choice for eternity is being made today while you are still on this earth.** I've tried to make this as clear as I possibly can. Much is available in the millennial reign, but the kingdom of God is also available now. It is your choice.

Chapter 26

Summary

In the first five chapters of this book, we looked at the different dispensations of God's kingdom. Even though there are differences in each manifestation of God's kingdom, it is important to remember that the basic rules of conduct are the same. Regardless of whether you are looking at the past, present or future, God is in charge of his kingdom. He has established the principles by which his kingdom operates, and **you must live by those principles if you want to abide in his kingdom.**

<u>Settle the Lordship Issue</u>

God's kingdom is set up with Jesus as Lord. Although I have stressed this point many times throughout this book, it bears repeating. You cannot be lord of your own life and abide in God's kingdom. **You must submit to the Lordship of Jesus Christ if you want to abide consistently in the kingdom of God.** This will qualify you to remain there now, and it will also ensure that you will rule and reign with Christ later. God's standard of righteousness has never changed nor will it ever change. If you want to be part of the kingdom of light, you must abide by its rules.

If this decision is not settled within your spirit, I suggest that you stop right now and spend some time meditating on this issue. Everything you have learned in this book will be meaningless unless you actually apply it to your life. The Lord is calling you to be part of his kingdom. Will you answer him?

Moving Into the Kingdom of God

Chapters 5 through 14 of this book focus on the kingdom of God now. If you need additional instructions on how to make Jesus your Lord and all the benefits of that decision, go back and study these chapters in detail. In addition, I again suggest that you read *My Sheep Hear My Voice*. It will teach you how to get to know the Lord and abide in the Spirit.

Highlights from chapters 5 through 14 are detailed below so that you can review them in your mind and heart. These summaries will enable you to find out which chapters you might need to refer back to for additional study and repentance.

Chapter 5

God doesn't change. His standard remains the same. The kingdom of God is available in part to God's children now. You can know God in an intimate, personal way. Luke 17:20 and 21 state that the kingdom is in you (in your hearts) and among you (surrounding you). The Spirit was sent so we can live in God's kingdom.

John 14:23 says if you love Jesus and keep his commandments, he and the Father will fellowship with you. Lordship is the one condition for this fellowship. Getting into Christ through submission to him is the key. You must be able to hear his voice and obey him. It is not enough to have the Spirit in you. You must also abide in the Spirit. If you are obeying God because you love him and your life is filled with joy that is not affected by external circumstances, you are living in God's kingdom now.

Matthew 6:33 explains God's priorities. Seek his kingdom first and all the other things you need will be added to you. Righteousness comes only through Jesus' shed blood and his forgiveness. Make his ways and his righteousness your first priority. Now is the time to get prepared as Christ's bride. This preparation can only take place if Jesus is the literal, functional

Lord of your life. Humble yourself before him and obey his commands rather than your sinful nature. If you walk in the Spirit, you <u>cannot</u> fulfill the lusts of the flesh. (Galatians 5:16) Mortify your flesh by refusing to submit to it. Remember to obey Proverbs 3:5 and 6.

Chapter 6

The only place of security for a Christian is within the kingdom of God. You can abide in the Spirit (in the kingdom) or move into the flesh where satan can have access to you. If you find that you have taken over lordship, simply repent from your heart and God will forgive you. That will move you back into his kingdom.

God's standards of righteousness do not change. We are called to be blameless and without blemish in a wicked world. (Philippians 2:9-16) Salvation includes being kept safe from the enemy, with the ultimate salvation being our deliverance from this earth into God's eternal kingdom. You can move into the kingdom of God now by submitting your whole heart to the Lord. God's promises are for us as we abide in Christ.

Chapter 7

The first requirement for living in the kingdom of God is being born again. (John 3:3-5) However, being born again doesn't automatically qualify you to live in the kingdom. Your heart attitude must be like that of a little child. (Luke 18: 16 and 17) **You must trust the Lord with <u>all</u> your heart.** If you trust him, seek his kingdom and repent of any sin in your life, you can move into the kingdom of God. You can enjoy his presence and abide in him.

The definition of trusting God with all your heart is found in Proverbs 3:5. It means that you refuse to lean to your understanding and acknowledge him instead. This is the foundation of submitting to the Lordship of Jesus Christ. **If you are not**

bowing your knee to the Lord daily, you are in rebellion. Life is so much better when he is in charge!

1 Peter 5:5 says God resists the proud (being lord of your own life) but gives grace to the humble (submitting to Jesus as your Lord). God wants you to submit to him so that he can exalt you in due season. (1 Peter 5:6)

Sin is the only thing that will move you out of the kingdom of God. You can't walk in the Spirit and in the flesh at the same time. Make the choice today to submit to the Lord! Repent quickly if you make a mistake. Embrace the conviction of the Lord when he reveals sin to you.

Chapter 8

You are righteous when <u>nothing</u> separates you from the Lord. You become righteous by receiving God's gift of cleansing through Jesus' blood.

Mark 9:35 says if you want to be great in God's kingdom, you must learn to be the servant of all. God wants you to serve him so he can bless you. He wants to give you peace and joy. Philippians 4:6-8 gives instructions on how to enjoy God's peace. God will keep your heart and mind if you will stay in Christ. You can cast your cares on him. (1 Peter 5:7) Again, Lordship is the key.

The kingdom of God is positional. It is in the Holy Ghost. In the kingdom, you are given eternal life. John 17:2 and 3 explains eternal life as the opportunity to know the Father and the Son. As you walk in the kingdom and abide in the Spirit, eternal life will begin to manifest in you. Continual fellowship with God is available as he rules your life and you obey out of love.

Chapter 9

Living in the kingdom now is required for you to become a son of God. This will greatly affect your future. John 1:12 says that those who receive Jesus are given the power to become the sons of God. Romans 8:14 says that all who are led by the Spirit are the sons of God. Again, this is a conditional promise. You can't walk in the kingdom without being led by the Spirit, and you can't be led by the Spirit unless you submit to the Lord and mortify your flesh.

Romans 7:18b reminds us that there is nothing good in our flesh. This is hard for many of us to face. Righteousness is in Christ alone. **The only way to be righteous is to abide in Christ.** All sin, the desire to sin, and the temptation to sin are in the flesh. You have to separate yourself from your carnality and subdue it by appropriating the power of God within you. Otherwise, your flesh will constantly move you out of God's kingdom. The flesh is sense and reason without the Holy Spirit according to Romans 8:6 in the Amplified Bible. You will never be able to please God if you continue to operate in the flesh.

You have a choice. In fact, you are making choices every moment of every day as to whether you are living in the flesh or in the Spirit. If you are living in the Spirit, he is directing and controlling your life and your daily decisions. You can't become a son of God if you don't learn to walk in the Spirit. If you don't walk in the Spirit, you can't live in God's kingdom now.

Becoming a son of God (by walking in the Spirit consistently) opens the door for many future benefits. You become an heir with Christ and you qualify to reign with him in his literal kingdom when it is established. You become part of his bride.

You must be willing to suffer for Christ, but the present sufferings are not worthy to be compared with the future glory God will reveal to us! 2 Timothy 3:12 tells us that we must be willing to suffer in order to reign with him. Don't resist persecution if God allows it in your life. God's grace is sufficient for anything he may allow. (2 Corinthians 12:9)

Every work you do in this life will be judged. 1 Corinthians 3:13 is the test. Unless love for God (which is defined as obedience to Jesus in John 14:15) is your motive, it profits you

<u>nothing</u> and <u>you are nothing</u>. If you want rewards in heaven, you must walk in the kingdom and be led by the Spirit. The Lordship issue is the very foundation of it all!

Now is the time to repent. You must yield your life to Jesus' Lordship now if you want to become a son of God. Now is the testing time for receiving future benefits and blessings from God. He wants you to share in the inheritance he has ordained for you.

Chapter 10

The main reason God's children do not have knowledge of the kingdom of God now is because they have substituted the natural for the spiritual. **Satan has deceived many with the lie that you can operate in the natural and achieve spiritual results.** This is a way that seems right which has kept many believers from the truth. This is sometimes known as "spiritualized flesh", which is when you try to do "good" out of your carnal, fleshly nature.

Satan loves to tempt us to operate in the natural, because God and his kingdom are in the spiritual realm. All the blessings which are found in Christ are in the spiritual realm. In the natural, you cannot even perceive that which is spiritual.

The only way to understand God's works and his Word is if the Author of the Word opens your understanding. Only the Spirit can lead you into truth. God is seeking for those who will worship him in spirit and in truth. You can only worship God by abiding in the Spirit and hearkening to the Lord's voice.

God loves you but he will not excuse your flesh. You will give an account for <u>every</u> deed done while in this life. However, you can humble yourself, repent and begin to obey God by walking in the Spirit. Your life of obedience will move his heart!

You can choose <u>today</u> to serve the Lord. You can set your heart on spiritual, eternal things and refuse to operate out of your fleshly nature any longer. Take the time to repent right now and begin to enjoy the blessings of kingdom living.

Chapter 11

Satan rules the kingdom of darkness and he wants to destroy anything that is part of God and his kingdom. Satan tried to destroy Jesus and he wants to destroy his followers. Satan tried to tempt Jesus in Matthew 4 but he was unable to draw Jesus into disobedience to the Father. He also tried to kill Jesus numerous times during his ministry.

Satan continues to function in the earth now and he has been coming against the church for centuries. We can be kept safe from his destruction if we continue to abide in the kingdom of God. Those who are in Christ overcome the devil by the blood of the Lamb and the word of their testimony.

The only way satan can get access to you is if you leave the kingdom of God by yielding to your flesh. This limited access is given by your own choice! Satan's kingdom survives by what it steals from believers. He cannot steal from you if you abide in the Spirit. He wants to steal your heritage by keeping you in the flesh where he can get to you.

God does not intend for you to ever leave his presence or his kingdom. It is only when you listen to a lie from the devil that you leave God's presence. Don't listen to satan's temptations to operate in the natural. That one thing will keep you from receiving all the blessings God has for you.

Chapter 12

If you realize you have been yielding to your flesh and satan instead of Jesus, it's time to repent. God will forgive you regardless of the mistakes you have made in the past.

You have gifts and callings in your life that have lain dormant. Stir up your faith in God and let him begin making changes in your life. Choose this day to serve the Lord.

If you realize you have been lukewarm by alternating between walking with God and walking in the flesh, now is the time of decision. In order to be hot, you must submit to Jesus' Lordship with your whole heart. **Now is the time to obey God with a right attitude and pure motive.** If you draw near to God, he will draw near to you. (James 4:8) When you make a mistake, be quick to repent and move back into the Spirit. If you will yield to God and love him, you will learn how to live in his kingdom now as well as throughout eternity.

Chapter 13

Living in the kingdom of God now will dramatically change your life for the better. You will become a new creature in Christ. (2 Corinthians 5:17) Remember that Lordship is the foundation of kingdom living. (I have said this repeatedly because it is so crucial!)

Be eager to embrace change. If your character has been influenced by your flesh as well as satan, carnality and selfishness have become a way of life. When you repent of being in the flesh, God will begin to change your character. The Lord will create a new nature within you. You will move into right standing with God and begin to walk in his righteousness, peace and joy. His love will fill your heart to overflowing and you will become unselfish. You will walk deeper and deeper into fellowship with God as you allow Jesus to control your life.

God will begin to change every area of your life for the better as you submit to him. He will give you revelation on how to do your work, how to enrich your home life, and how to walk in his blessings in every part of your life. He has a good plan for everything you do!

Chapter 14

If you choose to reject what God is making available to you now, it will drastically affect your future. As in the story of Esau, choosing your flesh over obedience can have very negative consequences. (Genesis 25 and Hebrews 12:17) Do not sell your birthright as he did!

Matthew 25:1-13 relays the story of the ten virgins. All were waiting for the bridegroom but only five were prepared. Procrastination is a very dangerous thing. Having good intentions will not save your inheritance but faithfulness will. Now is the time to repent if you have been in the flesh rather than the Spirit.

You can live in the kingdom of God now if you will meet God's conditions. There will never be a more convenient time to obey God. Today is the day of salvation. **Don't let satan tell you to put this decision off a little longer!** God's kingdom is available to you now.

God's Plan for You

Chapters 15 through 17 elaborate on the fact that God has a plan and a place for you in his plan. **Jesus is the author and finisher of God's plan for your life.** The kingdom of God is available now, and the millennial kingdom has a place for you in it. It is important to accept this truth personally and not read this book as if it is for someone else. You must come to the point that you believe in your heart that you can be part of God's plan for this lifetime and in his future kingdom.

Chapters 18 and 19 explain how to get started. It is not complicated! Humble yourself and deal with the Lordship issue. Trust the Lord and start obeying him out of love. It is really quite simple. Chapter 19 details how to get into Christ and grow up in him, which is the foundation of living in the kingdom of God now.

Chapters 20 through 25 elaborate on what it takes to qualify to rule and reign with Christ, as well as the blessings this will bring. It is important to realize that there are consequences for the decisions you are making now. It is critical to understand that living in God's kingdom now qualifies you for the future. What you do now will determine whether or not you will reign with Christ during the millennium and throughout eternity.

Chapter 27

Conclusion

<u>It's Time to Get Started</u>.
It is important to remember that you don't <u>grow up</u> and get in the kingdom of God. You <u>get in</u> the kingdom first and then grow up. **This is critical.** Review chapters 18 and 19 on how to get started. The opportunity to live in the kingdom of God is part of your heritage, but it does have conditions. This is too important to take lightly. Meditate on each scripture. Ask the Holy Spirit to make the truth clear to you. **God never lies and he never changes.** If you find that you don't line up with him and his Word, you must change.

Satan is a thief. In order for him to steal your heritage, he must keep you ignorant of the truth and convince you to believe his lies which are disguised as truth. Satan did not want this book written and put in the hands of God's children. He resisted this work in numerous ways, but he was defeated. Now this book is in your hand. What will you do with it? I pray you will wake up spiritually and escape from the snare of the devil.

With the evidence presented in *My Sheep Hear My Voice* as well as this book, you really have no excuse for being ignorant of what God requires in your life. There is no excuse for not knowing who you are and the standard God requires of you.

Jesus is Lord. He was Lord before the creation. He is Lord now and he will be Lord when the new heavens and earth are created. It is imperative that you recognize this truth and learn to bow your knee before him and walk in his Lordship now. If you will submit to this truth, there will be a dramatic change in your life. If you do not walk in this truth, you cannot really walk in anything God has to offer you. Get to know him and develop a relationship with him. Find out about your place in God's kingdom. If you want to abide with Jesus and the Father, you must move into the kingdom of God and live there consistently.

Parting Thoughts

I have opened my heart to God and to you. I have endeavored to put in writing the words God has given me on this subject. I know that many things in this book may seem like "hard sayings" to you. Nothing in me wants this to be hard for you. The Lord promises that his yoke is easy and his burden is light. (Matthew 11:30) I have found this to be true in my life, now that Jesus is truly my Lord. However, the yoke was not easy nor the burden light when I was being lord. Only after I had bowed my knee to his Lordship did my life begin to change dramatically.

God loves you and wants you to enjoy the benefits of his love. Draw near to him and he will draw near to you. No matter how many times you have failed in the past, God still loves you and will give you a fresh start every time you truly repent.

Make the decision to walk in God's kingdom today and stick with it. Remember, God sees in fullness. Get in his kingdom now and begin to grow up.

God bless you!
J. C. Hedgecock

Additional Books by J. C. Hedgecock

My Sheep Hear My Voice Expanded Edition

Are you a Christian? Do you desire to go beyond your salvation and know your Lord and Savior Jesus Christ in a more personal way? Would you accept the opportunity to hear the Lord speak directly to your spirit, leading you daily in every detail of your life? If the answers to these questions are "yes", then this book is for you. It will give you clear, detailed, easy to understand instructions on how you can have an exciting and fulfilling walk with your Lord Jesus. This is a vital message to the church, teaching a relationship instead of a method from experience, not theory.

(123 pages) ISBN 0-945255-21-7

My Sheep Hear My Voice
(Children's Edition)

Patricia Ross has edited *My Sheep Hear My Voice* to provide children with the opportunity to have a relationship with God and hear his voice. This is easy to read and can be understood by children of all ages. It can be used by parents as a tool to train children in the ways of the Lord.

(21 pages) ISBN 0-945255-05-5

My Friends Obey My Voice

This book has been written as a sequel to the book, *My Sheep Hear My Voice*. It is primarily for those who have heard the first teaching and have studied it many times. If you are not walking in the fullness of the first message, this book will provide help in understanding why you don't obey when you have heard the Father speak.

(66 pages) ISBN 0-945255-09-8

The Manifested Sons of God

Describing the fruit found in those called "sons", this book was written for the children of God who have a desire to grow up and be productive in the kingdom. It describes in detail how to come to maturity and be a vessel of honor. Regardless of the perversions, ignorance and unbelief surrounding this title, the Word of God is very plain on the subject. At the closing of the church age, in the last days, there will be a manifestation of the sons of God. The only question you have to answer at this time is, will you be one of them? Now is the time to prepare. Just because satan has produced some counterfeits, using people who are immature and prideful, doesn't mean God is not going to have real manifested sons who are mature and humble. We are living in a glorious age. Don't miss the tremendous blessings and opportunities that God is presenting to his children. Seek him with your whole heart and you will find him. This book will give you a wide view of how to come to maturity and what our future is as sons of God.

(216 pages) ISBN 0-945255-13-4

Light, Light, Light

Light, Light, Light is a book which sheds God's light on twenty-three key areas including faith, authority, judgment, the five-fold ministry, the anointing, and the three infallible witnesses that you are hearing God. It was written for the children of God who are lights in a world of darkness and who desire to shine even brighter. Jesus said in Matthew 5:16, *"Let your light shine before men, that they may see your good works, and glorify your Father which is in heaven."* When we receive revelation from God, it lights up our spirits and minds. Ignorance and darkness flee before revelation and light. In obedience to our Father, Pastor Hedgecock has shared some of the light he has on a variety of subjects. This book will encourage, challenge and equip you, and add to the light you already have. Jesus said he who has, to him more shall be given. Many key truths await you in this book.

(136 pages) ISBN 0-945255-17-9

Sound Doctrine

Sound Doctrine is an in-depth series of teachings on corrupted doctrines or the ways that seem right and how to walk in the kingdom of God now. It deals with how satan has corrupted our doctrine, teaching and even our method of learning. There is a literal kingdom coming and we have the opportunity to rule and reign with Christ. Now is the time of qualification. If you have ears to hear you will realize the kingdom is here now.

(302 pages) ISBN 0-945255-50-0

The Gilted Prison

The Bible says that to those who have, more will be given. This book speaks primarily to those who are serious about walking with God and don't have any intention of being deceived. Those who aren't yielding to the lust of the flesh or consciously walking in sin may realize in their hearts that they aren't growing at the rate they should grow and don't know why.

If you are confused and frustrated at times because everything seems to look so good but at the same time you know there are problems you can't find the answers for, this book will help you see more clearly the tactics of the enemy and how to rescue yourself from them.

(77 pages) ISBN 0-945255-57-8

How Love Grows

How Love Grows is a pocket booklet that sets out in detail a teaching on how to allow God's seed of love to grow in your life. God not only wants you to be filled with his love, but he also wants you to have an abundance to share with others. The greatest way we can be effective ambassadors and children of God is to manifest his character, which is love.

This book will take you step-by-step through the process that will bring you to an abundance of love. It's your heritage. Don't let anyone steal it from you.

(56 pages) ISBN 0-945255-74-8

Three Infallible Witnesses

As you begin to be sensitive to the Lord's voice within you, there are many obstacles to overcome in regard to discernment of the difference between the voice of the Lord, satan or self (the Adam nature). We must be able to test every thought to see if it is from God or not. We need infallible witnesses. The Father, Son and the Holy Spirit are those witnesses.

This book teaches how you allow the Godhead to become witnesses to each and every thought which enters your mind and how to take those thoughts captive. This is a valuable teaching in how to consistently walk with God.

(39 pages) ISBN 0-945255-73-X

In addition to the books described on the previous pages, individual teaching cassette tapes, study guides and other materials are available.

For more information contact:

In North America:

J. C. Hedgecock Publications
P. O. Box 702981
Tulsa, Oklahoma 74170-2981 **U.S.A.**
e-mail: aaron.of.solm@juno.com

In Europe:

Dr. Keith Jenkins
2 William Road
Stapleford
Nottingham **England NG9 8ES**
e-mail: kajenkins@solm.ndo.co.uk

NOTES

NOTES

NOTES

NOTES